ARN 0288

D1548296

WITHDRAWN

THE ATHENE SERIES
An International Collection of Feminist Books
General Editors: Gloria Bowles, Renate Klein, and Janice Raymond
Consulting Editor: Dale Spender

MEN'S STUDIES MODIFIED The Impact of Feminism on the Academic Disciplines
Dale Spender, editor

WOMAN'S NATURE Rationalizations of Inequality
Marian Lowe and *Ruth Hubbard*, editors

MACHINA EX DEA Feminist Perspectives on Technology
Joan Rothschild, editor

SCIENCE AND GENDER A Critique of Biology and Its Theories on Women
Ruth Bleier

WOMAN IN THE MUSLIM UNCONSCIOUS
Fatna A. Sabbah

MEN'S IDEAS/WOMEN'S REALITIES Popular Science, 1870-1915
Louise Michele Newman, editor

BLACK FEMINIST CRITICISM Perspectives on Black Women Writers
Barbara Christian

THE SISTER BOND A Feminist View of a Timeless Connection
Toni A.H. McNaron, editor

EDUCATING FOR PEACE A Feminist Perspective
Birgit Brock-Utne

STOPPING RAPE Successful Survival Strategies
Pauline B. Bart and *Patricia H. O'Brien*

TEACHING SCIENCE AND HEALTH FROM A FEMINIST PERSPECTIVE
A Practical Guide
Sue V. Rosser

FEMINIST APPROACHES TO SCIENCE
Ruth Bleier, editor

INSPIRING WOMEN Reimagining the Muse
Mary K. DeShazer

MADE TO ORDER The Myth of Reproductive and Genetic Progress
Patricia Spallone and *Deborah Lynn Steinberg*, editors

TEACHING TECHNOLOGY FROM A FEMINIST PERSPECTIVE
A Practical Guide
Joan Rothschild

FEMINISM WITHIN THE SCIENCE AND HEALTH CARE PROFESSIONS
Overcoming Resistance
Sue V. Rosser

RUSSIAN WOMEN'S STUDIES Essays on Sexism in Soviet Culture
Tatyana Mamonova

TAKING OUR TIME Feminist Perspectives on Temporality
Frieda Johles Forman, editor, with *Caoran Sowton*

RADICAL VOICES A Decade of Feminist Resistance from *Women's Studies
International Forum*
Renate Klein and *Deborah Lynn Steinberg*, editors

THE RECURRING SILENT SPRING
H. Patricia Hynes

EXPOSING NUCLEAR PHALLACIES
Diana E.H. Russell, editor

THE WRITING OR THE SEX? or why you don't have to read women's writing to know
it's no good
Dale Spender

FEMINIST PERSPECTIVES ON PEACE AND PEACE EDUCATION
Birgit Brock-Utne

THE SEXUAL LIBERALS AND THE ATTACK ON FEMINISM
Dorchen Leidholdt and *Janice G. Raymond*, editors

WHENCE THE GODDESSES A Source Book
Miriam Robbins Dexter

NARODNIKI WOMEN Russian Women Who Sacrificed Themselves for the
Dream of Freedom
Margaret Maxwell

FEMALE-FRIENDLY SCIENCE Applying Women's Studies Methods and Theories to Attract Students
Sue V. Rosser

SPEAKING FREELY Unlearning the Lies of the Fathers' Tongues
Julia Penelope

BETWEEN WORLDS Women Writers of Chinese Ancestry
Amy Ling

THE REFLOWERING OF THE GODDESS
Gloria Feman Orenstein

ALL SIDES OF THE SUBJECT: Women and Biography
Teresa Iles

CALLING THE EQUALITY BLUFF: Women in Israel
Barbara Swirski and Marilyn P. Safir, editors

KEEPERS OF THE HISTORY

Women and the Israeli-Palestinian Conflict

Elise G. Young

ATHENE
SERIES

TEACHERS COLLEGE PRESS
Teachers College, Columbia University
New York and London

Extracts from Paul Cossali and Clive Robson, *Stateless in Gaza* (London: Zed Books, 1986) reprinted by permission of the publisher.

"Intifada," by Peter Boullata, reprinted from *Intifada*, edited by Zachary Lockman and Joel Beinin, with permission from the publisher, South End Press, 116 Saint Botolph St., Boston, MA 02115 USA.

Published by Teachers College Press, 1234 Amsterdam Avenue, New York, NY 10027

Library of Congress Cataloging-in-Publication Data
    Keepers of the history: women and the Israeli-Palestinian conflict / Elise G. Young
        p.   cm.   — (The Athene series)
    Includes bibliographical references and indexes.
    ISBN 0-8077-6262-8 (alk. paper) — ISBN 0-8077-6261-X (pbk. : alk. paper)
    1. Jewish-Arab relations—1949-   2. Intifada, 1987-   3. Women, Palestinian Arab—Israel.   4. Women, Jewish—Israel.   I. Title.   II. Series.
    DS119.7.Y68   1992
    305.4′095694—dc20   91-33277

ISBN 0-8077-6261-X (paper)
ISBN 0-8077-6262-8 (cloth)

Printed on acid-free paper

Manufactured in the United States of America

99 98 97 96 95 94 93 92   1 2 3 4 5 6 7 8

To my mother, Sylvia Beigel Young,
and my father, Maurice Yanovitch Young

The crimes committed against women because they are women ar-
ticulate the condition of women. The eradication of these crimes, the
transformation of the condition of women, is the purpose of feminism:
which means that feminism requires a most rigorous definition of what
those crimes are so as to determine what that condition is.

Feminism requires precisely what misogyny destroys in women:
unimpeachable bravery in confronting male power. Despite the impos-
sibility of it, there is such bravery: there are such women, in some periods
millions upon millions of them.

Andrea Dworkin
Right-Wing Women

Contents

Acknowledgments   xi

Introduction   1

CHAPTER

1   The Intifada: Women on the Journey Through Colonization   26

2   Historical Precedents: Women Supporting Women's Survival   75

3   In the Modern Era: Women's Rights and Interethnic
    Relations   108

4   Consequences   158

Epilogue   199

References   205

Index   215

About the Author   225

Acknowledgments

This book began to take shape in the summer of 1985. On a research grant from the University of Massachusetts, Amherst, I met with Israeli and Palestinian educators in Israel and in the West Bank. At Bir Zeit University I engaged with Palestinian women and men, sharing histories, politics, daily lives. At Kalendia Refugee Camp, I spoke with Palestinian women and began to learn what occupation meant to them. Over the past 5 years, my engagement with this subject has deepened through contact with many women whose unfailing courage and commitment to liberation have sustained and fueled my own.

The 1985 research grant was made possible by the unfailing support of Dr. Meyer Weinberg. Dr. Weinberg's work in the field of desegregation is respected globally. As an educator and historian, his wisdom, his insistence on the plain facts, his impatience with fabrication and romanticism, made my education as a historian, and as a Jew, possible.

Dr. Janice Raymond's scholarship and friendship provided the ground from which this book took seed. Her patience and tenacity, her "two-sights seeing," have inspired, and continue to inspire and make possible, my work and my daily life. Her contribution to feminist scholarship makes vision reality.

My understanding of the necessity for, and possibilities of, historical research owes its germination to Anita Weigel. She has shown me that the path of resistance to easy answers is the only one that makes sense. Her skills as a librarian, and her generosity and perisistence in making sure the books I needed appeared at my doorstep made this work possible.

Special thanks to Dr. Barbara Reinhold; to Sally Koplin, whose assistance was critical in the final stages of this work; to Lois Ahrens, who inspired, listened, read, and critiqued; and to Fran Schwartzberg. Thank you to Dr. Aaron Berman for continuing support, and to the librarians of Hampshire College.

I want to thank Chaya Shalom for five years of letters and visits detailing every stage of the Israeli women's peace movement, for her courage in defying injustice, for her constancy in friendship.

I also want to thank the late Betty Geringer. On Rosh Hashanah you always found me, and on each new year I remember.

Thank you to Rose Yanovitch Rosen for her poetry and historical commentary. Thank you to Peggy Yanovitch Finstein and to the late Sarah Hanovitch Lotto . . . Yiddishkeit is your culture, " 'not a thing of nations,' not grand or exalted but associated with family, nurturance, and survival" (Meyerhoff, 1978, p. 96).*

With gratitude, I thank for their constancy and support my parents and sisters, Maurice and Sylvia, Ilene and Enid. Our conversations always leave me with renewed belief in the promises of dialogue, of education, of hard work, of renewal. "Perhaps the deepest impressions of life are where the roots are set . . . " (Meyerhoff, 1978, p. 57).

---

*Barbara Meyerhoff, *Number Our Days* (New York: Simon & Schuster, 1978).

KEEPERS OF THE HISTORY

Women and the Israeli-Palestinian Conflict

Introduction

May 20, 1990. Day breaks over the narrow alleyways of Jabalya Refugee Camp in the Gaza Strip. In the dim light, Palestinian women and men wait for buses to take them over the border into Israel. Once in Israel, they will stand in places commonly known as slave markets, hoping to find unskilled or semiskilled jobs at wages far below minimum standards, and without the benefits accorded Jewish workers. Women will labor in fields once owned by their families and worked by their grandmothers; men will work as day laborers in construction or in factories. Some of the women are professionals, trained in universities as doctors, lawyers, and teachers, but are now prohibited from utilizing their skills.

Nabila is not among those leaving; her arduous day's work, for which she receives no pay, will take place within the confines of the camp. There she will cope with crowded living quarters, unclean water, sick children for whom there are no doctors. She is already at work heating water she spent hours hauling the day before, waking children, watching her husband walk off to find transportation. Five nights a week, Nabila's husband, like tens of thousands of Palestinian workers, sleeps illegally in Israel, where recently three Gazan day laborers burned to death in their hut next to the construction site where they worked.

Follow the men now down the long winding roads leading to Rishon Lezion, a slave market outside Tel Aviv. They are standing in the early morning sunshine when a young Israeli wearing army fatigues and carrying an automatic rifle approaches them. He asks them to show their identity cards, which all Palestinians are required to do. As the men pull the cards out of their pockets, the Israeli lifts his gun and begins to shoot.

In a shattering moment of flying blood and flesh . . . as she bends to light the stove, he loses consciousness.

In a matter of moments, 17 more Palestinians are splayed across the pavement—7 dead and 10 wounded. This is what the media will report: one Israeli driving by stops his car, jumps out, and dances around their bodies.

Within 3 days, 850 more Palestinians are lying dead or in hospital beds, gassed and wounded for expressing their grief and outrage.

1

In North America, what are the responses of Jews and others to these most recent killings in the third year of the popular uprising in the occupied territories, the intifada?

For some, it is outrage, grief, and frustration. For others, it is terror, confusion, fear. Images of shattered flesh flying through the plate glass windows of a bus driving between Jerusalem and Tel Aviv. For others, memories of Holocaust violence flash in a sequence of pictures that forms a range of responses: withdrawal, contraction, revenge or connection to world suffering, a promise to eradicate the means and ends of genocides.

Images of a Palestinian, masked and dangerous. Images of an Israeli, armed and dangerous. Images of a Palestinian, proud and defiant—bent and broken. Images of a Jew, proud and defiant—bent and broken. Flesh torn open: Jew, Palestinian, Arab, Jew.

Increasingly, in cities and towns all over the country Jews and others gather to express their outrage. While there are those who are indifferent, while there are those who support the killings, there are others who are seeking solutions—demanding an end to violence. Their actions and words have precedent in a vital but for the most part unrecognized history of Jews who, with others, have protested Palestinian suffering at the hands of the Israeli state apparatus—who connect crimes against Jews with racist policies worldwide.

For those who seek an end to the Israeli-Palestinian war, the urgent and central question is: What kind of political movement do we need to break this spiral of violence?

THE ISRAELI-PALESTINIAN WAR

Causes and Explanations

To address this central question—what kind of political movement do we need to break this spiral of violence—begin by examining the incidents of May 20 described above, what happened, and how it was characterized.

The murders are a consequence of occupation. The victims are casualties of a nationalist struggle for control of land. They are day laborers—that is, their labor, their very bodies, are being utilized by the occupier for his own gain. They have no rights because they are not citizens of any state. They must carry identity cards in order to exist. In this instance, as they pull out their cards, they are shown what that identity is worth by a "deranged" Israeli who pulls the trigger. The media reports that the murderer is himself a victim— of unrequited love. He told his girlfriend that if she would not take him back, he would go out and kill. Palestinians and women became confused in his mind.

Palestinians are asking for the right to self-determination, for an end to occupation. The intifada is the courageous struggle of a people to define its own borders, its own legal system, economic system, system of social organization; in short, to preserve its traditions.

The Palestinian resistance movement is waging a struggle against a people who themselves have been struggling for the right to self-determination in the face of systematic terror against them throughout history.

This is how the story is told. Two peoples, two opposed nationalities—Arab and Jew—are locked in an either-or struggle for survival. There will be a winner and a loser. Or there will be negotiations and compromise. Who will benefit? Who will lose? What will be gained or lost? What is left out in this characterization of the conflict, and why; what are the consequences?

Arabs and Jews are said to be two peoples between whom a natural antagonism exists. The natural antagonism is both specific to them and general—endemic in the human condition, a natural antagonism between human beings locked into a drive for self-interest and power. This is the conceptual framework informing characterizations of the Israeli-Palestinian war and structuring the political work related to resolving the conflict.

But it is a conflict that can never be fully resolved as it is conceptualized, since it describes conflict as biological. The underlying assumption is that there is an inherent greed and power-seeking in humankind; this fact becomes the justification for the nation–state. The ostensible purpose of the state is to define and to ensure justice for all its citizens and to punish those who do not conform to its beneficent rules. Today in the Israeli state, who controls the seats of justice? What does justice look like in terms of the day-to-day lives of Israeli citizens? Who does not benefit from, and who does not conform to, its beneficent rules?

It is a conflict that can never be resolved as it is conceptualized because it assumes a biological, inevitable enmity between Jew and Arab.

The Israeli-Palestinian conflict is not the result of a supposed "eternal hatred" between Arab and Jew. On the contrary, relations between those peoples who are Arab and Jew are rooted in a complex history that is ignored and misrepresented in Western discourse.

In Israel–Palestine, there are not just two peoples, Arab and Jew. Rather, there are European Jews, Palestinian Jews, Jews from other Arab countries—Syrian Jews, Yemenite Jews, Iraqi Jews, North African Jews, for example—and Israeli Jews. There are Muslim Arabs, Christian Arabs, Druze, Bedouin. Because relations—historic and current—between all these peoples are interconnected and multifaceted, in what sense are we talking about eternal enemies? Binary oppositions, positing a "one" and an "other," leading to and/or assuming a good and a bad—two sides, two views—reduce and render invisible those issues that are most central to understanding the Israeli-Palestinian conflict: gender, race, and class politics. Not only is the Arab and Jew of popular discourse male; he is also monolithic. This dualistic reductionist conceptual framework fuels the notion that all Arabs are and think alike, and that all Jews are and think alike. Thus, one is on, or must take, the side of one over and against the other, within the framework of two sides to the question. Distinctions of geography, social status within a range of class frameworks, social constructions of gender, violence against women, victimization of colonized men, violence against nature—all are obliterated.

The peoples of Israel–Palestine are women as well as men. The women, however, do not have the same relationship to the land of Israel–Palestine as do the men. Women's relationship to the land is structured by world domination of land by men as prescribed by gender, race, and class formations within historic and geographic context. Women's relationship to the land can be understood only within the context of a close study of these factors. The history of women in every known area of the world is a history of struggle in the face of appropriation by men—of women's bodies, labor, resources, associations, visions. This history is central to the current Israeli-Palestinian conflict: in all its permutations, this struggle informs the current situation. Feminist analysis is therefore central to possible resolution of the conflict.

From the Vantage Points of Women

Friday, May 25, 1990. Day breaks over the ancient stone walls of Jerusalem. An Israeli woman awakens with a sense of urgency, gathers her tools, and carefully fills in the letters on the poster before leaving for work. In the afternoon, she rushes home to finish preparations for the day's activities. She dons a black shirt and black slacks.

In 21 cities throughout Israel, Women in Black gather for a silent vigil. They are from cities, agricultural and industrial settlements, small towns, and villages. They are one of a number of women's organizations that are addressing the Israeli-Palestinian conflict from the vantage point of women who come from a range of historical, class, and cultural experiences. They are the grassroots community organizer, the establishment spokeswoman, the housewife, the businesswoman, the lawyer. They are Israeli Jews, Ashkenazi, Sephardi, Jews from Arab countries, Palestinian Muslim, and Christian. They are building a political movement addressing the cycle of violence.

On that same day in the West Bank, Palestinian women gather at meetings of the Working Women's Committees to discuss strategies in response to the most recent closing of a local school. And at Bir Zeit University, one of the women faculty is missing: she is on a hunger strike in response to the killings of the Gazan day laborers. From all social classes, and within the context of the resources and skills available to them, Palestinian women risk their lives daily and are daily humiliated and killed, resisting occupation.

In what ways are political movements of women significant in the Israeli-Palestinian conflict? In what ways are political movements, created from the vantage points of women, significant for possible resolution of the conflict?

A central premise of this book is that violence against women, inextricably linked to violence against nature and to violence of race and class politics, is the implicit, unstated axis upon which the Israeli-Palestinian conflict turns. Mainstream theories and political movements from right to left are therefore inadequate for resolving the conflict. A feminist analysis, that is, an analysis of the intrinsic connection of violence against women in its relation to nationalism and to nationalist struggles, is necessary to both understand and resolve the Israeli-Palestinian crisis.

Globally, women struggle against, accommodate, and survive violence directed against them daily: rape, battering, economic hardship, vilification, objectification. Feminists document and analyze the ways in which women are utilized to support male hegemony within all economic systems, including capitalist–patriarchy. Nonetheless, popular and academic discourse and movements ignore feminist critique, treating the question of women, if at all, as derivative; that is, as attached rather than central to the Israeli-Palestinian conflict. The basic realities of women's lives, and the connection of those conditions to the suffering of both Jews and Palestinians, are overlooked by the prevailing analyses.

One critical consequence is that the conflict appears to be insoluble. In this sense, the politics and historiography—or politics of writing history—support that which they ignore. By continuing to marginalize women they implicitly condone violence against women, against the earth, against colonized peoples internationally. This is the war that is fueling the war. As long as the underlying misogyny of commonsense discourse is ignored, there can be no end to war in the Middle East.

Androcentric historiography appropriates and renders invisible the multifaceted and complex relations of women to, and within, historical developments leading to the Israeli-Palestinian conflict of the 20th century. But it is precisely within that exploration that possible resolution—an end to the spiral of violence—must be sought.

A political movement that can hope to end the spiral of violence in Israel–Palestine must develop a new conceptual framework taking the emphasis off Arab versus Jew. A feminist conceptual framework can critique terms such as *peace, justice,* and *equality,* asking what the terms of this peace are; asking "equal to whom and to what?" Whose figure is it that is the measure of equal? A feminist critique can analyze the underlying framework supporting official definitions of justice. Justice is morality as defined by a ruling class of men. Justice unfolds within a dualistic hierarchical framework of ruler and ruled, powerful and powerless, those who mete it out and those who must struggle for it. Within historic and geographic contexts it is critical to look at who fills the seats of justice and who waits in the corridors to be let in.

The basic understanding of feminism, that the fate of all women is interconnected, is a bridge between Israeli and Palestinian women, polarized by

those forces that have brought Jew and Arab to this battlefield. This understanding allows us to see that for every woman who is privileged, another
is downpressed. The occupation of women's bodies is the spiral of violence
of class and race politics. The purpose of this book is to bring into the foreground critical connections between gender, race, and class as they inform
historic and current developments of the Israeli-Palestinian conflict. Women
are "keepers of the history": feminist critique is the basis for politics that can
transform the deadlock between Israeli and Palestinian, "Jew" and "Arab."

WOMAN, THE OCCUPIED TERRITORY

One of the purposes of feminist analysis is to free women from the confines of male theoretical assumptions. Because language has itself been
colonized, it is necessary to wrest language from the bonds of phallocentrism.
What then is the *self* of self-determination, the term so widely used to describe the goal of nationalist struggle? And what is the *right* that women struggle
for within the boundaries of a language that reproduces and reinforces the
right of male hegemony? These questions form the background of any analysis of women's participation in the intifada; in the Israeli-Palestinian conflict.

Women struggle for the right to equal access to male constructs: to economic systems, justice, and education. They struggle within a social system
and social reality defined and controlled for the benefit of those men with
the most direct access to male power. In the process of that struggle, many
women reinterpret, redefine, and re-envision those constructs. Because the
self of self-determination is prescribed by men, women are challenged to re-
envision the meaning of self-determination from a feminist perspective.

How do women survive within phallocracy? Given that a system of forced
dependence and co-optation sustains women's place, self-determination implies clarity about the ways in which that system operates. The process can
be observed in nationalist politics designed to ensure national identity and
nation–state hegemony. In Israel, the breakup and destruction of villages and
towns, accomplished through land confiscation, deportations, and resettlement, is carried out by alliances of men as Israeli officials buy off local *mukhtars*, or heads of villages. In the Gaza Strip, a Palestinian woman describes
a similar process:

> . . . Now drugs are coming into the Strip; every day more of our young men
> are in a daze of drugs. You know how the drugs come? From the sea, smug-
> gled. Three groups of men aid this, by direct support or by closing their eyes:
> the smugglers, the Israelis, *and the mullahs.* The smugglers gain money, the
> Israelis gain a drugged-out male population, and the mullahs gain power and
> dependency by being the connections. This must stop! And the women are the
> ones who will stop it! (Morgan, 1989, p. 257)

This collusion maintains the state of conflict ensured by the co-optation
and dependence of Palestinians. In another example, some Orthodox Jewish

women and fundamentalist Muslim women support the state of conflict as they gain power by supporting nationalist boundaries. Self-determination for women is a complex and multilayered question and event.

When we use the tools of the phallocracy, when we assume the language of the phallocracy, we become convinced of the reality of "woman." We become convinced of woman's "natural" dependence, frailty, and powerlessness, and of the necessity, therefore, for male rule and for military might. The colonized woman lives within and against assumptions that distort our view of history. We become mesmerized by accounts of men's exploits—diplomacy, wars, goals. It becomes both possible and acceptable to describe the killing and sacrifice of women, children, colonized men, as the "elimination of a terrorist stronghold."

Nationalist ideology characterizes women's role in nationalist struggle by what feminist author Andrea Dworkin names the "woman-superior" model of antifeminism informing political discourse (Dworkin, 1983). Woman is the model of good, of chastity, of morality. Nationalist movements utilize this model to achieve their goal of social control. " . . . she must be in her person the example of good that will civilize and educate man and make the nation moral" (Dworkin, 1983, p. 207). This view of woman disempowers women by seeming to empower her. "She cannot become merely a human in the muck of life, morally flawed and morally struggling, committing acts that have complex, difficult, unpredictable consequences . . . " (Dworkin, 1983, p. 206). This view of woman is a distortion of history that in turn disempowers women's actions to change history, to change the definition of "woman."

The following editorial chronicles and celebrates the crucial role of Palestinian women in the intifada:

> From the Occupied Territories to Lebanon to the diaspora, the Palestinian woman is the backbone of her history, her society, and her national struggle for self-determination.
> Her role is one that she shares with all women who struggle for peace and justice in their respective areas of the world. While equal rights may not have been reached in these societies (as we in the West understand the concept), the fact that these women are soldiers, wives, mothers, educators, and professionals tells us that in some ways at least, they may have surpassed women of the First World. (Palestine Aid Society, 1989, p. 1)

The women of this editorial are characterized as "heroes." This idealization of women is a danger signal. Putting "woman" on a pedestal, men occupy her body: they foreclose women's participation in the world of daily decision making. From that position it will be difficult for women to enter the foray of events once the war has ended and to continue to take control over their destinies.

Within the geographic, economic, and psychic boundaries defined by nationalist struggle, women continue to produce the ways and means, against all odds, of sustaining their societies. At tremendous risk to themselves, Palestinian women in the territories are daily tortured and humiliated, as they attempt to transform a historical tragedy.

This editorial extols the central role of women in the struggle against occupation, and for self-determination: without their participation the struggle cannot succeed. Control of women's reproduction, as they are the "guarantors of the future of this nation" (Mies, 1986, p. 194), and of women's labor, as men are fighting the war, is critical to the struggle against a foreign aggressor. Sociologist Maria Mies puts it this way:

> Apart from their unpaid housework, they [women] have to keep agricultural and industrial production going and thus provide the requirements of the people at home and the men at war. Without women's responsibility for the continuation of the economy, no successful liberation war can be fought. . . . The need to mobilize large masses, if not all women, of a "nation" for these patriotic tasks requires the foundation of national women's organizations. (Mies, 1986, p. 195)

Women participate in nationalist struggles that promise them access to basic needs: shelters, health care, the ability to read and write; this in spite of the fact that women who are citizens of nations all over the world suffer deprivation of basic needs as members of a "despised" race or class. Still . . . without national rights, woman is anyone's prey.

And without woman's services, society cannot function. Palestinian women are creating the infrastructure for the new state through the Women's Work Committees, which have made survival possible during the intifada.

This work of providing basic services, of advocating for basic services, is not new. It is women's work. The occupation is a paradigm for the situation of women. For the "woman" of history is already occupied. She knows the conditions of occupation well. Her skills are attuned to survival within the occupation.

Nationalist ideology extols women, drawing upon phallocratic myths that sustain the reality of women's colonization. He calls his country "she." She is his domain. Within his domain, she stumbles over her occupied body, carrying the flag. The flag promises that she will be rewarded for her suffering. Her role in carrying the banner earns her the possibility of being counted. She is a citizen, deserving a livelihood, however meager. The flag earns her the possibility of protection. It also earns her rights and the right to advocate for rights. Without that, there can be no peace and justice.

Palestinian and Israeli women, continuing to insist upon a part in creating and maintaining a social order that will provide them equal access to resources, are women who believe in peace and justice; who have given up believing in peace and justice; who never believed in peace and justice, because peace and "justice" for them have always meant rape, incest, pornography, starvation, dependence, co-optation, murder. These women have their own hidden agenda. Daily they risk their lives—building stone barricades, resisting torture—to restore women, to restore the earth, to redefine national goals within a feminist context. Pitted against one another, competing in male ideology and reality, as "First World" and "Third World," they are the backbone of the nationalist struggle.

Does the fact that these women are soldiers, wives, mothers, educators, and professionals tell us that they have achieved self-determination? Is this editorial yet another attempt to co-opt women's work, or an affirmation of their co-optation?

Whatever lies outside the boundaries that are acceptable to the official nationalist struggle is branded as prey. "As she is 'nature,' 'sin,' she must be permanently under his guardianship . . . " (Mies, 1988, p. 90). As the colonized peoples are "nature," "sin," wild and unpredictable, they must be permanently under the guardianship of the colonizer. Because control of women and of land is the basis for the masculinist system of capitalist exploitation, women must be convinced through force and through coercion, to give up their relationship to their "evil" selves and to "wild" nature.

In describing what characterizes women's relationship to themselves and to nature, Maria Mies points out that:

> In the course of history women observed the changes in their own bodies and acquired, through observation and experiment, a vast quantity of experiential knowledge about the functions of their bodies, about the rhythms of menstruation, about pregnancy and childbirth. This appropriation of their own bodily nature was closely related to the acquisition of knowledge about the generative forces of external nature, about plants, animals, the earth, water, air. (Mies, 1988, p. 74)

Mies goes on to note research substantiating ways that women appropriate their own generative productive forces, passing their experiences on to their daughters. For example, Egyptian women, using vaginal sponges dipped in honey and acacia tips that contained a spermicidal acid, regulated the number of children they bore (Mies, 1988).

Self-determination implies control of one's generative forces—thinking, analyzing, acting, reflecting, passing on knowledge, giving birth.

Women are well known to have been the first agriculturalists; as such they developed a productive relationship to nature characterized by reciprocity, rather than by predation or control.

> . . . they were not *owners* of their own bodies or of the earth, but they cooperated with their bodies and with the earth in order "to let grow and to make grow." . . . As producers of new life they also became the first subsistence producers and the inventors of the first productive economy. This implies, from the beginning, social production and the creation of social relations, that is, of society and history. (Mies, 1988, p. 76)

Colonization of women (control of their generativity) and colonization of those peoples populating mineral-rich areas of the world depend upon militarism, the structure by means of which men make, control, and utilize the armaments of war. Mies traces the predatory relationship of men against nature and against women. Men's productivity and relationship to nature is mediated through tools whose purpose is to destroy life. Men who hunted had power not only over animals but eventually over communities they raided in order to acquire surplus wealth. Female slaves, women captured in these raids, were the first forms of private property (Mies, 1988). Further, the coercive domestication and breeding of animals to increase wealth may have paralleled establishment of patriarchal lines of descent and inheritance to control domestication of women, that is, women as breeders. "Women were also subjected to the same economic logic and became part of the moveable property, like cattle" (Mies, 1988, p. 83).

The paradigm is occupation; the occupier–occupied relationship governing all areas of life where, for those who are occupied, self-determination has become but a shadow on a stone wall.

Occupation

History convinces us that occupation, the invasion and subsequent maintenance of control by force, of territory, of bodies, is inevitable. History documents predation: wars, diplomacy, social control. To study history is to become convinced that the occupier–occupied model in all its guises, citizen–pagan, king–subject, man–woman, is inevitable.

Thus, we frame the conflict between Israelis and Palestinians, between Jews and Arabs, as the inevitable clash of two opposed nationalities, two eternal enemies. This characterization of the conflict perpetuates the notion that nationalism is a gender-neutral concept. It perpetuates the myth that the nation–state serves both men and women equally. In reality, women and men, with differing relations to the means of production, do not participate in nationalist movements with the same power, privileges, goals, and/or visions. Similarly, the culture that nationalism purports to sustain and to protect appears to be gender neutral. Culture has become a catchword for a set of customs, beliefs, and traditions of a people. But men's relation to culture is not the same as that of women.

Culture

The action or practice of cultivating the soil; tillage; also, the raising of plants or animals: these activities are what culture is. Culture—a particular relationship to the earth mediated by the tools of cultivation, by the methods utilized to control growth, production, distribution, sale. Ownership— Mediated by the tools of domestication; the action or practice of cultivating the soil, plants, and animals to enhance his store. His wealth. His kingdom.

Culture. The word signifies changing hands. Hands that are calloused with working the soil; hands that are studded with gems to signify whose soil it is.

The histories of cultivation of the soil and of sexual exploitation are interwoven. Culture is the range of historical relationships of men to the earth; to the domestication of women. Culture is the range of historical relationships of women to the earth and to the culture of men, mediated by the tools of domestication.

Cultural survival, then, is the perpetuation of systems of exploitation of the land, of animals, of women, of enslaved men, as well as the struggle against that exploitation. All socioeconomic political systems that perpetuate exploitation of the land, of animals, of women, of colonized men, are ultimately self-destructive. Ultimately, all such structures contradict cultural survival by destroying those systems and relationships to the land that ensure the continuation of cycles of growth and renewal in nature.

Thus, whether invader or invaded, ruler or ruled, a nationalist struggle for control of land is not the same struggle for women that it is for men; nor is it the same for all women. Women's struggles in relation to nationalism unfold in relation to the politics of survival as "woman."

The concept of nation has already left women out. If we look at nationalism as patriotism, this becomes clear. Patriotism is derived from the Greek for fatherland, land of one's fathers. In supporting nationalism one becomes a patriot. Nationalist–imperialist movements appropriate women and land, reducing both to their "use value." This critical connection between the struggle for control of land and the struggle for control of women as it shapes historical events leading to the current Israeli–Palestinian conflict has not been named. The concept of Jews versus Arab, of Jew and Arab as eternal enemies, is a smokescreen concealing these central issues. Political discourse has itself been occupied.

THE LEGACY OF NATIONALIST IDEOLOGY

Intifada

the land of Palestine shook
until the very stones loosened

and were gathered up by you
as other children, innocent, have picked flowers

your rocks blossomed blood-red
against a conspiracy of years

of having your every breath, heartbeat observed constrained
until you could not breathe, every gasp a battle

the way you suffocate under a veil
of teargas, chambers of death
your own homes, streets, gardens

you said you have had enough
and started an earthquake

drawing down a shower of hailstones
against a sinful nation

the occupation officers have hit a stone, been struck
by the steadfast hardness
of a people willing
to die on their feet
rather than live on their knees

you love your lives enough
to struggle
against the constraints

bound, as you have been
all your lives

you are loosening the bonds now
casting off what has kept you down
you are bound for glory
shaking, shaking until you are free.

Peter Boullata (1989, p. 4)

Intifada means shaking loose. The children of the stones are the carriers of resistance, shaking loose 20 years of occupation, and 20 more of invasion, killings, destruction of homes and properties, alienation from land, military regulations circumscribing their living and their dying. They are women and men, from 6 months old to 100 years old. On December 9, 1987, young Palestinians responded to the killings of Gazan laborers by an army military vehicle. Their weapons were stones, organized demonstrations, courage, and despair. The current stage of the intifada had begun.

War Against Women and Against Nature

From a feminist perspective, Boullata's poem speaks to the intrinsic connection between sex and race ideology in the history of expropriation of land. Women of despised races, women across race, class, geography, "suffocate under a veil/of teargas, chambers of death . . . ." What we are witnessing with the Israeli-Palestinian war is the ongoing process of violent expropriation of nature, women, people of color, that is necessary to capitalist-patriarchal hegemony in the 20th century.

Historically men have controlled land and the basic means of production through disruption of women's relationship to nature and through expropriation of women's sexuality. In ancient history accumulation of captive women was a sign and a goal of military victory; capture and distribution of women signified political power and status. As early as the third millennium B.C.E., sexual regulation of women accompanied consolidation and formation of classes (Lerner, 1986). Feminist historian Gerda Lerner's analysis of the Middle Assyrian Law 40 shows the connection between the ability of the state to control property rights and to control women's sexuality. State power depended upon negotiation for control of the patriarchal family:

> The patriarchal head of the family at the time of Hammurabi was still somewhat restrained in his power over his wife by kinship obligations to the male head of the wife's family. By the time of the Middle Assyrian Laws he is restrained mostly by the power of the state. Fathers, empowered to treat the virginity of their daughters as a family property asset, represent an authority as absolute as that of the king. Children reared and socialized within such authority will grow into the kinds of citizens needed in an absolutist kingship. . . . The archaic state was shaped and developed in the form of patriarchy. (Lerner, 1986, p. 253)

This negotiation between state and patriarch informs socioeconomic political systems to the present. Lerner's thesis that sexual regulation of women undergirds class formation and undergirds state power can also be applied to racial formations. Sexual regulation is a key component of racial segregation, and institutes a range of written and unwritten laws circumscribing women's lives. For example, because religious courts have jurisdiction over marriage and divorce in Israel, there is no legal basis for intermarriage between Jew and non-Jew. State policies reward Jewish women for having Jewish sons, particularly if they are *Ashkenazi* (a term meaning German–generally used to refer to Jews born in central Europe and their descendants).

In the 20th century, nations are carriers of gender and racial formations. While nationalist ideology has become a symbol of freedom from domination, of self-determination, it is critical to examine the "free" of this freedom, of this self-determination. Within capitalist–patriarchy, freedom is free enterprise. But competition within a system of free enterprise is circumscribed by a legal system that benefits those who control that system. Property rights, the right to territorial expansion, the right to control basic resources, are all assumed by the "free" of free enterprise to belong to the men of the ruling classes.

Similarly, "peace," "justice," and "equality" are cited as the goals of the nation–state, and of those supporting resolution of the Israeli-Palestinian conflict. But it is critical to examine those concepts within historical context, for the concepts themselves are occupied.

The history of man's relation to nature is connected both to the social construction of gender, and to race relations. Historian Carolyn Merchant has shown that the changing metaphor of nature in the 16th and 17th centuries in western Europe supported the interests of a rising class of entrepreneurs and industrialists. The new mechanistic view of nature, connected to the emerging view of "male–female biological generation where the female and the earth are both passive receptors," sanctioned the manipulation of nature and of women, and "could easily become sanctions for exploitation as the organic context was transformed by the rise of commercial capitalism" (Merchant, 1980, p. 16). The view of matter as inert, rather than as informed by an "animating spirit," supported manipulation of nature to suit the needs of industry. Merchant points to consequences of separation of nature and culture in traditional historical accounts. Androcentric history conceals the contiguity of the rise of democracy, the politics of capitalist economic institutions, and the exploitation of nature, of women, and of the colonies. Structural violence against women, and structural violence against the colonies, is the process of the "ongoing primitive accumulation of capital" (Mies, 1986, p. 170) of class and imperialist relations. "Women and colonial peoples were defined as property, as nature, not as free subjects. . . . Both had to be subordinated by force and direct violence" (Mies, 1986, p. 170).

Demonstrating that control of women's relationship to nature—to birth and to healing—was integral to the development of capitalist modes of production in 17th-century Europe, Carolyn Merchant shows that women's work was expropriated, as the emerging nation–state—in league with entrepreneurs, merchants, industrialists, and academicians—took control of the means of production. In this process, millions of women, midwives, and healers were burned as witches and heretics. As nature was put in constraint through the technologies of industrial development, so were women increasingly put in constraint, forced into economic and psychological dependence. Separating nature and women from culture, academicians and others justified development of methods designed to subdue both. Zionists would capitalize on this distinction, extolling the virtues of tilling the soil to justify exploitation of nature:

> The mysticism of tilling the soil, plowing mother earth to implant seed in her and make her fruitful once more, was exclusively male. And its masculine bias was natural to a generation born and bred in the shtetl and exposed, in the Jewish Enlightenment of the time, to such influences as Freud, Nietzsche and Weininger, with their stereotyped images of women as passive receptacle, contaminating weakness, or base necessity. Their overlay of socialism, with its credo of equality, was powerless against a deeply entrenched psychology of sexism and the men's painful sense of unmanliness to be redeemed. (Hazelton, 1977, pp. 93, 94)

Feminist philosopher Sarah Lucia Hoagland traces the emergence of enlightenment notions of equality to the rise of mercantilism and industrial capitalism (Hoagland, 1988). She connects enlightenment philosophy with the dualistic hierarchical split of Platonism, attributing the rational to the soul and the irrational to the body. Plato associated women with the appetites; men were able to achieve enlightenment because of a natural propensity toward the good, the moral, the rational, the just. Hoagland shows how the assumption that the "natural" state of humankind is "violent, aggressive, egoistic, and solitary" allows men to "maximize their self-interest if they were to give up some of their natural rights such as the right to pillage and plunder their neighbors to a central authority which could regulate pillaging and plundering, thus creating order and cooperation" (Hoagland, 1988, p. 250). Under "cooperative values" the state protects the hegemony of those in power; justice, then, maintains a system of hierarchy supporting male ruling class hegemony.

Merchant's work supports this thesis, showing that 17th-century "democratic" theories "based on atomistic equality for each individual in reality meant equality for middle and upper class property holding males" (Merchant, 1980, p. 214). She notes the work of Thomas Hobbes who, in the 17th century, maintained that the antidote to the natural state of anarchy that characterizes humankind is "peace," "order," "control" through a legal system prescribing the conduct of each citizen; prescribing in fact, who is a citizen. These laws, promulgated in the interest of ruling-class men, "promoted the peaceful, rational, civil behavior necessary to the conduct of business, industry, trade, navigation, arts, letters and culture" (Merchant, 1980, p. 214). Women, however, whose "lesser nature" makes them less fit for rational conduct, have to struggle for entry into these domains. In their struggle for equality, women remain under the authority and dominion of men.

The figure behind equality then is male. The figure behind justice is male. Peace prefigures war: that is, behind the figure of peace lies the continually warring nature of humankind that must be subdued. This humanist conceptualization becomes the justification for expropriation of and violence against nature and against women, and for unending accumulation of capital. It is justification both for violence against Palestinian women and men in the 20th century, and for a resolution to the conflict that will benefit the interests of those in control of capital accumulation.

In the name of cultural survival, the Israeli government is attempting to maintain an upper hand in control of natural resources—land, water, women— in the ongoing competition that characterizes misogynist economics. Given that violence against women is intrinsic to this "ongoing primitive accumulation of capital," the "fastest and most 'productive' method if a man wants to join the brotherhood of the free subjects of owners of private property" (Mies 1986, p. 170), it also becomes critical to examine what the "liberation" of the Palestinian liberation struggle will mean for women when its goals are realized.

In the 20th century, women are the backbone of the world industrial complex—the cheap labor force, on the assembly line, in the brothel, in the home, sustaining an outpouring of capital gains for the ruling classes. Nature's resources and women's bodies are endlessly exploitable mines. Disruption of woman's relationship to the land and expropriation of woman's sexuality and control over her body are the backbone of nationalism as it has emerged throughout history. The historical subjugation of nature and of women is intrinsically tied to the development of the modern nation–state as a carrier of misogynist economics. This book explores this history in order to show the ways that Jews and Arabs have participated in this process across class, gender, geography.

The phrase "Palestinians struggle for control of land" must be understood within the context of class, race, and gender. For example, Palestinian elites have a different historical relation to the land than do Palestinian peasants. The goals of differing groups of elites and of peasants for control of land may or may not overlap, both within and between class strata. Women within race–class and social–class context have different histories and sets of assumptions, visions, goals, possibilities, and privileges in relation to control of land. How those goals are conceptualized, and whether or not their respective visions can be realized, depends upon global politics. It depends upon how the Israeli-Palestinian conflict is resolved within the context of an international race, class, and gender division of labor, upon access to basic resources, and upon the prevailing view of nature, as that view supports social-economic-political organization.

ANTI-SEMITISM AND ANTI-FEMINISM

The language of imperial politics is sexual politics. The dualistic hierarchical separation of Arab and Jew parallels separation of world geography and world historical developments into an East and a West, as well as a North and a South. North American discourse hegemonizes western Europe and itself and elevates the European peninsula as if it were the center of the world (Hodgson, 1974). It associates the West with morality, advancement, good. The East, defined in relation to and from the perspective of the West, is associated with loose morals, backwardness, evil. These hierarchical dualities reflect antifeminist ideology propagating degradation of women, and fear of women's "evil powers" and "loose morals." Anti-Semitic ideology, applied to both Jew and Arab, effeminizes that which it seeks to destroy. The Semite is inherently evil and must be controlled. The first evil is woman. The first good is the God of the man in whose image man is created.

In the 17th century, as noted, the emerging class of industrialists seeking control of land and resources accumulated capital by robbing poor women of their means of subsistence and of their lives, characterizing them as evil, as witches whose mores were inimical to the social good (Merchant, 1980). Similarly, rulers in western Europe subjected Jews to cycles of expatriation in the process of accumulating capital to build the nation–state. The dissolution of the Ottoman Empire, connected to both internal and external factors, testifies to the imperial project of reducing the East to an exploitable land and resource base controlled by the then great powers of the West. Like nature, woman must be tamed: She is reduced to a virgin nature whose "chastity" is then "protected" by the men who, by planting their seed, inherit the right of descent or succession.

Harriet Goldberg's (1979) study of antifeminism and anti-Semitism in Hispanic literary tradition focuses on accusations of excessive sexuality, treachery, and demonism of Jew and women.

> The three principal areas are: lasciviousness, treachery, and involvement with the devil. First, both groups were thought to be sexually insatiable, practicing the ancillary sins of intemperance, gluttony, and drunkenness. They were thought to be treacherous, disloyal, and frequently deceitful in their dealing with others, which often led to their being stingy, avaricious, envious, and covetous. Both groups were said to be arms of the devil, and in consequence sacrilegious; they were practicers of witchcraft and capable of remarkable depravities. . . . Other similarities will emerge, but the central one is that both groups represented perils that threatened to weaken, damage, or even destroy the faith of a good Christian man. (Goldberg, 1979, p. 87)

Jews were also "given to overeating and overdrinking with the result that they were all obese" (Goldberg, 1979, p. 90). That is, Jews were fleshy, corporeal, earthy, like women—a sin against spirit; an ever-present temptation to violate God's (man's) ways.

If Jew and woman are by nature oversexed, then they must be desexed, subject to genital mutilation, castration, genocide. Goldberg points out that Christians admonished Jews, who practiced polygyny, for their marriage and lax divorce laws. While a man's prestige was heightened by the number of wives he had, it is also true that in many instances polygyny allowed more freedom for a woman, who was not under the constant surveillance of her husband. From this perspective Jews are indicted as men who cannot control their women. Independent women are a threat to national hegemony: "She also undermined the structure of society when her unquenchable desires led her to deceive her husband, since obviously no one man could bring her to a state of satiety" (Goldberg, 1979, pp. 92, 93).

The antifeminism of anti-Semitism is reflected in injunctions in the western Christian church against Semitic peoples, whether of the heterodox eastern Christian churches, Islam, or Judaism. Historians Helen and Alan Cutler maintain that an ignored but critical aspect of Christian anti-Semitism was the association of Jew and Muslim. Quoting church dogma, such as the statement by Peter the Venerable in the 12th-century Toletano-Clunia corpus, "A Jew is not a Jew until he converts to Islam," they cite evidence supporting the view that many medieval western Christians considered the Jew an ally of the Muslim and an Islamic fifth columnist in Christian territory (Cutler & Cutler, 1986, p. 2). Woman, Jew, Muslim are backward, irrational, mysterious, violent, exotic, manipulative, and preoccupied with controlling the world.

Antifeminist anti-Semitism of official Western discourse characterizes the Arab as wealthy sheik, deceitful, corrupt, secretly plotting to control the world, terrorist, rootless nomad, primitive. Similarly, the Jew is portrayed as deceitful and untrustworthy, with a mission to control the world. Jew, Arab, woman—all are blamed for economic hardship and all are variously punished across time and place.

In the 20th century, the recurring image of the ever-present threat of the petroleum-rich Arab nations to the industrialized West is an example of how antifeminist anti-Semitism conceals male bonding and the expropriation of basic resources by men. Janice Terry notes that:

> . . . the impression that the petroleum-rich Arab nations should be brought firmly under control of the industrialized west distorts the bilateral symbiotic or mutually dependent nature of petroleum exporting countries and large multinational companies. (Terry, 1985, p. 88)

Economic warfare between groups of men conceals the fact that all groups of men profit from the traffic in women undergirding a worldwide phallocentric economic–political system.

The prevailing view of the Palestinian propagated by the Israeli state is informed by anti-Semitic antifeminist ideology. "Palestinian," as does "woman," implies backward, deceitful, primitive, corrupt. The Jewish male, assumed to be European, then places himself on the opposite side of the duality, retrieving his masculinity. Jews from the Arab world, characterized as "Oriental," are considered primitive, in need of westernization and enlightenment. As such, they, along with Palestinian Arab Israeli citizens, are the largest segment of the poor within the class structure of Israeli society. The barriers that divide Israeli women unfold from the dualistic language used to describe them: European and Oriental; civilized and primitive; advanced and backward.

IDENTITY POLITICS: ANDROCENTRIC DISCOURSE

Those who consume stereotypes agree with them by the very act of taking them in over and over. Repetition of the same structure, meaning, and often, words, literally impresses upon the consumer of those messages, a type. We learn to think in types. This learning to think in types itself undergirds or creates identity politics . . . a language of repetition by means of which characteristics are ascribed and reified. The type becomes the goal, concealing (and congealing) the subject-as-actor. The subject is objectified, reified, identified, made over. This modality, "the language produced and spread under the protection of power" (Barthes, 1975, p. 40, in Wexler, 1982, p. 294), serves the needs of state control, by fostering hegemonic belief systems.

The use of the generic term *man* underlines all stereotyping: It is the classic explication of "enratic language (the language produced and spread under the protection of power)" (Barthes, 1975)—a language of repetition. The generic "man" is repeated in every structure of the language we use: language becomes androcentric discourse. The "I," the "we," the "people;" the logic—subject–verb–object—all repeat the "power over" of man.

Identity politics presumes a fixed set of characteristics that do not substantively change over time. Identity politics romanticizes the past, and romanticizes culture, encouraging and maintaining loyalty to a people, or to an idea of a people, or to a set of ideological presuppositions supporting a particular view of reality.

Current discourse in the West about the Israeli-Palestinian conflict is informed by the fixed idea of identity. Jews and Arabs as fixed identities view one another and themselves through this lens. Many Jews, for example, support and are supported by an identity rooted in a notion of history that describes the Jews as a people in exile. Some Jews support an identity based on concepts of justice inherent in Judaism: treat the stranger as your brother. These Jews often disclaim the acts of the Israeli government as "un-Jewish." From this perspective, or position, it becomes difficult if not impossible to take note of and learn from the range of political activities engaged in by Jews throughout the centuries. The assumption is that one has already taken responsibility for history by virtue of being a Jew. Furthermore, this position collapses all aspects of experience into the category "Jew," a strategy employed by Zionists to garner support for the Zionist project.

Another danger of an identity politics is the reduction of all historic-geographic experience to one aspect of historical experience. For example, persecution of the Jews has become the basis for an identity that often excludes rather than includes a sense of connectedness to others suffering persecution. The particular historical experience, if it belongs to a people in the sense of shaping an identity, can inhibit rather than encourage action both to analyze and to put an end to the causes of that suffering. It can inhibit the understanding that persecution is one aspect of a larger plan with a variety of motivations and victims. In this sense the end of this line of thinking is ahistorical, because it lifts oppression out of history, out of the context of time and place, and makes one particular set of experiences absolute.

Two points made by Israel Shahak, Israeli professor, Holocaust survivor, and political activist, illustrate the impact of identity politics, with its ahistorical reductionism, on the attitudes of many Israeli youth toward the Holocaust and toward Palestinians in the territories. Shahak notes the proliferation of Holocaust jokes among Israeli youth:

> . . . devoid of the tiniest conceivable bit of historical understanding, referring merely to abstracted features of the annihilation camps, like the gas, the ovens, the tattooed numbers or the electrified fences. . . . If quoted out of context, they would be regarded by an average foreign reader as products of some morbidly anti-semitic minds outside Israel; in reality, they are products of the minds of Israeli-educated youngsters, usually from good Jewish families of European descent, more upper or upper-middle-class than otherwise. (Shahak, 1989, p. 81)

Shahak's analysis of these jokes is that the youth are expressing scorn for their parents, many of whom are Holocaust survivors, and delight in profaning the "sacred" (i.e., victims of the Holocaust) (Shahak, 1989). In addition, their identities are shaped by association with the strong oppressor against the weak victim. This identification reflects the effects of a universally ingrained chauvinism reflected in polls that find significant numbers of Israeli youth supporting "racism, xenophobia and jingoism, together with . . . appetite for either expelling or exterminating 'national enemies' and, incidentally, grabbing their property" (Shahak, 1989, p. 81).

Many Israeli youth believe that because a Holocaust was perpetrated against Jews, Jews have the right to perpetrate a Holocaust against others. They are supported in this by the ahistorical view, assumed in the educational approach toward the Holocaust, that all Gentiles are enemies of all Jews. This approach can only be effective, even when it criticizes stereotyping, by attaching a set of fixed characteristics to a people. The no-win result of this is evidenced by the disdain that the Israeli youth cited above have for both Jews and Gentiles alike. In their minds, both have become caricatures.

Shahak also comments on a report by journalist Tom Segev about a kibbutz that became a center for research and documentation on the Holocaust, including a museum detailing Jewish armed struggle against the Nazis. The museum had been reserved one day a week for men enlisted in the army; but the army decided to discontinue this practice for two reasons. Follow-up interviews with men who toured the museum established that some soldiers "were inclined towards even greater racism and brutality when on duty in the occupied territories" (Shahak, 1989, p. 80). Others, on the contrary, were swayed toward refusing to carry out orders in the territories.

> . . . some female officers who had conducted the tours and the follow up talks with the soldiers made a convenient scapegoat for, allegedly, misguiding the soldiers by connecting the Holocaust "too much" with present-day politics. (Shahak, 1989, p. 80)

According to Segev, the army arranged the tours in order to utilize the Holocaust as combat motivation as well as to:

> . . . learn something about respecting other human beings, about the rights of minorities and about the limits of obedience—all this without telling the soldiers explicitly what kind of attitudes are expected from them. (Shahak, 1989, pp. 80, 81)

In fact, Israeli youth who defy the psychology of utilizing the Holocaust as combat motivation, face denigration and imprisonment. The Israeli army is the breeding ground for an identity politics that enforces the "inevitability" of the dualisms of winner and loser, conquerer and victim, strong and weak. The army supports phallocentric policies; men are brute force and have license to utilize whatever means necessary to prove it: "In the [Israeli] army . . . the properly trained sadistic impulses of both young and older men are given totally free rein" (Shahak, 1989, p. 83). Israeli and Palestinian women, victims of violence in the home and in the streets, bear witness to this fact.

In 1987, 20 Jews broke into an apartment of two Arabs following a quarrel in the streets of the Tel Aviv suburb where they lived. They threw one of the Arabs out of a second-story window and later returned to burn the apartment building. In recounting this use of brute force, Middle East commentator Joel Beinin points out a tragic irony of identity politics:

> In a bizarre twist underscoring the mythological character of the politics of national identity, evidence presented at the trial of the Jewish assailants two years later revealed that according to Jewish religious law the two Arab victims are actually "Jews" because their mother is a Jew and their father is an Arab. (Beinin, 1989, p. 214)

Identity is utilized by the state to maintain the loyalty of its citizens. To have an identity is to belong in a system that rewards those who accept and support state rules and punishes those who defy them. Middle East scholar Edward Said makes this point, asserting that the state creates terrorists by proclaiming who is within acceptable bounds (of identity) and who is outside those boundaries:

> Terrorism in short must be directly connected to the very processes of identity in modern society, from nationalism, to statism, to cultural and ethnic affirmation, to the whole array of political, rhetorical, educational and governmental devices that go into consolidating one or another identity. One belongs, either to one group or another; one is either in or out; one acts principally in support of a triumphalist identity or to protect an endangered one. (Said, 1988, p. 54)

The state-created "terrorist," whose political convictions, whose impulses to act to save herself or himself from destruction, are rendered invisible by the ahistorical propaganda of the state, is without meaning—other than as terrorist. She or he is reduced to a form of state property.

To the Israeli government Palestinians are, in this modality, like women everywhere, terrorists who are acceptable by virtue of their identity cards. Those who are caught without an identity card are arrested, detained, beaten. All over the world, women carry around the identity card of dress code, accepted association with men, manners, politics. Women are the permanent terrorists who subsume their actual experience under the guise of complicity, of allegiance to "womanhood."

WOMEN'S ASSOCIATIONS: CROSSING BOUNDARIES

Life in the Middle Eastern lands has been shaped by the creative impact of cultural assimilation among and between women, both within and outside the parameters of social constructions of ethnicity, race, and culture. Behind the Arab and Jew of androcentric history vibrates a genealogy (as defined by feminist scholar Janice Raymond) of associations among women ". . . an ongoing testament and testimony of women as acting subjects who, in relation to their vital Selves and each other, have created passion, purpose, and politics" (Raymond, 1986, p. 21).

In her philosophy of female friendship, Janice Raymond describes the intent of genealogical tracing of female friendships. This tracing counters the "cultural or historical relativism whose effect is to divide women from their Selves and each other" (Raymond, 1986, p. 24). According to Raymond, "The most blatant obstacle to female friendship is the prevailing patriarchal adage that 'women are each other's worst enemies' " (Raymond, 1986, p. 151). Capitalists also have a history of perpetrating an ideology of hatred between ethnic and racial groups, fostering divisions as a means of controlling labor. These two facets of capitalist–patriarchy are related: separation of women, whose survival is dependent upon the men with whom they are associated, disrupts a central focus of intercommunality. In both cases, biological determinism is utilized as a mode of social control. The notion of intrinsic enmity between women and between ethnic and racial groups—the conceptual framework of Jew versus Arab, dualistic and hierarchical and assuming an eternal and biological enmity—serves the institutionalization of economic systems supporting the interests, power, and gain of ruling classes of men. The "principal men" inherit the earth.

"The task of Gyn-affective scholarship is to save Gyn-affective women and deeds from the futility that comes from oblivion—oblivion not only from lack of recognition but from the wrong kind of recognition" (Raymond, 1986, p. 147). Raymond defines Gyn-affection as "personal and political movement of women toward each other" (Raymond, 1986, p. 8). Focusing on women's relation to the ancient and current history of Israel–Palestine brings into the foreground those issues most central to the possibilities and limitations between Palestinians—Jews, Muslims, Christians, and others—and European Jews. Resolution of the current crisis must begin with rejection of all ideologies that declare women and nature the property and domain of, and adjunct to, men. Resolution can come about as industry, science, education, and the state are transformed by the forces they seek to objectify and control. Speaking about the connection between destruction of the ecosystem and violence against women, environmentalist Patricia Hynes puts it this way:

> The same mechanisms used by science to control nature are used to dominate women in science and by science. They are hierarchy of being, objectification, fragmentation, devitalizing and silencing, elimination of diversity, pitting the economy as the indicator of the "well-being of mankind" against the integrity and well-being of women and nature" (Hynes, 1989, p. 25).

ANDROCENTRIC MAPS

The ancient kinship of Jewish, Muslim, and Christian Arab in the Middle East is ignored and misinterpreted in the West. Educational materials on the Middle East tend to be "oversimplified, naive and distorted" (Griswold, 1975, p. 1). Eurocentric biases in education are reflected in the lack of information and the distortion of the historical relation of those women and men most central to the Israeli-Palestinian conflict. It is crucial to examine, then, the extent to which nationalist ideology creates, fosters, and utilizes those distortions.

For example, the Zionist movement propagated the Eurocentric myth that Palestine was barren before the Jewish settlers of the early Zionist movement arrived. This notion, popular among Jews in North America, reduces Jewish history to the history of Jews in Europe. It is also a form of historic genocide in that it renders Palestinians invisible.

This mythology reveals two interrelated aspects of phallocentric politics. The Jew, insofar as "he" has been "effeminized" by anti-Semitic ideology, proves his virility by planting his seed. Here nature is defined as woman, and woman as a nature whose "salvation" is the "coming" of man.

Second, the notion that Palestine was barren before the Zionists arrived renders invisible women who for centuries have inhabited the geographic area of Palestine–Israel. Whether affiliated with Hebrew tribes, with women's cults within or outside those tribes, with the many sects of early Christianity, or with movements supporting or refuting Islam, women have been a central force in shaping the course of historical developments affecting the region.

The Palestine of today is a territorial unit created to facilitate control of the region by Britain, France, and now, the United States. Ancient Palestine, once part of the province of Roman Arabia, is now divided among five nations: Egypt, Israel, Jordan, Saudi Arabia, and Syria (Bowerstock, 1988). Historiography reflects the imperialist perspective. For example the land of Canaan, according to most Jewish historians, was invaded and subdued by the Israelites. The Book of Joshua describes how a confederacy of Yahwist tribes subdued the peoples of Transjordan through the central hill regions to the north of Galilee (Reuther, 1989). This historical "fact," informed by the superior/inferior model of dualistic hierarchy, serves the evolution of Jewish identity politics. On the other hand, theologian and historian Rosemary Reuther notes that the invasion of Canaan was probably an ancient peasant revolt that included the Canaanite peoples (Reuther, 1989). Tribal unity was created by allegiance to the sole cult God, Yahweh, and represented a power struggle among rival tribal monarchies that took place gradually, and that took hold only after a long period of time (Reuther, 1989).

Androcentric maps tell the story of men's exploits from the perspective of the ruling classes. In a cave in the Judean desert, Israeli archaeologist Yigael Yadin discovered documents describing harmonious relations between Jews and Arab tribes in the region south of the Dead Sea. Yadin's discoveries were kept from the public for 25 years. The 35 documents detail, over a period of 40 years, the legal affairs of a Jewish woman named Babatha, who fled into the wilderness during the Jewish revolt against Roman rule in the reign of Hadrian (132–135 C.E.). Babatha and her family witnessed the transition of the province of Arabia to a Roman province. The documents attest to the "social coherence that mirrored the administrative and geographic unity" (Bowerstock, 1988, pp. 185, 186).

There is a connection between suppression of this material and the fact that the Israeli state might have an interest in preserving the theological-historical notion of Jew and Arab as abstract groups and as eternal enemies (Bowerstock, 1988). Suppression of materials that give us insight into women's lives of this period serves a related purpose, contributing to the theological-historical notion of male superiority by the continued repetition of male visibility and female invisibility. Distortion of the historical relationship between Arab and Jew is supported by suppression of women in history and of women's associations that supported intertribal, intercommunal relations. Nationalist history, the progression of ruling empires, warring factions, and ethnic-racial rivalries prevail as a way of viewing geography.

Throughout history, the effects on women and on women's participation in the struggle between rival empires for control of Palestine, have been central to relations between Israelites and other Arab tribes. To give a brief overview, as early as the third millenium the land of Canaan was controlled by adjacent empires in Egypt or from the northeast, Assyria, Babylonia, Persia, and then from the northern Mediterranean, the Roman–Byzantine Empire. The ancient province of Rome, known as Arabia Petraea, in the southeastern corner of the Mediterranean, encompassed the Sinai peninsula, Negev desert, both sides of the Jordan River, southern Syria and the Hejaz, northeast Saudi Arabia (Bowerstock, 1988). In the second century, the Roman emperors gave the name "Palaestina" to the parts of Arabia Petraea known as Canaan and Judea. The Roman–Byzantine government divided Palestine into three units: Judea and Samaria and southern Jordan Valley; eastern and central Galilee and parts of the Jordan Valley; and southern Transjordan, the Negev and Sinai (Porath, 1975). The Arab Muslims administered the provinces of Palestine from the imperial centers of Baghdad, Damascus, and Cairo. For 200 years Palestine was subject to the Crusaders: it was ruled by the Mamluks from Egypt from 1291 to 1517. From 1517 to 1918, the Ottomans, or Turkish Muslims, ruled the eastern Arab provinces, including Gaza, Jerusalem, and Nablus, in the province of Damascus.

Arab chiefs were first recorded by Assyrians in alliance with Israelites in an expedition in 854 B.C.E. against the king of Damascus (Abbott, 1941). Israelites and other Arab tribes were affected by changes in ruling empires, and alliances were formed both in resistance and accommodation to external intervention. Located in the Syrian desert, settlements of Arab tribes were a buffer between Rome and Persia, which manipulated tribal animosities to win allies. For example, from the 3rd century until 602, Jewish communities at Hirah near the Euphrates were controlled by the Lakhmids, Arab vassal princes of

Sassanian Persia (Baron, 1983). Wars between Empires stimulated rivalry between tribes for wealth through control of important trade routes.

Records from the seventh century B.C.E. note the activities of Arab queens, as well as kings, of the North Arabian Arab states. Arab queens influenced developments among and between tribes and ruling empires. They founded and administered states and led armies in defense of their domains. The Judaic-Islamic world was shaped by traditions of ancient Babylonia, Egypt, and Persia; by the administrative language of the Assyrians, Aramaic, as well as by the customs and practices of Hellenism. It was shaped by the visions, practices, and customs of women creating, reacting to, and sustaining traditions in concert and in contradiction to the tenets of rival male rulers within and outside their domains.

This book is not a comprehensive history of the Judaic-Arabic-Islamic heritage. My purpose is to develop a feminist interpretation of historical developments informed by recognition that women are central to those developments as actors and as instruments in the advance of phallocentric politics shaping the course of current relations between Arab and Jew. What is presented here is a call for an urgently needed revisioning of political discourse and historiography in regard to the Israeli-Palestinian war.

Chapter One
The Intifada: Women on the Journey Through Colonization

I sat through the video with anguish. Steve York travels with a medical health team on one of their regular excursions into a village in the West Bank. The road is blocked by huge boulders put there by the Israeli army; villagers cannot leave for treatment. The team makes the arduous climb into these rocky hills hoping soldiers won't confront them, but they do. It takes two hours of negotiations before they are allowed in.

There are two women and three men with this team. They treat complications from tear-gas inhalation and gunshot wounds from live ammunition, as well as from rubber and plastic bullets manufactured in the United States. Often, because Palestinians in the West Bank do not have access to medical care, these injuries have gone untreated for too long and are far more serious than they would have been if treated promptly. One team member gives first-aid information to a group of women. The women are given kits with bandages and antiseptic solution to help with immediate care. In the discussion of treating tear-gas inhalation, the women make it clear that they have learned how to deal with tear gas out of necessity.

York takes us with the medical team into a hospital. The victims are men with fractured arms and legs and bodies covered with dark bruises from beatings. One man had lost his leg because an Israeli hospital released him without proper treatment. Patients are repeatedly released too soon and without adequate means of caring for injuries. Twenty-two percent of the injured are women, with the same types of injuries. On several occasions this medical team, like others, has been detained and its members arrested. Today, driving home in their van, they are singing about freedom.

In January 1988 with over 40,000 injured, the need for emergency medical treatment in the occupied territories was critical. The Union of Palestinian Medical Relief Committees (1988) created Emergency Medical Relief Committees and in the first year of the intifada, treated more than 80,000 Palestinians, including approximately 4,000 with injuries caused by shootings, beatings, and tear-gas inhalation. They distributed 17,000 medical kits throughout the West Bank and Gaza (Union of Palestine Medical Relief Committees, 1988).

On the return trip, the van is flagged down by a man whose son has an injury that had been stitched but is now swelling and painful. The army forced their way into his home and broke everything in sight. The soldiers turned to the women, struck them, and then pulled down their pants, exposing themselves. The father says, "Shameful, they are shameful."

DISMEMBERMENT AND OCCUPATION
A VIEW FROM ABOVE: EFFECTS BELOW

The goals of Israeli occupation today continue the process of dismemberment, fragmentation, and co-optation that governed the San Remo Conference in 1920, when Great Britain and France divided up the geographic areas of Greater Syria, Mount Lebanon, and the areas east and west of the Jordan River. West of the Jordan River the British created a new geographic entity, the "mandate," under their control until it became the state of Israel. The area east of the Jordan River was designated Transjordan, and administered by the government of King Faisal from 1918 to 1920, when it was given to his brother, Abdullah, subject to mandatory control. Geographic boundaries between Iraq, Palestine, and Transjordan were delineated by Anglo-French agreements in 1920 and 1922, arbitrarily dividing Arab communities from one another (Antonious, 1946; Hourani, 1946; "Palestine," 1947).

After the 1948 to 1949 Arab–Israeli War, Abdullah annexed East Jerusalem and those areas of central Palestine not in the hands of the Israelis, designated as the "West Bank," to the state he now called the Hashemite Kingdom of Jordan. During the 19 years of Jordanian rule, there was a high rate of unemployment in the West Bank and no significant industrial development. Captured in the 1967 war by the Israeli army, the West Bank continues to this day to suffer from policies implemented to deter independent economic development. They include confiscation of land and water, deportations and resettlement, discriminatory tax laws, trade restrictions, prohibition of industrial developments, and military hegemony in the name of security.

The Israeli Defense Force maintains the territories as "defensive outposts," a means to ". . . alter the hostile intentions of our Arab neighbors" (Ma'oz, 1984, p. 62). With these aims in mind, in October 1978 after the Camp David accords, the government produced a comprehensive 5-year plan for settlement of "Judea" and "Samaria" (the biblical names used by some Jews to refer to the West Bank). Their objective was to create Jewish enclaves among the 800,000 Palestinian inhabitants. The result has been massive loss of land by Palestinians and their replacement on that land by tens of thousands of Israeli and American Jews attracted by subsidized housing and supported by pioneer zealots. Statements of government officials since 1947 make it clear that the issue of security is a smokescreen for expansion. In a December 1948 diary entry, David Ben-Gurion wrote that ". . . an Arab state in Western Palestine (that is, West of the Jordan) would be less dangerous than a state linked to Transjordan, and maybe tomorrow to Iraq" (Chomsky, 1990, p. 52). In 1990, 6,000 to 7,000 Israelis moved to the occupied territories, bringing the settler population in the West Bank and Gaza Strip to over 90,000 (Brinkley, 1990).

Laws operating in Israel do not apply to Palestinians in the occupied territories who since 1967 have been subject to Israeli military regulations based on the Defense Emergency Regulations, instituted by the British in 1945 against Jews and Arabs. These regulations sanction detention without charge and trial by military tribunal. Detainees can be held for a year without review, and then their detention can be renewed. Detention centers are tent camps with open sewers and a lack of food, medical care, adequate clothing, or access to legal assistance. Despite the fact that these regulations have been declared illegal by the Geneva Convention Relative to the Treatment of Civilian Persons in Time of War and by the United Nations Universal Declaration of Human Rights, the Israeli government continues to sanction their use.

Palestinians living in refugee camps in the territories suffer squalid and dangerous living conditions: overcrowding, inadequate shelter and food supplies, lack of sewerage systems, and lack of support facilities. In addition, Palestinians in camps are subject to constant military surveillance, demolition of homes, separation from family and friends, detention, imprisonment, and deportation.

Between December 9, 1987, and September 30, 1990, 851 [sic] Palestinians, including 96 women, died at the hands of Israelis. Of this number, 708 were shot, 64 died from nonbullet causes, and 89 deaths were tear-gas related. An estimated 101,550 Palestinians were injured. Most injuries resulted in life-long disability. More than 10,000 Palestinians, including 2,000 women, were arrested and detained. In the West Bank, 3,955 days of curfew were imposed; in the Gaza Strip, 3,888. Over 92,000 trees were uprooted. More than 1,000 houses and structures were sealed and demolished (Palestine Human Rights Information Center, 1990).

While soldiers were previously allowed to shoot only masked youth armed with knives, axes, metal bars, or other weapons, in August 1989 soldiers were ordered to shoot Palestinian youth who ignored calls to halt once warning shots had been fired. Along with plastic bullets, a high-velocity "improved" bullet had been introduced, which contains a metal marble rather than a rubber bullet. Both bullets are fired from tubes attached to rifles that were introduced in March 1989 and are capable of firing 16 bullets at a time at speeds much more dangerous than conventional rifles. Over 250 Palestinians, some as young as 4 months old, have lost eyes from rubber bullets, and many have lost their vision as a result of head injuries (Lempert, 1990).

In June, July, and August of 1989, in a pattern that has been escalating since the beginning of the Intifada, more than 57 Palestinian women were denied resident status and deported. Over 200 children were expelled with them or separated from their mothers (*The Other Israel*, 1989). Women are often rounded up in the middle of the night and given no time to collect belongings or notify relatives. They have been denied the Israeli identity cards necessary for residency in the occupied territories. These cards were available through the family reunification program, but the Israeli army has stopped processing applications for them. Women in their 80s have been deported to Jordan; many have no relatives there and are unable to read or write.

Hundreds of thousands of Palestinians in villages, refugee camps, and cities are daily placed under curfew and are unable for hours, sometimes weeks, at a time to obtain food and water. Livestock cannot be fed and are left to wander. Villagers are not allowed to harvest crops, which are left to rot.

Since the start of the intifada, universities and elementary schools have been closed. Kindergartens operated by Working Women's Committees have been tear-gassed and closed down.

Health problems in the occupied territories are exacerbated by these conditions. Most villages, for example, have no source of clean water. While water is piped to settlers, the water source used by Palestinians is open and must be used for cleaning as well as drinking.

Women are a target of policies designed to demoralize, dispossess, harass, and destroy Palestinian Arabs in the occupied territories. More than 2,000 Palestinian women were arrested between 1967 and 1979, before the current stage of resistance, the intifada (Antonious, 1980). These women, including school-age children and elderly women, were arrested, detained, interrogated, sexually abused, humiliated, and tortured (Antonious, 1980). In the current stage of resistance, the detention, interrogation, and torture of Palestinian women is routine. By the end of 1989, 78 women had been killed, many in demonstrations, some as they were outside hanging their wash, or on their way to school.

WHAT IS LIBERATION FOR WOMEN?

Women and Health: Occupation

Salwa Najjab is a Palestinian and Muslim, born in Ramallah on the west bank of the Jordan River. Tonight she is speaking to a group in western Massachusetts, one stop in a 2-month tour on behalf of the organization of Israeli and Palestinian Physicians and the Union of Palestinian Medical Relief Committees. She is a gynecologist and a founder of the Women's Health Project.

Najjab received her medical education in the Soviet Union. In an effort to restrict the population of Palestinians, Egypt closed universities to them after the 1967 war. Palestinians then attended universities in the Soviet Union and other socialist countries, where they were welcomed. Najjab studied economics until a Jewish woman, her professor, encouraged her to pursue medical training for the benefit of her people. With this training, she participated in creating an independent health-care system with services for the first time designed to meet the needs of women.

In her "Notes on Women and Health in Occupied Palestine," Najjab explains the critical need for a health-care system designed for women. Because most data on health conditions do not distinguish between men and women, the particular problems of women remain invisible. But, clinically, women suffer from more disease, and women and children, who comprise 70% of the population, are more at risk of disease and dying (Najjab, 1989).

Najjab analyzes the situation of women within the context of nationalist struggle and within the context of class and gender exploitation. What are the health conditions of Palestinian women living under military rule?

Primary health-care services, already deficient, have deteriorated under occupation. Outside the green line (an unofficial designation for the boundaries of Israel before the 1967 war), there are no basic health services for women. Health care is available only to those who can afford the high costs prevailing within the Palestinian private sector, excluding most women who live in rural areas and refugee camps, where 70% of the population lives (Najjab, 1989).

During periods of curfew imposed by the military, women often risk their lives getting food and water for themselves and their families. Access to health facilities is prohibited. Homes are demolished daily. Anyone suspected of resistance activities—and this includes the entire Palestinian population—can expect to lose shelter, food, and basic survival needs. Soldiers detain and arrest women whether or not they are involved in nationalist activities: they attempt to locate husbands and sons by torturing wives, sisters, daughters. The tactics of the army make it clear that women are at risk because they are women, as well as for the "crime" of being Palestinian: the two are linked.

Reports from the Women's Organization for Political Prisoners (WOFPP) are published monthly. Formed in Tel Aviv in May 1988 to ". . . defend the human and democratic rights of Palestinian and Israeli women imprisoned because of their social and political activity in the legitimate struggle against the occupation" (Women for Support of Political Prisoners, 1989, p. 3), this organization of Israeli women in alliance with Palestinian women has taken on the critical function of documenting crimes against Palestinian women under occupation. The largest detention center for women from Jerusalem and the West Bank is the Russian Compound, run by Jerusalem police. In a 1990 report, *B'tselem*, the Israeli Information Center for Human Rights in the occupied territories, detailed conditions in the Russian Compound ". . . which do not meet the most minimal requirements of humane imprisonment" (American-Israeli Civil Liberties Coalition, Inc., 1990, p. 5). The Security Service or SHABAK, housed at the Russian Compound, carries out investigations involving forced confessions, isolation, torture. Detainees, often not allowed to see their lawyers, are pressured by verbal and physical assault to sign documents written in Hebrew, a language most women do not know. Women are hostages of the security forces, often detained as bait to capture husbands or sons or brothers, or because they live in poverty and cannot pay fines imposed on children. WOFPP addresses itself to the detainees' ". . . personal and physical well being, defending their human rights and personal dignity," as well as supporting families and bringing cases to the public (Women for Support of Political Prisoners, 1989, p. 3).

The connection between military conquest and sexual conquest, hidden and undefined in most accounts of the nationalist struggle, is nowhere more evident than in these reports. They are the testimony of war as rape and of the link between rape of the earth and rape of the daughters of the earth. Land and women torn asunder, exploited, desecrated in the name of progress, are nationalism's products.

In a similar manner, violence perpetrated to "protect" the "purity" of the nation is one of nationalism's products. Soldiers expose themselves in front of Palestinian women on the streets, in home searches, and in demonstrations to scare the women off. A soldier removes his pants and places a Palestinian flag on his genitals in front of a group of women (WOFPP, 1989, May). A gathering of women is a show of strength to be targeted and dissolved.

Nablus, March 25, 1989. Six soldiers beat a 14-year-old girl on her breasts and genitals. One of the soldiers tells her that he would do whatever he wished to her if she screamed or tried to run away (WOFPP, 1989, May).

On May 12, a 70-year-old Palestinian woman sets out for Jordan on pilgrimage to Mecca. As she approaches the Allenby Bridge she is surrounded by soldiers, arrested, undressed, and her body searched. For 8 days she is held in the Russian Compound in solitary confinement in a tiny, filthy cell. This woman, 70 years old, is hit on the chest, thrown on the floor, and kicked in the stomach. She is accused of hiding a note in her vagina. She is told that she will be thrown into a large sewer. She is made to listen to suggestive remarks about her sexual organs and those of her husband. Her family does not know that this is happening, and under continuous curfew, they could not help if they did (WOFPP, 1989, June).

At 2 and 3 a.m. soldiers raid villages: over the loudspeaker they blare sexist oaths and curses. Daily, border police attempt rape, beat and sexually intimidate Palestinian women.

Five Palestinian women file a complaint against border policemen who beat and sexually assaulted them on October 19, 1988. From the time of filing the complaint they are continually harassed. One woman suffers a miscarriage during administrative detention. Her husband is arrested and her house disrupted daily by soldiers. A medical report detailing the injuries of the women is missing (WOFPP, 1989, June).

Prison officials hold a 16-year-old, Layaly, threaten her with rape, beat her on her breasts and genitals. They try to push a club between her legs and tear the zipper of her trousers. They handcuff and shackle her. She is singing with her friend, Jamila; as punishment, her tooth is broken. Later Jamila is removed from her cell and told that Layaly is dead. She persists in asking about her friend. For the crime of friendship, she is tied to an iron bar and beaten. Then they transfer her to another prison to await trial (WOFPP, 1989, June).

Mariam Ali Musa Isma'il, 27, is a Palestinian woman from the village of al-Khader near Bethlehem in the West Bank. She is secretary-general of the Palestinian women's committees for the Bethlehem area. For the crime of organizing in an effort to provide basic survival needs for women, she is detained at a roadblock, held for 31 days in detention, tortured, and served with a 6-month administrative detention order. Under administrative detention she is not allowed to leave her home; she is under constant surveillance (WOFPP, 1988, May).

Palestinian women insist upon visibility. With Israeli women they defy policies prohibiting speech, prohibiting intra- and intercommunal association among women. How will their words be read? Will women and men rise up in outrage, rise up to support and to defend them, to stop this spiral of violence?

One response to that question lies in the cover stories of newspapers and periodicals in the United States as these words are being written. In another courtroom, perhaps not so far removed from the Israeli courtroom, the "faceless" Central Park jogger is helped up to the witness seat where she will testify to a crime so brutal that her psyche has erased all memory of it. But the memory lives on in her unsteady gait: she has lost her ability to balance herself as she walks. Sex crimes often penetrate the body leaving the brain numb; knowledge is buried under layers of protective devices saturating a woman's words, actions, possibilities, daily life. A 21-year-old woman, not Palestinian, but "white," jogs through Central Park in New York City on an April evening. Though worlds apart from her Palestinian sister perhaps, like her, she had gone out to breathe cool night air, to weigh the strength of her body against the closure that restricts women all over the world from free access to the night. Maybe she allowed herself to feel joy in the steady rhythm of the running, not away from, but in search of health and harmony. Does her breath change, stop for a moment, when for a lightning second she faces a death with no mercy . . . when suddenly she sees a gang of soldiers, of men, lurching toward her: before she is suddenly struck in the back with a bullet . . . when for a lightning second she realizes once again, or for the first time, or perhaps for the last, that she is target; that she is prey?

She is attacked by a gang of men who beat her senseless with a lead pipe, who rape her repeatedly. The New York City police, notorious for their racism, as most police forces are, arrest three African-American men who "confess" to involvement in the crime. Now it appears that the country is not sure whether this is a crime of sex or of race. Some reporters, defending the men against a history of racist accusations of crimes, put it this way: she could have had sex in her apartment before she went out to jog. Is this the same rationale as: Jews went willingly, passively, into the ovens?

In a November 7, 1990, *Guardian* editorial, "Jogger rape: Ask a Black feminist," feminist scholar Barbara Smith points to the predominantly racist reaction of the media, while making the following point:

> The fact that the racist media leapt in with their lynch-mob mentality, however, does not mean that there is nothing more to examine and that sexual violence in the Black community does not need to be addressed. It is true that the media ignores rapes and murders of women of color (some of which happened on the very same night as the Central Park attack), but what this indicates is not just the racism of the white establishment, but that the ruling class views all violence against women as trivial.

She critiques those whose focus on the racist reactions to the April 1989 rape, for which three African American men were convicted, leads them to ignore the consequences and the causes of violence against women in the Black community.

The Central Park jogger is a woman alone; globally, she is prey. Yet, had the issue not been white against black, her trauma would not have been front-page news. Janice Raymond underscores this point in a May 25, 1989, editorial in the *Greenfield Recorder:*

> In the national media during this same time period, we have been treated to the story of battered Hedda Nussbaum, the nine serial rape killings of women in New Bedford, the recent rape attack of a woman in Central Park, and the rape brutalization of a Harlem woman atop a housing project, who was then thrown off the roof and somehow lived to tell about it. Perhaps you missed that last one since the woman was black, and the media covered it as a one-time story on page 16. (Raymond, 1989, p. 8)

Dust settles in Rafah Refugee Camp, in the town of Nablus, in the city of Akko. A 21-year-old Palestinian woman lies beneath a clothesline, blood trickling from her body. With each bullet, each beating, each threat of rape, white male supremacy triumphs. Not as nature, but as act. Not all men everywhere, but each man in the act of pulling the trigger, of waving the banner of the phallocracy in her face.

With each WOFPP report, new detainees. Samira, 19, from Silwan, a neighborhood of Jerusalem, stands outside her home visiting with neighbors. Soldiers driving by see "a crowd of Palestinians." For the crime of engaging with one another, she is sprayed with rubber bullets. She sustains seven bullet wounds in her legs, is hospitalized, treated, and returns home a day later. Three hours after she returns, she is back in prison, accused of throwing stones at soldiers. Is she unsteady as they lead her to the witness stand . . . has she lost her ability to balance herself as she walks?

Establishing Health Projects

What are the health conditions of Palestinian women living under military occupation? What are the health conditions of women globally living under occupation? What services are available to them? Who is listening to, hearing, responding to, their words?

The consequences of occupation on the health status of women are documented by the Women's Health Project. One of the organizers is a Palestinian woman who states that women's health depends upon recognition of connections between three factors: nationalist struggle, poverty resulting from class oppression, and gender oppression (Najjab, 1989). Girl babies suffer from health problems that are not experienced by their brothers. Mothers who neglect their girl children have, according to Najjab, learned that when it is a question of limited resources, the men come first, since it is they who have access to economic power. Men have the ability to provide for their mothers in their old age. Under occupation, with no state benefits, no social security benefits, this problem is exacerbated (Najjab, 1989).

When visiting a village to treat the population for tear-gas inhalation and a range of wounds sustained in the conflict, Najjab speaks with women who come to her complaining that their husbands, having other wives, treat them badly. Najjab, understanding this as another critical aspect of women's health, advises them that this is a situation they do not have to accept.

The Women's Health Project documents that the incidence of cancer among Palestinian women is rising, as it is among women globally. In the small town in western Massachusetts where Najjab speaks, a 27-year-old woman dies an agonizing death of ovarian cancer. An incest victim, she asserted to the end that this crime is what killed her. Within a year, two more cases of womb cancer strike this woman's community.

Denial, numbing, torpor, neglect, defense of institutions that protect women's purity: all forms of dis-ease that pervade women's lives under occupation. Living in the colonizing divisions, the fabrication of a politics seemingly divorced from gender politics, divorced from spirit, women read newspapers that tell them: race or sex, the one or the other, Jew or Arab, Palestinian women or Jewish women, protect the home by staying off the streets.

Women are socially at a disadvantage in Palestinian society, notes Najjab. Women, the newspapers do *not* note in reporting the trial of the Central Park Jogger case, are socially at a disadvantage in every society living under the terrorism of male supremacy, of androcentric rule.

Against the background of daily terrorism, the Women's Health Project began establishing health projects for women in the West Bank and Gaza Strip. Within two years they had developed the following:

- Provision of primary maternal and child health services as a matter of course
- Education for mothers to improve their health status and that of their children, especially girls
- The right to easily accessible basic health services at affordable costs for women, not just for those who live in urban areas and who can afford good service
- Pap smear testing
- Training of village women to become community health workers with access to women in remote rural areas and refugee camps
- Prenatal and postnatal services, and family planning
- Education of communities about the importance of caring for their daughters' health and education
- Collection of baseline data on health conditions in various sectors of Palestinian society.

Sexual Subjugation/Seizure of the Land

While these projects of the Women's Health Project are ongoing, so is the brutal subjugation of the Palestinian body—targeted through sexual subjugation and seizure of the land. A statement by a 20-year-old Palestinian woman about her experience at the Moscobiyeh interrogation center encapsulates the tactics utilized:

> One time an interrogator put his legs on the chair on either side of me and boxed me on the ears until I couldn't hear any more and brought in my father and told him to strip and make love to me. "She isn't your daughter, she's your wife, go on, sleep with her." My father screamed and they beat him till he lost consciousness; blood was pouring from my mouth and nose and I couldn't hear any more. . . . Another time they stripped me and took me to a room where men were suspended from the ceiling. They handcuffed me to the hooks in the ceiling—it was a pulley system which could be raised and lowered—and they chained my feet to the ground, wide apart, and raised me so only the tips of my toes touched the ground. They said they had been going to rape me but I was too dirty for them and they would instead get some prisoners who hadn't seen a woman for a long time. I used to curse them as long as I was conscious. (Cox, 1984, p. 26)

The technology of torture makes use of pornography, of sexual fantasy based on the helplessness of the child against the power of the father; woman as crime, as dirt, as victim, as whore; all speak to the sexualization of race that characterizes male supremacy. By the time that she is 23 years old, one Palestinian woman born into a refugee camp in the Gaza Strip will have witnessed and experienced the demolition of her parents' house by the Israeli army who brought charges against one of her brothers; the murder of her husband; arrest, along with her two children, on a charge of aiding members of an illegal organization and illegal possession of firearms; constant interrogation, sexual harassment, severe beatings; deprivation of sleep for five to six days; being systematically choked four to five times a day over a period of three days. She is removed by one interrogator to a separate room with no policewoman present (in violation of regulations—policy is that women police women), forced to sit in a corner with her head wedged between the interrogator's legs while he touches her, verbally abuses her, threatens her with rape, and evidently reaches sexual climax. On another occasion a different interrogator exposes himself in front of her, this time with both another interrogator and a policewoman present (WOFPP, 1989, February). These tools, these strategies, are legal, are what the legal system protects. These tools and strategies are what defines who she is. They are sanctioned because sex as conquest is sanctioned, glorified, condoned, allowed, assumed, in defense of "democracy." Yet in democracies, men protect the women they possess. The degradation of Jewish women in the Holocaust is evoked, sanctioned, and glorified in the pages of an Israeli magazine. Interviewed in *The Jewish Advocate*, Gail Dines-Levy, an educator who served as media consultant for the Israeli Ministry of Education from 1985 to 1987, notes:

> The most astounding example, however, is what the Institute has labeled the "Holocaust Fashion Spread." It is a fashion photo sequence advertising women's underwear. Women are shown running from a World War II vintage freight train, as well as being posed next to objects such as a furnace and a light-fixture resembling a showerhead. In another photo a woman is standing next to a fire extinguisher and immediately to her left is a blazing oven. "The last time we saw Jewish women portrayed this way was in Nazi Germany. Now Israeli men are doing it to Israeli women." (Antonelli, 1987, p. 1)

The terrorism of masculinity as sexual power was the underlying rationale for Hitler's expansionism. The territory he sought to control was both land and women. Jews were the symbolic and actual metaphor and target for the war he waged: the demonic, voracious Jewish male whose castration was the "natural" outcome of his sexual appetite. Andrea Dworkin brings into the foreground the meaning of the genocide of the Jews that is most often ignored:

> The concentration camp woman, a Jew—emaciated with bulging eyes and sagging breasts and bones sticking out all over and shaved head and covered with her own filth and cut up and whipped and stomped on and punched out and starved—became the hidden sexual secret of our time. The barely faded, easily accessible memory of her sexual degradation is at the heart of the sadism against all women that is now promoted in mainstream sexual propaganda: she in the millions, she naked in the millions, she utterly at the mercy of—in the millions, she to whom anything could be and was done—in the millions, she

for whom there will never be any justice or revenge—in the millions . . . (Dworkin, 1989, pp. 144, 145)

If, as Dworkin asserts, ". . . the male of the racially despised group suffers because he has been kept from having her, from having the power to make her" (p. 145), the Israeli Jew takes back that power both in vilifying Israeli Jewish women and in taking the power from Palestinian men "to have" Palestinian women. Control over women of the despised race through physical terrorism is a characteristic and a tool of nationalist rationales for expansionism. Control of women of the "superior" race through strategies of co-optation, underscored by physical terrorism, is a characteristic and a tool of nationalist rationales for expansionism. Israeli journalist Leslie Hazelton notes: "The Hebrew for penis is zayin, which is also the word for a weapon. The phrase for Israel's armed forces can thus translate as "an army equipped with penises," and the verb meaning "to take to arms" also means "to have sexual intercourse" (Hazelton, 1977, p. 96).

The use of penis as weapon is linked to penetration of the earth through modern military and industrial technology; armed forces in alliance with the industrial world complex gave Hitler the base from which to control and subdue production and reproduction: "In fact, in creating a female degraded beyond human recognition, the Nazis set a new standard of masculinity, honored especially in the benumbed conscience that does not even notice sadism against women because that sadism is so ordinary" (Dworkin, 1989, p. 145).

As ordinary as this: A 20-year-old Palestinian woman, pregnant, was sentenced to six months in prison based on a confession given under torture and threat of rape. Over several days she vomited, refused to drink or to wash herself. She was not allowed to see a doctor. Finally the prison doctor demanded she have an abortion. When her own doctor examined her, he found the embryo underdeveloped and recommended improved diet, continued medical supervision, exercise. She continued to receive an ordinary prison diet: no vegetables, calcium, or protein (WOFPP, 1989, February).

Who will notice? This is the "ordinary" consequence of war, of the struggle for the survival of the fittest; of the imperative of male biological superiority. Pregnant women, extolled as carriers of the race, of their nationalist duty, tortured and shot as carriers of the race, of their nationalist duty, are conditioned to loss of control over their bodies. They "belong" to the medical profession, to the industrial world complex, to the state, to the men who father their children. "Her belly is his phallic triumph" (Dworkin, 1989, p. 222), whether in prison or in the legal system that controls her choice. If, as men who make war on women assert, and as men and women who support that war actively or passively assert, women are what pornography says they are, then who will respond to the outcry of Palestinian women? Who will respond to the outcry of Israeli women?

RESPONSE TO THE OUTCRY:
LIMITATIONS AND POSSIBILITIES

Women's activities in relation to nationalist movements and to women's organizations within and outside these movements are chosen and lived out in the context of class struggle. Economic class, social class, race class, sex class, are interrelated aspects of women's historical oppression. The Israeli occupation has had a critical impact on the class–gender structure of Palestinian societies. Interviews with women living in the Gaza Strip, published in 1986 by teacher and activist Paul Cossali and Clive Robson, a development worker, reveal the impact of the interlocking factors of economic class, social class, race class, sex class, on women's possibilities and limitations.

Amal—". . . women suffer more from occupation. . . ."

In her 50s, described at the time of her interview in 1986 as an intellectual, an activist, and a fierce secularist, Amal asserts that women's lives will not change with the formation of an independent state in the Gaza Strip. She acknowledges that while some women are very active in the struggle, most are "shut at home mopping their men's brows" (Cossali & Robson, 1986, p. 33). Because of their social class status or, as Amal puts it, the social restrictions they face, women suffer more from occupation: "It's hard to become independent at a stroke" (Cossali & Robson, 1986, p. 35). While the occupation is, according to Amal, a politicizing factor, even women who are economically independent face restrictions. For example, the extended family decides who the daughter will marry. Amal notes that Palestinian men, like men everywhere, are threatened by signs of women's growing freedom. Because they are humiliated and oppressed, they tend to clamp down on women as a way of saving face. For both men and women, the occupation can become the impetus to ". . . stick to the ancient culture" (Cossali & Robson, 1986, p. 38). "If you ask men why they won't let women have more freedom, they say, 'What is left for us? We don't have land, homes or identity—at least let's have our honour' " (Cossali & Robson, 1986, p. 38). Amal concludes that it is up to women to change these attitudes and that people must accept that women cannot fully participate in nationalist struggle because of social restrictions. "We must start making our own decisions and see the importance of demanding social change, irrespective of what the Israelis do or don't do in their own society. We need a separate movement for social change which is no less important than the nationalist movement" (Cossali & Robson, 1986, p. 39).

Nabila—"The victory was ours."

Born in Jabalya Refugee Camp, which would become legendary in the early days of the 1987 uprising, Nabila made her own decision to join the resistance, for which she served two long prison sentences. She finds it more difficult to challenge the occupation of her own society than the occupation of the enemy: "But it's harder to defy the people of your own society who have the same aims of liberating our homeland. If I impose a siege on myself and stay at home, I won't be able to take part in the struggle" (Cossali & Robson, 1986, p. 34). Nabila runs literacy campaigns and discussion groups to strengthen the ability of women to shape their lives: economic independence is the basis of social independence. The successes of women in Lebanon are her inspiration (Cossali & Robson, 1986).

Nabila has links with Israeli women in Women Against Occupation and Democratic Movement for Israeli Women. Groups outside the territories provide some protection, particularly through publicity. Israeli women support demonstrations and publicize strikes in prison. Delegations from Europe visit the Working Women's Committees in the occupied territories (Cossali & Robson, 1986).

According to Nabila both sides tend to oversimplify and reduce the other: Gazans collapse Judaism and Zionism, and Israelis ". . . say that we are just out to destroy them" (Cossali & Robson, 1986, p. 116). Nabila seeks out progressive elements within Israeli society; while she cannot work with Zionist organizations such as Peace Now, she welcomes Israeli women who are questioning Zionism. She describes the possibilities for building alliances in prison. Though opportunities arise, they are limited: "There was one girl who was in for killing an Israeli soldier—it was some sort of love tiff. She came in a confirmed Zionist but we managed to bring her round to supporting our cause" (Cossali & Robson, 1986, p. 116).

Given her history in struggle, it is surprising that Nabila seeks contact among Israeli women. As a young child she participated in demonstrations, making sure that kids in her area of the camp harassed soldiers with stones and slogans when the camp was put under curfew. As she got older, she was one of the women who supplied *fedayeen* (fighters) with food, weapons, and medical aid. On one occasion she utilized traditional mores to escape capture. Bringing supplies to fedayeen hiding in a citrus grove, she was stopped by soldiers. When they moved to search her, she protested; as a Muslim woman, she could not let a man search her. She asked that a woman soldier be brought, knowing there were none nearby. Luckily, they relented and let her go (Cossali & Robson, 1986).

But that was the last time she was to get off so easily. When Nabila finally moved from support work to military action, she was shot and lost an arm in a grenade attack on a military position. She was arrested three times, in the course of which she was interrogated, tortured, and released until she was captured again. Her first sentence was 7 years; her family's house was demolished and her mother, father, and aunt were arrested. Nabila was released after 5 years because the doctors gave her only 2 months to live. Again in 1977, she was released after 2 months because she was so ill (Cossali & Robson, 1986).

During her third confinement in 1981, Nabila organized a strike with other women when the prison governor, a woman from Russia, and the governor's deputy, an American woman, ordered the prisoners to serve the guards, to prepare their food and wash their dishes (Cossali & Robson, 1986). The "high-up" officials were all Ashkenazi, and the deputy governor was known for her hatred of Palestinians and adherence to the hard-line Begin government. In response to the strike, prison guards took away all the women's personal belongings and finally confiscated and began to destroy their books. The women continued to resist, singing patriotic songs. Soldiers rushed at them with clubs and guns. Then they removed all the Jewish prisoners, shut the windows, and sprayed tear gas. After three tear-gas attacks, women lay on the ground unconscious, with skin burns and with hair burned off. Nabila suffered from muscle convulsions, gas burns, and nervous fits. For days after coming to consciousness, her voice was hoarse, she had pain in her larynx and eyes, and general exhaustion in her joints and limbs. When Felicia Langer, an Israeli lawyer known for her defense of Palestinian political prisoners, and others heard what had happened and came to witness the devastation, the soldiers moved the women to another cell. Finally, in November 1983, Nabila was released. Those kept inside continued the strike for 4 months, and finally won. They got back their library, did not have to serve jailers, and were allowed to have visits every 15 days instead of every 2 months. "The victory was ours" (Cossali & Robson, 1986, pp. 143, 144).

Faiza—"Liberty is not about refusing to serve men."

Palestinian resister Faiza connects political activism with resistance to the Israeli occupation: liberation for women is providing fighters for the nationalist struggle. She asserts that ". . . when it comes to getting jobs, there is no distinction between men and women . . ." (Cossali & Robson, 1986, p. 34); and that if a family is unable to educate all the children, the man must be chosen ". . . because he will be the breadwinner and the head of a household" (Cossali & Robson, 1986, p. 35). "What is women's liberation anyway? The freedom for women to choose? But how can I choose to be educated instead of my brothers during this time of occupation? Women's liberation means something different in our society. Can a woman who joins the resistance support her children? Liberty is not about refusing to serve men" (Cossali & Robson, 1986, p. 35).

Majda—"... the clothes of chastity ... protect me from ... social strife ..."

A student at the Islamic University of Gaza who wears full Islamic dress, Majda accepts the fundamentalist perspective on who and what women are: "But with God's help, I hope to be the good Muslim woman that He wants me to be" (Cossali & Robson, 1986, p. 40). When she first decided to put on the full Islamic dress, "... it was like putting on the clothes of chastity which protect me from the social strife caused by wearing vulgar dress" (Cossali & Robson, 1986, p. 40). Protection is the aim and goal of her dedication to God, who rewards those who are pious. For Majda, serving men is the way toward peace, toward opposing our enemies:

> Our role as women is clear. It is said that we are half of men, but I believe that we are the whole society because on women's well-being depends the well-being of society. We are able to raise scores of courageous men who know themselves and their duty towards their society. Woman can fulfill this role in the home which is the position to which God assigned her—and it is the woman's obligation to bring up her children in the true Islamic way—to spur them on to Jihad in the path of God to elevate the glory of their religion. (Cossali & Robson, 1986, p. 41)

Salwa—"I'm interested in discussing and studying wider issues."

A practicing Muslim and a teacher for the United Nations Relief and Works Agency (UNRWA), Salwa was raised by parents who would have preferred that she become a doctor: "They said a good qualification would give us independence if our husbands died young." For Salwa, Islamic dress represents protection, as it does for Majda: "If I wear Islamic dress then people, especially men, must relate to me as a person which gives me confidence" (Cossali & Robson, 1986, p. 42). Salwa turned to religion for confidence when she failed her exams: "I just couldn't understand it, then I came to see it as a punishment from God for my laziness and free life" (Cossali & Robson, 1986, p. 42). Unlike Majda, Salwa doesn't approve of the Islamic University; she would prefer that it include Christians and nonbelievers (Cossali & Robson, 1986). The Islamic University of Gaza was created in 1978 by the Saudi Arabian government; the fundamentalist Al Azhar University in Cairo refuses to accredit it. The Israelis did not permit a group of Gazan scholars to found a secular university (Morgan, 1989). According to Salwa, the university exploits Islam to achieve its aims, as men "... exploit their version of Islam to achieve control. That's the reason why I don't go to any of the Islamic women's groups here, because they only talk about Islam and I'm interested in discussing and studying wider issues" (Cossali & Robson, 1986, p. 43). For Salwa the occupation suffered by women in their homes touches her more than that of the outsider: "It's difficult and it faces me more strongly and more often than occupation does" (Cossali & Robson, 1986, p. 43).

Maha—". . . occupation forces everything that is reactionary. . . ."

Maha, a middle-class woman from one of Gaza's best suburbs, was 19 at the time of her interview. She notes that the occupation reinforces everything that is reactionary in Gazan society: "I don't think Palestine will be liberated without the women being liberated first. I mean how can our society be called progressive enough to defeat Zionism if half of that society is enslaved inside the home?" (Cossali & Robson, 1986, p. 44). She rejects the ways men utilize Islam against women in order to ". . . justify their domination and their supremacy. For example, men say that women can't become judges because they're not in control of their feelings and emotions!" (Cossali & Robson, 1986, p. 44).

Maha fought against male supremacy in her home, an act of resistance that she feels must come before involvement in politics outside the home:

> I mean if I want to fight and struggle for anything, how can I say that women have the right to do things if I don't have this right inside my own home? I must start in the house challenging the attitudes of my brothers and all the restrictions imposed on me. My home is my base, and when my base is strong, then I can think of working outside in politics. (Cossali & Robson, 1986, p. 33)

The home is also the base in terms of providing social services denied to Palestinians under Israeli occupation. Again, those services depend on the structure of male dominance. As Dr. Nabil, a Gazan from the Jabalya camp notes:

> Certainly the family provides services which should be the government's responsibility, such as mental health care, unemployment benefit, educational grants and so on. But more than this, the preservation of the extended family reinforces the strict male-dominated hierarchical nature of Gazan society. The family's sanctions are all powerful. (Cossali & Robson, 1986, p. 46)

Mona—"So we put our hope in God . . ."

The mother of nine children, Mona lives in Khan Yunis Camp in the Gaza. Her husband works in an Israeli factory, staying in Israel five nights a week. But when he is at home, he makes decisions about what they will do, who will come to visit, what she will do. Life is regimented by the "etiquette" of male–female relations:

> When my husband comes back, he's usually very tired after six days in Israel working long hours. So I get the mattresses and pillows ready for him and ask him how things are. He usually just says: "Praise be to God," washes his face and hands and sits down. I give him ten minutes to relax, then bring his tea, supper and fruit if we have any, and we chat about the family and friends and things. Sometimes he likes to stay in to be with the kids which gives me a chance to go and visit friends, and sometimes he has to go out to see some people himself. I always ask my husband before I do anything, and won't do it if he's against it, although sometimes I try hard to persuade him. Usually he's pretty flexible

and listens to what I have to say, but sometimes he comes back from work and his mind is as hard as a stone and it's best not to ask him things when he's in that mood. Sometimes he shouts at the kids. I just wait and listen till he's got the anger out of his system, then I say, "Ya Ibn al-Halal, not like that." (Cossali & Robson, 1986, p. 37)

Mona looks toward a Palestinian state: she is poor and doesn't qualify for help from UNRWA. "So we put our hope in God and ask Him to look after our children, provide for them and make them good citizens" (Cossali & Robson, 1986, p. 38).

WOMEN SUPPORTING WOMEN

How are these and other Palestinian women, alone or involved with the range of women's organizations—grassroots, official, named and unnamed—realizing their needs, visions, goals, and perspectives? The following sections outline several responses.

Summer 1982

Israeli women form Women Against Occupation (WAO) in response to the Israeli invasion of Lebanon. They campaign against town arrests; they support Palestinian women prisoners in Neve-Tirza prison who strike for 9 months for better conditions. They initiate contact with women's organizations in the occupied territories.

September/October 1983

Dozens of women demonstrate in front of the Neve-Tirza women's prison, where Arab prisoners were severely punished after they refused to cook for the guards (*The Other Israel,* no. 3, p. 2).

March/April 1986

The women's faction of Taudi (affiliated with the Communist Party, Rakah) holds a Jewish–Arab rally in demonstration for peace, and against occupation (*The Other Israel,* no. 21, p. 3).

January/February 1987

Members of a new group, called Women Against Violence, hold a vigil in downtown Jerusalem, calling for an end to violent acts in the city. Their banner reads: "Solutions, Not Victims" (*The Other Israel,* no. 24, p. 3).

March/April 1987

Members of the Women's Committee for Peace and Equality picketed the Defense Ministry in Tel Aviv, to protest the treatment by the military authorities of Siham Barguty, a West Bank woman who has been a leader in organizing the Women's Work Committees. Her husband was deported to Jordan, and she is denied permission to visit him unless she agrees not to return for 3 years. This method is used to force emigration from the occupied territories (*The Other Israel*, no. 25, p. 5).

1987

The Women's Committee for Peace and Equality organizes Jewish and Arab women in opposing the Iron Fist policy of increased repression in the territories. This organization has been active since 1975 in lobbying for passage of laws prohibiting discrimination against women.

March 1988, Na'amat

The women's section of the Israeli Trade Union Federation, Histadrut, collects hundreds of thousands of signatures calling for equality for women. "In an act unprecedented for her normally mild and 'uninvolved' organization, the Secretary-General links the discrimination of women with the occupation and calls for withdrawal of the army from the occupied territories. On the following morning a kindergarten belonging to Na'amat is found wreaked with the slogan 'Death to the Traitors' on its walls" (*The Other Israel*, no. 31, p. 7).

March 1988

In Lydda, women's groups from Tel Aviv and Lydda march in solidarity with Palestinians in the territories (*The Other Israel*, no. 31).

May 1988

In Ashkelon prison, a Palestinian woman who is pregnant does not eat for 2 days during Ramadan. (Ramadan is the month of the Arabic calendar when Muslims abstain from eating, drinking, and sexual activities from daybreak until sunset, in honor of Muhammad's first revelations of the Quran.) She is taken for a medical examination by a man who, posing as a doctor, grabs her and pushes her onto her stomach, forcing her to stay in his jeep in this position for two hours. Upon being returned to the prison she is thrown into a cell with a Jewish prisoner who demands she be taken to a hospital (*The Other Israel*, no. 32).

IS A PEOPLE'S REVOLUTION
A WOMAN'S REVOLUTION?

In Neve-Tirza, the Israeli civilian prison, Jewish and Arab women meet as prisoners. There a Lebanese political prisoner, Salwa, is able to establish some connection to a few of the Jewish women ". . . based on things they shared: missing their children, boredom with the monotony of prison food, oppression by patriarchal family laws. It surprised Salwa to find that traditional Jewish family law is in many ways more oppressive to women than the Muslim Shari'a" (Sayigh, 1985, p. 23).

Salwa is moved to a military base turned prison, later to become the detention camp of Ansar. Though the higher-level intelligence agents are Ashkenazi Jews, the others are Sephardic Jews. Thus their cultural ties with the Arab prisoners are deep, a fact that is useful in acquiring information from them. The women military police, drawn from the army, comprise the lowest level of prison administration. Most are Arabic speaking, from Arab countries. Their situation reflects the class system of the larger society; they are badly paid and share deplorable living conditions with the prisoners (Sayigh, 1985). The bond of race-class and gender-class oppression is the basis for friendship and mutual support. The policewomen and the prisoners sing Arabic songs together, ". . . with one of them [women military police] posted at the door to give warning of approach" (Sayigh, 1985, p. 29).

> At the end, when it was known that the prisoners were about to be released, prisoners and guards exchanged gifts, and tears were shed. One of the guards told Salwa that her dream was to buy a farm, and have both Israelis and Palestinians work together in it. (Sayigh, 1985, p. 29)

Associations of women—formal or informal; institutional or grass-roots; across a clothesline, a desk, a podium, or at the marketplace; whether or not one names such associations "feminism"—have a vital political impact on the societies in which women live. In the case of the Israeli-Palestinian conflict, women's associations, intracommunally and intercommunally, are prolific, and are critical to women's survival, as well as to the evolution of their respective communities.

The Palestinian nationalist struggle of the 1980s, the intifada, is a site for ideological debate and for day-to-day struggle regarding the status of gender relations (that is, women), and the relation between women and the state. Within the context of nationalist revolutions, the issue of women's role has consistently been utilized, both by the aggressor and by those aggressed upon, to achieve their goals. Women participate in those debates within and outside the context framed by the men who formalize the debates.

In an interview with Lina Mansour of the English feminist publication *Outwrite*, Dr. Rita Giacaman, Palestinian activist and journalist, describes the events preceding the current phase of the Palestinian women's movement:

> In the mid-70's, a group of active urban women workers and university gradu-
> ates got together in Ramallah to discuss the woman's issue as it relates to the
> national question; from that meeting were born the women's committees who
> form the Women's Liberation Movement. . . . We have set ourselves two tasks:
> one is to raise our consciousness as women socially, politically and economi-
> cally: and the second is to bring Palestinian women into the mainstream of Pales-
> tinian politics. (Mansour & Giacaman, 1984, p. 7)

As they began making connections with women in rural areas, some were
shocked by the poverty; providing physical relief became a priority (health,
water, nutrition) ". . . before attempting any form of feminist and political discussion groups" (Mansour & Giacaman, 1984, p. 7). Women's committees
were formed in villages, functioning autonomously, to make it more difficult
for the Israeli authorities to destroy the organization as a whole. When Israeli
soldiers ransacked the Ramallah center and closed it down for several weeks,
other centers continued to function (Mansour & Giacaman, 1984).

Basic Survival

Giacaman describes the difficulty of obtaining basic survival needs under
occupation and how those difficulties affect women. A central aim of the Israeli government's political policies in the occupied territories has been to
control water sources. Since the aquifers running under the West Bank are
a prime target for managing water, the government does not allow Palestinians to dig new wells; it has closed and taken control of most existing wells
and springs, and has denied access to others.

> Water collection is exclusively a woman's chore. And in most villages there is
> no potable water supply. Do you know how long, on average, it would take a
> woman, head of a six person household, to provide water for her family? Two to
> six hours a day. (Mansour & Giacaman, 1984, p. 7)

Giacaman's group decided to try to pipe water from an existing well into
a village so that women would not have to carry the water long distances.
They took their plan to the Israeli authorities for permission. For two years
women continued to haul water while they waited for a response. Finally,
the Israelis rejected their plan, ". . . because water, OUR water, is the property of the Israeli state" (Mansour & Giacaman, 1984, p. 7).

Women's committees train women chosen by the villagers to work in
health-care centers they set up; they in turn train other women. Lack of funds
from both Israeli and Arab sources, arrest and detention of involved women,
closing of centers and clinics, all slow but have not destroyed their work and
commitment.

One channel for contact between Palestinian women and Israeli feminists
has been the struggle to keep open the Bir Zeit University, a West Bank
Palestinian university frequently shut down by the Israeli government. But

Giacaman suggests that contact is limited by the Zionism of Israeli women who uphold ". . . the politics and ideology of our oppressors," noting also that the women's movement is split because Israeli women who are anti-Zionist also participate (Mansour & Giacaman, 1984, p. 7).

Giacaman asserts that until the occupation ends, meeting day-to-day survival needs takes precedence over "tackling the issue at its roots." At the same time, "Our consciousness raising and solidarity as women through our work is very important to us, and renders the issue of steadfastness, sticking to the land, not merely a physical process" (Mansour & Giacaman, 1984, p. 7).

Forming Committees

The Working Women's Committee and the Women's Work Committees formed in the early seventies, along with trade unions and other grass-roots organizations, have organized thousands of women in the occupied territories. Samar Hawash and other Palestinian women created the Nablus branch of the Palestinian Working Women's Committees to address issues of working women not addressed by the male-dominated unions. Sewing classes become a site for organizing and politicizing women who will attend women's committee meetings, but not meetings of the union.

Resistance organizations acquire power from the ways that women have historically made use of structures imposed by male supremacy. The Women's Work Committees, described by Giacaman and by one of the founders, Zahira Kamal, make use of segregation of women and men. They hold small informal meetings in camps and villages, knowing that fathers, husbands, and brothers often do not allow women to attend political meetings. Women decide what projects are needed, whether literacy classes, sewing classes, typing classes, or learning how to set up a cooperative. While the organization assists in getting materials, women are responsible for finding teachers and for passing on acquired skills. The organizers encourage women to "challenge the power structure in the family. And they do" (Morgan, 1989, p. 278).

Kamal describes the monthly gatherings at the seashore organized by the Women's Work Committees:

> . . . They talk. They compare notes. For the first time ever, maybe, they are meeting women from outside their own village or camp. Perhaps one group has finished literacy training and feels content. But then the women of that group learn that the women in the other group are learning how to type, or how to set up an embroidery co-op, or a co-op for processing and selling food. Marketing training. Lifting women's skills always performed free within the family out into the visible public world. Money to be earned from it—for themselves, for their children. For their own independence. Suddenly they are no longer content with literacy or socializing. Now they thirst for more. (Morgan, 1989, p. 278)

From Giacaman's perspective, nationalist struggle, defined as resistance to occupation, takes the form of daily acts of survival, a form of resistance

with particular implications for women because of how women's work is mandated within class context. For Palestinian women involved in the official nationalist movement, that is official party structures, the terms of the struggle
are mandated by official policies designed to define and control the Palestinian nationalist movement as a whole.

There are four women's organizations associated with official liberation
organizations. The first, the Women's Association for Social Works created
in 1988 by Yasser Arafat's Fatah branch of the Palestine Liberation Organization, defines its goals as uprooting ignorance, occupation training for women,
collecting donations, organizing strikes, and struggle on behalf of prisoners
(Fishman, 1989). The second organization, founded in 1981, is the Association of Palestine Women of George Habash's Popular Front for the Liberation
of Palestine. The Association of Palestine Women has 30 branches, 10 of them
organized since the beginning of the intifada in December 1987. They focus
on supporting economic independence on the West Bank; projects include
sewing workshops and small industries employing women to produce food
products and baked goods (Fishman, 1989). Third is the Association of Labor
Committees, formed in 1978 and linked to Nayef Hawatmeh and the Democratic Front for the Liberation of Palestine. It provides occupational training,
courses in first aid, lectures, and fund-raising bazaars. In addition to leaflets,
it publishes "The Woman's Voice" and "Who We Are," the latter a publication that appeared in English presenting the goals of the Association: "United
around a program based on a socialist and feminist perspective, the Association works to improve the economic and social status of women, and defends
their basic rights to work, education and self-advancement" (Fishman, 1989,
p. 9). The fourth organization, the Association of Working Palestinian Women,
has been affiliated with the Palestinian Communist Party since 1978. In
November 1988 the Palestine National Council in Algiers united all women's
organizations under a Supreme Women's Council (Fishman, 1989).

Women's Participation in the New State

In an interview with Suha Sabbagh, freelance writer and executive director of the Institute for Arab Women's Studies, Yasser Arafat, chairman of the
Palestine Liberation Organization characterizes the historical role of Palestinian women, comparing their suffering to that of Mary, mother of Jesus, a
Palestinian whose sacrifice of her son became her raison d'être. He notes that
the Palestine Declaration of Independence esteems women as the ". . . guardians of our existence and of our eternal fires"; a phrase ". . . derived from
ancient Arab tribes, for whom the fire was the symbol of warmth, of wealth,
and of hospitality" (Sabbagh, 1990, p. 10). While held up as "mothers of mar-
tyrs," and "keepers of the eternal fires," women constitute only about 6% of
the higher authority in the total organization of the Palestine Liberation

Organization (Sabbagh, 1990). In the army they hold 4% of the higher posts, while in the Red Crescent, a service organization in the occupied territories, they constitute 40% of the higher positions. Of 301 parliament members, 37 are women, according to Arafat, the highest representation among world parliaments. Um Jihad, whose husband Abu Jihad was assassinated by the Israeli military, is a member of the Revolutionary Council of Fatah, the largest faction of the Palestine Liberation Organization. She occupied the highest position held by a woman in Palestine resistance organizations, while Isam Abdel Hadi, a member of the Central Council and president of the General Union of Palestinian Women, has achieved the highest position in the Palestinian mass unions and syndicates (Sabbagh, 1990). Isam Abdel Hadi survived a torturous ordeal; she was arrested in 1969, held without charge, interrogated, and forced to watch Israeli soldiers beat her daughter (Antonious, 1980).

Arafat justifies the low participation of women in crucial decision making positions by pointing to the lack of women's participation globally and reasserting the misogynist argument of biology as destiny:

> This lack of representation is probably due to the traditional role of women as the ones who provide care for the children, a role which I hold in great esteem and which very few men can do equally well. I would say that in the new state female representation in parliament and official jobs will (be comparable) to the most advanced nations in the world. (Sabbagh, 1990, p. 11)

While asserting that women's organizations and the popular committees are forming the infrastructure of the new state, in that they have taken charge of education, agriculture, political action, protection, he notes only that ". . . women constitute roughly fifty percent of all committee members, and some participate in the committees that physically challenge the Israeli occupation by throwing stones at the army" (Sabbagh, 1990).

Sabbagh reiterates an oft-repeated concern that Palestinian women's participation, however minimal or however critical in the formation and ongoing evolution of the new Palestinian state, will be terminated as was that of Algerian women who, in post-revolutionary Algerian society, experienced a reversal of the freedoms they acquired through their participation in the war of liberation against the French (1954–1962). She asks Arafat what measures would be taken by the new state to ensure "equality of women under the law." Arafat rejects the parallel, ". . . because the nature of their participation differs and because Palestinian women have a higher rate of education, enabling them to occupy any professional position of their choice." On this basis, asserts Arafat, it is Palestinian men who must be concerned about their position, ". . . given the strength, the abilities, and the tenacity of Palestinian women" (Sabbagh, 1990, p. 11).

While Arafat's assertions are intended to comfort, they indicate in fact that the struggle of women for equality under the law will take place within the context both of mythification of women, with its implicit denigration, and within the context of competition for scarce goods that characterizes women's struggle for equality under the dual system of democracy and capitalist–patriarchy.

Social Restrictions

Alex Fishman's 1989 analysis of the future status of Palestinian women is based on interviews and on conclusions she shares with the "Ideological Meeting Circle," a group of Palestinians who held a symposium in 1988 on the status of women in the occupied territories as a result of the intifada. They found that limits set for women have not shifted in spite of their level of education and participation. Social restrictions remain intact. Women's place in the economy remains intact, in spite of the fact that Palestinian women are working outside the home. They receive lower wages, they are considered auxiliary, and their work possibilities and mobility are controlled for the most part by men, either within their families or contracted by their families for that purpose. While the intifada has helped to lower the dowry for women, has lowered the cost of wedding ceremonies, and has allowed for increased contact between men and women, most men still prefer to marry a woman who has not received a formal education (Fishman, 1989).

Palestinian women relate to limitations and possibilities in the struggle for self-determination from a range of perspectives and positions. Among women globally, movement toward self-determination has different meanings. Yussra Barbari, a member of the Palestine National Council, founded the Palestinian Women's Association in 1964, calling for full equal rights for women, but did not identify herself as a feminist. But other organizations, such as the Association of Women Academics in Gaza, chaired by Lily Saba, work at raising women's consciousness as women, while training women to enter the work force (Fishman, 1989). For some, the goal of equality under the law means equal access to education, jobs, professions, and decent pay. For others equality under the law means transformation of the meaning of *equality* and of *the law* so that women are not condemned, in the struggle to be equal, to acceptance of male definitions of womanhood, and to the implied inferiority of the equation. On the other hand, equal rights within existing frameworks supporting male rule can mean the woman's right to fulfill her destiny as woman, solidifying nationalistic boundaries. Amal Zamili identifies herself and her organization with the Moslem religious movement, Hamas. Her manifesto, published in August of 1988, supports traditional interpretations of Islam placing clear limitations on women's destiny:

> The woman's place is in the home of the fighter and in the fighting family. Her important role is taking care of the home, raising the children, and educating them in the values of Islam and in the fulfillment of its commandments, in anticipation of their role in the coming jihad (holy war). (Fishman, 1989, p. 10)

Like many women's organizations, Zamili's trains women in sewing, embroidering, and secretarial work; it encourages women to dress modestly and to remain in the home.

On the other hand, Robin Morgan's meetings with Palestinian women from camps and cities, with and without formal education, with and without affiliation with nationalist movements, reveal the extent to which Palestinian women utilize nationalist boundaries to transcend them. Time and again women affirm that ". . . a woman who gives birth to herself and is free to help her people and the world" is more crucial to the resistance than a woman with ten or twelve children not in control of their possibilities for survival (Morgan, 1989, p. 272). Women risk their lives and sustain severe injuries for statehood; in that process their lives are transformed by the act of speaking out. Women shun official politics, seeing as political whatever will help them not to have more children. Women follow official lines encouraging women to have children for the revolution, while bitterly rejecting their subordination in the hierarchy of party politics.

Supporting Resistance

Palestinian women are traditionally community organizers, seeing to it that the needs of their communities are met through informal as well as formal associations involved in sharing resources, skills, mediating family arguments, facilitating community decision making. This work has historically included defense of their communities from outside invaders. The work of Palestinian women in poor urban neighborhoods and in camps to mobilize their communities to support resistance is critical to the survival of their communities. Middle East scholar Julie Peteet advises that appropriation of women's informal community work by the nationalist movement could ". . . further institutionalize women's associations within the domestic sector by infusing it with national patriotic meanings" (Peteet, 1986, p. 24). At the same time, the fact that women are transforming the meaning of their domestic duties by carrying them into the resistance struggle is bringing widespread social change. Whether it is as part of a network of stone throwers, through tearing a child away from a soldier, warning a group of stone throwers of an impending attack, sneaking out under curfew to find food, or teaching sewing and other domestic skills, women's resistance is bringing into the foreground connections between women's subordination and ways that nationalist ideologies are utilized as tools of oppression.

Rita Giacaman and Penny Johnson characterize three stages of women's participation in the intifada (Giacaman & Johnson, 1989). The first two stages involved direct confrontation with the army and the consolidation of neighborhood and popular committees. When those committees were declared illegal and shut down, their flexible structure allowed them to continue to function. In November 1988 some women active in women's committees began to consider how the women's movement could utilize changes occurring as part of the uprising to improve the social and political status of women. In that process the third stage began, in which a range of sometimes conflicting strategies and perspectives emerged among different women's organizations.

Based on conversations with Palestinian women, Robin Morgan notes concerns among women in male-appointed leadership positions for achieving a Palestinian state. Women in UNWRA facilities she visited told her "Help us. We want to push no one into the sea. All we need is space to breathe, some food, some medicine, education, dignity" (Morgan, 1989, p. 285). Women in grass-roots organizations also communicated to her their vision of self-determination. Many women who are refugees in camps focused on achieving control over whether or not and how many children they will have. Palestinian women struggling for changes in the Shari'a advocate for civil laws granting them the right to equal inheritance, the right to own property, to travel, to vote, to have equal access to education. They address the burdens placed on women by gender division of labor, child care, and housework, and emphasize the need for state services.

While the uprising as a class rebellion is precipitating a shift to popular control and breaking down elite power structures, it is unclear whether or not a Palestinian state will consolidate those changes. Nor is it clear how women will benefit. While women living in poverty are leaders in resistance, middle-class women are more often in formal decision-making positions. Education is a requirement for women involved in official nationalist organizations; nonetheless, education does not always provide access to decision-making positions in the power structure. Many Palestinian women with university educations are unable to find jobs or to utilize their degrees. Women in affluent classes continue to hire poor women as domestics in order to create free time for political work.

Feminism intrinsically locates women's oppression in a class system. The ideology and practice of male supremacy constructs gender as a class issue. Female is inferior. The historical construction of race and sex is linked: white–black hierarchy, as a manifestation of imperialist ideology, justifies the subjugation of colonized peoples through the biological determinism of misogynist-racist ideologies.

Social constructions of gender, class, and race are interlocking systems shaping women's possibilities for self-determination. Insofar as resistance movements address gender, race, and class as separate and competing realms, women's strategies and goals will necessarily conflict. And those conflicts can destroy the impact of associations of women, as women find ways to survive and transform the direct and indirect manifestations of the war against them. Given the historical and ideological connections between race, class, and gender, liberation of any group of women is tied to liberation of all women. The notion of liberation of upper- and middle-class white women in developed Western societies is a false one, because that liberation is posited on the basis of continued exploitation of women without access to resources and power. Liberated middle-class women fulfill the stereotype of the fashion-conscious consumer, a "model" whose image serves to further entrench androcentric values. What are these women liberated to do? The liberation that is being spoken of is women's level of participation in a system that intrinsically is sexist, racist, and classist.

ALLIANCES AND DIVISIONS

Palestinian and Israeli Women Crossing Boundaries

At the Brussels Conference of May 1990, "Give Peace a Chance—Women Speak Out," Palestinian and Israeli women formulated a joint statement of seven paragraphs accepting " . . . the principles of territorial partition, the right to self-determination and sovereignty, and the right to be represented by the legitimate representatives." As women took a careful look at the document, problems emerged. Nava Arad, member of the Knesset and representative of the Labor party opposed the phrase "principle of partition," the use of the term "legitimate representatives" referring to the PLO, and the term "political process," based on the Labor party's official rejection of these terms (Galilee, 1989, pp. 27–29). The conference challenged women to overcome their polarization in terms of nationalist identity, a challenge which brought to the fore the difficulties involved in developing an analysis utilizing the existing androcentric framework.

The Brussels Conference was organized by Simone Susskind, president of the Jewish Secular Cultural Community Center, who responded, when asked "Why a women's peace conference?":

> Why only women? I remembered the courage and impact of the mothers of the Plaza de Mayo, in Buenos Aires. I thought about the Israeli women in the peace movement and about the Palestinian women, who play such an important role in the intifada. My idea was that women, who have dabbled less in politics and are less imprisoned by ideological concepts and less divided by psychological barriers, might be more prepared to listen and talk to one another without prejudice. (Galilee, 1989, p. 28)

Palestinian women acting as representatives of the PLO and of grass-roots organizations, and others—those who were able to obtain visas and overcome the dangers involved—met in Brussels with Israeli women from a range of official and unofficial party and nonparty affiliations and connections to the peace movement. While they came with unequal access to power, while they struggled with comparing injustices and suffering, they nonetheless forged new alliances. And while they were unable to confirm a joint document, at the final press conference

> . . . With practically no prior coordination, the Israelis and Palestinians gave each other complete backing. There were no accusations, no criticism. They presented a united front to the dozens of journalists. Aloni spoke of a "successful conference which created trust and friendship." Mikhail-Ashrawi declared, "The conference demonstrated responsibility and seriousness; the problem is semantic, not a matter of essence." And Sulafa Hijawa, the senior figure from Tunis, summed up: "We would have been happier if the formulation had been accepted unanimously, but the very fact of the formulation is an achievement." (Galilee, 1989, p. 29)

Palestinian and Israeli women attending the conference formed a committee to continue the work of the conference. Reshet (Network) is committed to reaching out both to women of the establishment and to poor women living in Israel's slums.

The Network has begun working with the many Israeli women's organizations affiliated under Women for Peace. At the beginning of the intifada, the Israeli army stopped 40 Israeli women from visiting refugee camps in the West Bank to " . . . see the situation for ourselves and express solidarity with Palestinian women" (Ostrowitz 1989, p. 14). But the women continued to insist upon exposing the censorship surrounding the treatment of Palestinians, and to tell the Israeli public the truth. On a busy Tel Aviv street, a group of women including Rachel Ostrowitz, architect and editor of the feminist magazine *Nova*, screened slides taken by journalists in the territories. Realizing that the Palestinian story was not being told, that censorship is a feminist issue, that there is a connection between the violence of the occupation and the fact that their voices as women are silenced in government and policy making, these women decided to put an end to the current version of reality. Exposing the violence of deportations, demolition of houses, administrative detention under inhumane conditions, also meant exposing the increase in rape and violence against women:

> . . . I have no doubt that it was the iron fist policy which created the atmosphere and legitimacy for this. In recent weeks, two women were beaten to death by their husbands in Israel. . . . A society which places strong emphasis on its military strength and heroism on its soldiers inevitably marginalizes women. . . . When we read every day about nameless dead Palestinians, we remember that women are often treated as persons without names. "Women are all the same," they tell us, "all Palestinians are the same." The voices merge. (Ostrowitz, 1989, pp. 14, 15)

Some Israeli women make connections between and reject financing of the military to control land and unequal pay for women; between the closing of schools on the West Bank and the historic exclusion of women from access to formal education. They insist that education is not only a matter of access, but of methodology: " . . . We must enrich the existing modes of education with a new concept—educating for peace" (Ostrowitz, 1989, p. 15). Their activism confirms that a political system that perpetrates discrimination, killing, and exploitation by race or class is intrinsically sexist.

Leah Shakdiel, a religious Israeli Jew, a member of the Israel Women's Network, the religious peace movement Oz V'Shalom/Netivot Shalom, and the first woman, after a lengthy court battle, to serve on a local religious council in Israel, notes that Israeli women, like Palestinian women, can " . . . manipulate a sexist myth in order to promote the cause of peace" ("Women and Peace," 1989, p. 31). She is referring to Women in Black who utilize the image of a widow or mother mourning the loss of her husband or son, to arouse compassion in the hearts of the 20,000 people who see them each week holding signs saying "End the Occupation." Standing in vigil on streets in Jerusalem, Tel Aviv, Haifa, these "widows," however, arouse more than compassion as they bear the brunt of woman-hatred. "People curse, spit, throw eggs and tomatoes, threaten us, and constantly remind us that we are only women, that our place is in the kitchen, that we are traitors" (Ostrowitz, 1989, p. 14).

Women's protest takes many forms in Israel, and involves associations between Palestinian women who are Israeli citizens within the green line, Israeli Jewish women from Arab countries, from Europe, and Israeli born. In January 1988, Israeli Arab and Jewish women initiated a project called the Peace Quilt. As many as 5,000 women from around the country sent in embroidered, painted, squares of cloth—imageries of peace. The quilt, created for the "peace table," was presented by 500 women at the Knesset, and is utilized at conferences and demonstrations. Women in the United States supported these efforts by contributing squares to the quilt.

Ashkenazi and Middle Eastern Jews, Palestinians, religious and secular, of all ages and class situations, activists and women who had never been involved in political protest, signed a petition, "Mapat Hashalom," asking the Israeli government to end the occupation and negotiate. The petition read: "Do not do unto others what you forgot others have done unto you," "Enough bloodshed," "Let's get out," "Do not turn our sons into murderers of women and children."

Israeli activists work with Palestinian activists in Shani—Women Against the Occupation—organized in Jerusalem at the start of the intifada. With over 250 members, Shani organizes study groups, lectures by Israeli women activists and Palestinian women from the territories, solidarity visits to hospitals and nurseries, demonstrations, and protests against the detention of Palestinian political prisoners and, with Palestinian educators, the closure of schools in the West Bank.

As early as 1948, Israeli Jewish women, Arab and Ashkenazi, began working together in defense of women's rights, children's rights, and for peace.

Tandi, the Movement of Democratic Women in Israel: " . . . sees the struggle for equal rights for women as inseparable from the struggle for a democratic society in Israel with equal rights for all: for Arabs, for different ethnic groups and for a separation of religion and state" (Women and Peace, Women's Peace Movement, 1988). Tandi is committed to ending manifestations of racism within the Israeli polity as it is connected to racism worldwide. They oppose the arms race and nuclear weapons. Tandi has branches in Arab villages and towns and in Jewish villages and towns, with day-care centers, nurseries, and cultural and educational organizing. They belong to the World Federation of Democratic Women with 138 branches in 124 countries (Women and Peace, 1988).

The Bridge (Gesher Leshalom), associated with the Women's International League for Peace and Freedom since 1980, was organized in 1975 by women who believed that women, as mothers and citizens, have a central role in forging links between Jews and Arabs in Israel. Their activities include discussions, lectures, conferences on Arab/Jewish coexistence, social and cultural activities honoring both cultures, press conferences, and some demonstrations including solidarity visits to leaders of the Arab sector in Israel and the occupied territories.

Women in Black vigils say "no" to occupation. It is two years after the first vigil was held in Jerusalem (1988). To participate as a Woman in Black has become increasingly dangerous. At every vigil, right-wing advocates of eradication of Palestinians from Israel–Palestine:

> . . . appear regularly . . . waving Israeli flags, which serve a dual purpose; they proclaim the super-patriotism of the bearers and also serve as clubs with which to beat the women standing in peaceful and silent vigils. . . . In contrast to the women, these arch-racists dress in white and try to provoke the black-garbed women with verbal obscenities and sexual jibes. (Khouri, 1990, p. 10)

Women in Black is a movement of associations of women considered dangerous by and to the state. The women come from a wide range of backgrounds and political perspectives. Some see their work as the only hope for continuation of the state. Others see a need to restructure the state, and some question the basis upon which the state was founded. Some are there because of the connection between what they suffer daily as women and state repression against Palestinian women and men.

Most Women in Black are Israeli Jews, both Sephardi and European. Some are Palestinians, living inside the green line as citizens of Israel, and living without official state identification outside the green line under military occupation.

Ibtihaj Khouri, a Palestinian, stands in vigil with Israeli Jewish women, in Acre, because:

> ... if a killer ... decides to open fire on our vigil, I would rather die for the cause of peace with Jewish and Arab women I love, than die alone in my bed at home. Standing with Jewish and Arab women Friday after Friday endows me with power and hope, just as my participation strengthens them.
> I believe a vigil of Jewish and Arab women constitutes power. Both Jewish and Arab women derive support from one another, feel stronger by standing together. By standing together we create a powerful image of Jewish and Arab women who oppose war and want peace, who have joined forces to fight against racism. Coexistence is part of our message. . . . (Khouri, 1990, pp. 10, 11)

Genya is an 80-year-old Woman in Black who stands in the square in Jerusalem wearing a wide-brimmed hat to protect herself from the sun and holding a sign with the words "No to occupation" glued on it. A taxi driver passes screaming, "You should be screwed, all of you, one by one." Beside her stands 14-year-old Yael who receives daily harassment from her friends who shout, throw empty cans, eggs, fruit, and garbage at the women.

Why do women join? One woman joined because she didn't have the courage to defend an Arab on a city bus. Another, because she linked her son's suicide with his ambivalence toward service in the army. Others, after reading about 60 babies in a refugee camp in Gaza injured by tear gas from a grenade thrown by an Israeli officer into a UNRWA clinic:

> You read about it in the newspaper and you feel uncomfortable, disturbed. The thought of a young officer, who "misjudged" an unbearable, impossible situation in which no judgement is possible, agonizes you. The thought of possible irreversible damage inflicted on the lungs of infants gives you the shivers. Perhaps that's your moment of joining other women, who through various experiences, have become sisters in the struggle against the occupation. Perhaps you, too, will now wear black every Friday and stand in the square, with the Women in Black.
> During the first vigils, the support you will feel coming from Genya or Daphne will give you strength. Several weeks later you'll realize that you are forming clear and eloquent political views. . . . (Khouri, 1990, p. 12)

At the conclusion of a conference sponsored by the women's movement in December 1989, "A Call for Peace—A Feminist Response to the Occupation," Jewish and Palestinian Israeli women voiced their joint concern that women's peace groups form a forceful political voice in Israeli society. Continuing the work of the Israel Women's Alliance Against the Occupation, initiated by 75 women who first met in January 1988, their objectives are to work for negotiations with the PLO in an effort to end the occupation, while strengthening the position of women in political decision making.

Common motivations surface as Israeli women describe the necessity for a specifically women's movement for peace. Defined as "other," and suffering oppression, women recognize the importance of self-determination. Women honor human life. Denied positions of power within the government,

women's networks of associations are a powerful vehicle for influencing political developments ("Women and Peace," 1989).

The powerful voice of Israeli women is multifaceted and fragmented by
a range of political perspectives informed by social-class, race-class, and sex-
class status. Lesbians from a range of backgrounds and political perspectives
have been in the forefront of the peace movement. Lesbians threaten the occupation not only as Israelis in defense of Palestinians, but also insofar as they
defy the wifely role, and often reproductive imperative, mandating women's
responsibility to the state. Lesbian associations supporting women's survival
against the boundaries of phallocratic social systems have long historical
roots. From their vantage point, limitations of vision within heteropatriarchy
are more likely to surface.

Economic and psychological intimidation keep lesbians downpressed.
Chaya Shalom, founder of the only formal lesbian organization in Israel, Community of Lesbian-feminists (CLAF), comments on the fragility of lesbian
organizing:

> In the only lesbian organization in Israel (CLAF—Community of Lesbian-
> feminists), because political issues are so controversial and so emotional, in or-
> der not to push women out, political issues are hardly discussed. This was an
> unofficial decision of the organizers who are strongly involved in the women's
> peace movement. There is so little room and space, and so much oppression
> on lesbians that we have to be realistic in order to keep the little we have, dis-
> cussions, social events, our own magazine, etc. (Chaya Shalom, Personal
> Communication)

According to statistical analysis by Shalom and others, lesbians make up
30% of Women in Black, and 20% to 25% of the planning committees. Shalom characterizes their participation as committed, radical, long term. With
the start of the intifada, many lesbians involved in battered women's shelters
and rape crisis centers shifted their energies to the peace movement:

> When we have conferences, meetings indoors and especially outdoors (like
> on the Kibbutz), it is a first for the lesbian community. It's like a major opportu-
> nity for us to meet, to keep track, to do networking. (Chaya Shalom, Personal
> Communication)

Lesbians bring to the peace movement feminist organizing skills that reflect opposition to hierarchical systems of social organization. From a feminist vantage point, possibilities for re-visioning social organization are more
likely to follow. Rachel Ostrowitz refers to one aspect of that "re-ordering":
"The grassroots women in the peace movement are women who have worked
for years in organizations where no hierarchy exists, where power is shared.
Thus the connections women make between peace and their own lives are
not surprising" (Ostrowitz, 1989, p. 15). New possibilities for making those

connections arise as women address the characteristics or forms perpetrated under and growing out of male supremacist ideologies.

Bracha Serri is a Yemenite Jew, an Israeli, a poet, member of East for Peace and Women in Black. At a conference sponsored by *New Outlook* and *Al-Fajr* in March 1989, "Road to Peace," she spoke in a panel of Palestinian and Israeli women. She voiced concerns that as women, as Arabs, and as members of the lower class, the voices of Sephardi women are not heard: "It's very courageous to join Women in Black, but a religious Sephardi woman with ten kids cannot leave her home Friday afternoons and go demonstrate. You cannot expect this" ("Women and Peace," 1989, p. 33). Her own political perspective evolved out of her experience as a Sephardi woman and as a mother, first as part of Gush Emunim in support of settlement:

> I didn't know that this meant killing Arabs. I changed my views because I came to understand and I took responsibility. If I was able to change, other people can too. It's just a matter of loving them enough, of respecting their fears, of speaking to them as equals—human being to human being, woman to woman. Of saying, we're all afraid, but let's stop sacrificing our children. ("Women and Peace," 1989, p. 33)

Serri sent her son to the United States, rather than send him to the army: her daughter also left in order to avoid conscription:

> I would be lying to myself by going to demonstrations on the one hand, and on the other, seeing my son come home with a gun. I understood that if I didn't want to lie, I'd have to send him away. If he decides to come back, it's then his problem. But I had to take some responsibility. Many women, even Likud women, say they would do the same. ("Women and Peace," 1989, p. 33)

Serri learned from the Lebanon war not to trust generals, whose peace only leads to more war. In Yemen, she explains, her father and brothers did not have to kill. She refutes the popular misconception of Jews from the East as being against peace. Because they are often taken for Arabs, Jews from Middle Eastern countries often try to disassociate from Arabs in public. Looked upon as inferior, they try to make themselves equal to the Ashkenazi, not because they hate Arabs, but to achieve a measure of safety. The problem is not unlike that of women whose allegiance to right-wing ideologies is an attempt both to prove their worth and to "take cover" under the banner of the phallocracy. Serri points to the problem within the peace movement, of racism toward Eastern Jews: "They feel they're not intellectual. They're stupid. To them Arabs are primitive, and Jews from Eastern countries look like Arabs. These people have a Western orientation" ("Women and Peace," 1989, p. 33).

Najat Arafat Khelil experiences a similar problem as a Palestinian exiled in the United States, of having to prove herself: " . . . We don't have horns. We don't have tails. We can talk. We are educated" ("Women and Peace," 1989, p. 33). A nuclear physicist, president of the Arab Women's Council and the Union of Palestinian American Women, Khelil was studying in the United States during the 1967 Arab-Israeli war. The Israeli government designated all Palestinians who were away during the war as absentees, and divested them of all rights to return to their homes. After meeting with women in the United States and at the United Nations Women's Conference in Nairobi, she believes that: " . . . if peace were in the hands of women, I'm sure we would have reached a solution much earlier"; and that women must come as equals with men to the negotiating table, just as Palestinians must come as equals of Israelis ("Women and Peace," 1989, p. 33).

Carmit Gie, who works in Israeli television as a news reader, characterizes equality this way: "On the face of it, women are equal in Israel: but they're not really so. What the men do is give us an opportunity to be like them, to be men, plus being mothers and housewives and so on; so we have to be superwomen" (Lipman, 1988, p. 110). The struggle for equality of Sephardim described by Bracha Serri as the motivation for attempting to be like Askenazim, for attempting to hide that they are Arab, can result in a more conservative politics. Similarly, as they struggle for equality, for the right to have what men are entitled to as men, women are trapped in a paradoxical cycle of gains and losses that affirm their womanhood by reinforcing their inferiority. The work of the peace movement against the occupation is frustrated by gender and race definitions that are what the occupation is. Redefining equality between Palestinian and Israeli, the peace movement must examine the inequalities of equality as it is defined by the modern liberal democratic state. In that process connections surface between imbalances in access to resources and to decision making between women and men, and between Israelis and Palestinians as peoples.

Painful consequences of the divisions between women living within and living out the definitions of race and gender of phallocratic politics, discussed by Bracha Serri and others, are revealed by an Israeli, Dalia Elkana. She characterizes the work of women serving in the army on duty at the Allenby Bridge between Israel and Jordan, as "inhuman and degrading." Women around the age of 22, many of whom were university students, are initiated into the job of performing body searches on Palestinian women:

> We passed the refugee camp at Jericho, all crumbling and wretched, on our way to the base, where we changed into uniform and were given instruction in how to be alert: to stop the smuggling in of explosives, to protect the security of the State, while retaining one's human face. After all, the Arabs returning from Amman to Israel are human beings. We were posted to the Allenby Bridge, where there are two checkpoints—one for Arabs and one for tourists.
>
> So I am now doing body searches. You, Fatma, are one of the women who descend from the bus that has just arrived from Amman. You are returning from a visit to your relatives, or perhaps your husband, or from the burial of an uncle or aunt. You may arrive with four or five kids or by yourself, you can be a student from Bir Zeit University, or someone who studied in the United States or

Britain. You may speak English, you are rich or poor, sometimes sick or blind and sometimes strong as an ox. Sometimes you smell of the land, you have strong, hard hands, and sometimes you smell of expensive perfume. In different circumstances, we might be sitting on the same bench at University. (Lipman, 1988, p. 36)

In these circumstances, the equality of Dalia and other Israeli women is that the Palestinian female body has become the object of a brutal investigation that characterizes the experience of women globally.

Here you wait until you are called by a soldier using a loudspeaker. She returns your documents once everything has been filed and found in order. We know who enters and who leaves, who returns and from where. We know everybody, and you must stand in a queue until your name is called, then it's on to yet another waiting room, where a sign says We Have to Perform Body Searches for Security Reasons. Sometimes up to a hundred women wait there for hours. . . . Then I act as the censor, while you take off yet another layer of clothes and shouts and crying can be heard from other cubicles. We both want to get it over. I take away all your letters, every scrap of paper, even if it contains only one word: every address will go into a plastic bag for examination. I hope it does not contain the address of a terrorist gang, I hope you are not a terrorist . . . I am sending all your family pictures to censorship. (Lipman, 1988, p. 38)

As the weeks go by, Dalia begins to lose her humanity. She becomes impatient and paranoid: "Gradually that job takes you over. You have difficulty remembering that these are women like yourself . . . " (Lipman, 1988, p. 40). Mistrust of both women and Palestinians arises simultaneously.

For Dana Arieli, the opportunity to serve her state, " . . . made me a feminist" (Lipman, 1988, p. 45). She learns to be tough, aware, mature . . . "first in everything." Her tenure in the army led her to focus on politics and gradually to doubt the validity of Israeli policy in Lebanon, and toward Arabs. While she deplores terrorism, she believes that:

It isn't true to say that only Arabs use terrorism . . . in fact before the establishment of the State in 1948 Jews were using it—look at the killing of Count Bernadotte by the Stern Gang, the murder of Arlosoroff, the Zionists killing De Haan when he tried to make peace with Abdullah. Who invented terrorism? There have always been extreme parties in Israel, with major disagreements about what they wanted for the country, but some of those actions early in our history had a big effect on the future State. (Lipman, 1988, p. 47)

Jews had to wear yellow stars under the Nazis; in Israel Arabs are identified by blue car plates. Arieli's shock at this and the level of hostility and dehumanization of Arabs that she observes among her Jewish friends, motivates her to join Peace Now (Shalom Akshav).

Founded in 1978, the goal of Peace Now is to " . . . influence public opinion towards a comprehensive peace in the region" (Lipman, 1988, p. 164). They advocate a settlement in regard to the West Bank that supports recognition of Palestinian national determination or self-expression. Peace Now is regarded as conservative by other organizations in the peace movement, and for Dana Arieli, joining Peace Now may provide an opportunity to challenge some policy decisions proscribing nationalist boundaries without challenging government policy, or nationalism, itself. For Janet Aviad, an active campaigner for Peace Now, obstacles to the peace process in Israel are " . . . settlements, Jewish terror, Jewish super-nationalism, chauvinism, racism, Kahanism—that's it" (Lipman, 1988, p. 164). She analyzes the situation in the West Bank as one of growing apartheid in a colonial situation—a contradiction of Zionism and Judaism.

> On the West Bank there are 40,000 Jews living now who expropriate land, who block wells and build roads through other people's agricultural lands. They put the Palestinians under restrictions—I would say that the settlers in effect live through violence and their ultimate goal is to strangle the Palestinians so that they'll leave, but peacefully. (Lipman, 1988, p. 167)

Among those 40,000 Jews are thousands of Orthodox women who put themselves on the front lines of the Zionist enterprise of reclaiming the biblical lands of "Judea" and "Samaria." Many see themselves as continuing the original goal of a Zionism that has been abandoned by the Israeli government. While not all Orthodox sects affirm nationalist goals of land reclamation and Jewish hegemony, many Orthodox women see their role as homemakers in much the same way as do many Muslim fundamentalist women. As bearers of the race and keepers of the hearth, they represent those traditions within Judaism that link racial hegemony with women's purity, Janet Aviad's "super-nationalism."

In this sense, Israeli Irene Hirschman's claim that patriotism and the struggle for women's rights are linked has particular significance. Orthodox women who see women's rights in the context of patriotism and who support the notion of a greater Israel including the West Bank and Gaza Strip as their sacred right, recognize the link between nationalism, male power, and the servicing of both by women. Beita Lipman puts it this way:

> Shoshana, Miriam Levinger, Shifra Blass whom I was to meet later in Ofra, Rachel—all wore the appropriate garments of the Orthodox second sex, their hair hidden under a scarf and arms and legs covered, whatever the weather. Like Geula Cohen, they took an active part in shaping their own lives and were often forceful members of their community. The paradox of being deliberately excluded from all town councils with as strong an Orthodox flavor as their own did not concern them, nor were they worried about their traditional roles as homemakers. As religious Jews they did not question the tenets of female humility and service within the home which have informed Jewish writing for centuries. (Lipman, 1988, pp. 19, 20)

These women are among those who would label feminists as, in Irene Hirschman's words, " . . . betraying the existence of Israel, if at a time of war they let themselves worry about their own problems. The rights of women are less important than the State of Israel" (Lipman, 1988, p. 50). But from Hirschman's perspective in time of war it is women who suffer the most: " . . . everyone expected the women to stay at home to look after the family affairs, to be a good mother, to be a good daughter, a good sister to the soldiers who are at war. That is much more important than her job in the Army" (Lipman, 1988, p. 49). The law, custom, the Talmud, all deny women rights and support men who " . . . will never give up power without a struggle" (Lipman, 1988, p. 50). From this perspective the occupation and suppression of a woman's right to determine her own destiny are linked, and what frustrates those who call for an end to occupation frustrates women whose goal is self-determination. For Hirschman, the crux of the matter is the ability of women who seek self-fulfillment to influence others: " . . . You just can't say that all the women can talk the same language; it's a multi-layered, multi-cultural, pluralistic society" (Lipman, 1988, p. 50).

A professor and headmistress of a girls' school, Alice Shalvi connects religious orthodoxy, militarism, and the inequalities of working women in Israel. The central role of women in the home and family as wives and mothers is used as a rationale for keeping women out of the job market, for lower wages, less benefits, fewer occupational opportunities. Kept occupied by duties as childbearer, childkeeper, and by their wifely responsibilities, women have little time for political involvement or protest. Yet, even egalitarian legislation won by women involved in politics, reinforces the proscription that the primary function of women is within the home:

> . . . It's only women who can take maternity leave . . . it's only women who are allowed time off as *their* sick leave when the child is ill; and working mothers are allowed to work an hour less than men. All this legislation, which at first sight seems so beneficial, has the underlying conception that only women do the parenting. . . . We women are then left in a trap. You have to make up your mind to give up preferential legislation and say No: we want to be completely equal . . . In Scandanavia, mother and father share the maternity leave; that's what you have to start going for, that sort of legislation. It really is ironic that so much of the new legislation, which was intended to help us go out to work, has boomeranged in this way: instead of protecting, it ensures that we remain at the bottom of the pile. (Lipman, 1988, p. 104)

Alisa Tamir, an executive of the Histadrut, Israeli Trade Unions Federation, describes the dilemma for women who, while they are two-thirds of the members of a pension fund, contribute only 35% of the fund, based on their earnings. And while the highest percentage of teachers are women, men are at the top of the hierarchy earning the top salaries. Alisa Tamir: " . . . Our society is controlled by men. They are our government, our Parliament, our trade union leaders, and all their thinking and their attitudes suit men and *their* lives" (Lipman, 1988, p. 107).

The connection between male supremacy in the name of patriotism, and women's poverty, powerlessness, and vulnerability, is beginning to be recognized within Israeli and Palestinian women's peace movements. But among Israeli women of all faiths and politics, among Palestinian women of all faiths and politics, and between Israeli and Palestinian women, the fact of exploitation is a source of both division and bonding. The exploitation of Palestinian women is central to the goal of occupation and is kept in place by the ways in which Israeli women collaborate with a system that assures women an uneasy truce when they are on the right side.

ECONOMICS AS OCCUPATION

The Gaza Strip as Paradigm

By 1973 the West Bank and Gaza Strip had become Israel's second largest export market. From 1969 to 1974, the number of Palestinian wage earners from the West Bank and Gaza working in Israel increased from 9,000 to 70,000 (not including the thousands who work illegally) (Hilal, 1977). By 1989, 40,000 refugees from the Gaza Strip alone crossed the border to work in Israel. One-third of those workers were women, most of whom worked without permits. To this day, they work as charwomen, or in fields their families may have once owned. They often have no means of transport other than hitchhiking or " . . . haggling for whatever space is available for a fee in men's busses or trucks" (Morgan, 1989, p. 254). Some of them are professionals with formal education at the university level who are unable to acquire work in Gaza. Many who find employment in Gaza work in sweatshops created to service the Israeli garment industry. In the West Bank, approximately 15,000 women, half of the women in the labor force, work in the garment industry, in local sewing shops or at home doing piecework for Israeli contractors, as well as in Israeli textile factories (Palestinian Federation of Women's Action Committees, 1989, p. 4).

Repression in the wake of the intifada has compounded the exploitation of Palestinian women in the work force within the territories and within Israel. Low wages have been further reduced, and are paid by the day; general strikes mean loss of wages. Women on their way to work face the dangers of having to cross army checkpoints. With no benefits or protections, they can be fired at any time. Often women find employment through a local contractor hired by their families to keep track of them and collect their wages, reducing what minimal control they might have over their own labor. Under these conditions, women contribute to the economy of the occupied territories not, as Alex Fishman and others point out, because of economic development, but because of economic distress (Fishman, 1989). The decline of industry in the occupied territories, as Israelis have moved in with their own industry, and of agriculture, as Israelis have confiscated land (24,000 Israelis occupy 19 subsidized and irrigated settlements using 96% of the water and one-third of the land [Morgan, 1989]), has forced women into the service sector, secretarial work, and seasonal agricultural work confined to sorting and packing (Fishman, 1989). Palestinian women with formal education working in the occupied territories are dentists (13%); pharmacists (30%); physicians (8%); journalists (7%); lawyers (6%); agronomists (8%); engineers (4%) (Fishman, 1989 [union figures]). Fifty percent of agricultural workers in the West Bank are women, and 35% are in services. In Gaza, 13% work in agriculture and 65% in services (Fishman, 1989).

Since 1967, expropriation of the labor power of Palestinian men has left Palestinians with dangerous and substandard living conditions (no electricity, no running water, inadequate shelter), unemployment, low wages, job harassment. The incorporation of Palestinian men into the Israeli economy as a cheap labor pool concentrated in manual labor is dependent upon women's "invisible" labor. The work that women do within the home and in support of men's work is not acknowledged as labor and has no assigned value.

Rural women in Palestine have for centuries supported subsistence economies through their work on the land. In the 18th and 19th centuries, European imperialists, with elements within the government and indigenous population, began the process of incorporating Palestine into a world market. Destruction of subsistence economies, continued by the Israeli government, has exacerbated women's vulnerability, increasing their dependence on a male-dominated labor force. While Palestinian women continue to have full responsibility for family domestic labor, they work for lower wages outside the home. The unpaid labor extracted from women increases as women, now refugees, struggle with the chaotic, dangerous, and unsanitary conditions in refugee camps and in poor towns and villages often under curfew.

The Gaza Strip is a signpost of imperial dominion created in the aftermath of battle, a piece of the dismembered body. Located at the intersection of the Mediterranean on the west, Sinai on the south, and Israel on the north and west, the Gaza Strip is approximately 5 miles wide and 28 miles long. Close to 400,000 of the population of more than 525,500 are refugees from the 1948 and 1967 Israeli-Arab wars, making the Gaza Strip one of the most crowded areas in the world. During the period of the British Mandate (1919–1947), Gaza served as a port for grain from southern Palestine. Egyptian rule after 1948 turned Gaza, with much of its cultivatable land and trade links lost, into a market city dominated by small shops (Rockwell, 1985).

Israeli occupation since 1967 has compounded an already complicated class structure within the Gaza Strip. While tensions often exist between Gazan residents and refugees, they also surface between refugees. Some who came as refugees in 1948 managed to acquire houses, shops, and even small factories, while others live in depressed and dangerous conditions in camps. Refugees or original residents who became the new bourgeoisie between 1957 and 1967 through petty trading and smuggling, worked in industry, agriculture, and services in Israel after 1967. As working conditions in Israel deteriorated and inflation brought down their wages, they became a proletarian class. Israel's introduction of a monopoly capitalist system in Gaza has destroyed local industry and resulted in complete dependence of the working class on Israeli enterprises (Cossali & Robson, 1986). Those Gazans who have become agents for Israel and for Western corporations, along with those who continue to run the few remaining large factories, tend to support rightist forces in Gaza, and to exploit workers who, under these conditions, sometimes prefer to work for Israeli employers.

Research by economist Sarah Roy and others substantiates that occupation has brought about "de-development" in the Gaza, and economic dependence on Israel. Roy defines de-development as " . . . a process which undermines or weakens the ability of an economy to grow and expand by preventing it from accessing and utilizing critical inputs needed to promote internal growth beyond a specific structural level" (Roy, 1987, p. 56). Roy goes on to debunk the myth that Israeli occupation has brought economic prosperity, describing the severe consequences of lack of growth in both the industrial and agricultural sectors. In brief, Sarah Roy has found that (1) the government has not substantially invested in either social or economic development inside Gaza; (2) discriminatory tax laws inhibit the ability of the Palestinian producer, particularly in terms of economic bargaining power, leaving the Palestinian producer unable to compete with his Israeli counterpart; (3) strict trade controls have inhibited access to foreign markets; (4) creation of industrial zones, union organizing, establishment of factories, cooperatives and other business enterprises, development of credit facilities and other financial institutions, all have been prohibited; (5) lack of political, economic, and social linkages between Israeli and Palestinian elites further prohibits the establishment of an economic infrastructure; and finally, (6) the continuing dispossession of the Palestinian people from their land robs them of the resource most essential to economic growth (Roy, 1987).

De-development exacerbates the exploitation of women marked by expropriation of their labor, that is, of their bodies, that women experience within capitalist–patriarchy. The expropriation of the land of Palestine by those classes and forces aligned with, representing, and supporting incorporation of Palestine into industrial capitalism's global market, culminated in the formation of the Israeli state. As major loss of land has destroyed the traditional work of Palestinian women on family farms, women are forced into the wage labor market as exploitable labor. Job opportunities are restricted, so that as unskilled workers " . . . women usually engage in one 'step' of a production process, and are prevented from accumulating skills and wage increases" (Rockwell, 1985, p. 120).

The displacement of women from the land has changed forms of gender inequality and created increased opportunities for structural as well as physical violence against women. The new wage labor system introduced reforms in gender roles, destroying some forms of unequal interdependence, and retaining others. Palestinian men, as the new proletariat, still receive higher wages than women for the same work. Rockwell notes that Palestinian factory owners reportedly justified paying men twice what they paid women, because men ". . . traditionally head the household and need higher wages" (Rockwell, 1985, p. 120). At the same time, women's subsistence production, reproduction, maintenance of daily life, and, under occupation, ". . . female production of basic commodities at the periphery of the formal sector," enable Palestinian men to accommodate to the low wages paid to them by Israeli employers (Rockwell, 1985, p. 119).

Israeli authorities utilize the indigenous exploitation of women to take control over women's labor and lives. Factories within the green line subcontract to factories in Gaza. This allows Israeli employers to utilize cheap female labor in the face of proscriptions against women traveling to work in Israel. Women's role as a cheap labor force in small, subcontracted sewing factories, conversion industries, and seasonal food industries (citrus and ice cream packaging) keeps the minimum level of industry left in Gaza operable (Rockwell, 1985). The factory is the second "household" she must now maintain. Rockwell documents one factory owner who admits that ". . . workers are actually paying him, since their daily wage of 500 shekels ($10) was covered by the first three hours of work, giving him five hours of free labor" (Rockwell, 1985, p. 120). Given the even lower wages of women, factory work can be considered a form of violence against women, and not, as the colonizer perspective maintains, an indication of how development benefits women.

Under occupation, Palestinian men, targeted as the "despised race" and forced in large numbers into the "despised" class, lose access to and/or control over the basic means of production—land, land resources, tools to build an economic infrastructure, women. Many work in Israeli factories earning hourly wages 50% to 60% of hourly wages of Jewish factory workers (Rockwell, 1985). The fact that women function as marginal workers, doing unpaid labor confined to the home and low-paid labor outside the home, allows Israelis to depress wages paid Palestinian men. As the condition of more and more Palestinian workers becomes increasingly depressed, class polarization in general is emphasized. As men attempt to retain control over women through restrictions on their movements, control of their wages, wife abuse, and honor murders, the link between class hierarchy and misogynist social ideology and social organization becomes increasingly clear.

As more women must seek work in the newly defined formal sector in Israel, many men react by attempting to reinforce gender hierarchy within the indigenous community. Maintaining the family structure is critical within the new socioeconomic system, not only to ensure the position of women, but also to provide much-needed support and social services. Women's role as reproducer of the community and as keeper of the hearth—of tradition—is emphasized in the name of national unity and cultural survival. Isolating women in an attempt to minimize their exposure to Israeli society reinforces those aspects of the culture that serve male domination. Rockwell documents an increase in honor crimes in the Gaza Strip and violence against, some- times murder of, women accused of sexual promiscuity (Rockwell, 1985). Absorption of Palestinian women into the Israeli economic sector, and the subsequent exposure of Palestinian women to the "loose morals" of Israeli society, threatens the tradition of protecting family honor through controlling women's sexuality—that is, the enforcement of the patriarchal code. The increase in violence against Palestinian women as a result of the occupation thus has its roots both in the patriarchalism of the indigenous culture and in that of the invader.

An increase in violence against women, then, is one result of the Palestin- ians' overall loss in political status since 1948. Control of Palestinian women is central to nationalist ideology of the Israelis, for whom women as the reproducers of the despised race are a target of control. During the intifada, evidence of the Israeli military tear-gassing a nursery in Gaza and of pregnant women aborting from tear gas thrown into their homes, indicates a strategy designed to reduce the Palestinian population through brutalization of women. In September 1990, for example, 13 women miscarried after being tear-gassed (Palestine Human Rights Information Center, 1990). In addition, the role of the Palestinian woman in the nationalist struggle for self-determination is crit- ical for Palestinian men who cannot win the struggle without them since patri- archalism depends upon her co-optation and cooperation. The daily survival of Palestinian women depends upon walking a fine line between the threat of the invader and the demands of the internal struggle. Palestinian women have a critical stake in winning the nationalist struggle for self-determination of their people, particularly because they bear so much of the burden of lack of state services. The deplorable conditions of refugee camps strain women's capacities and imaginations, since they have the daily task of providing meals, clothing, and health care for their families. Without a state and a passport, professional women have been unable to obtain jobs in other Arab countries. Travel, already restricted for women, is often impossible for political reasons: Arab countries restrict Palestinian immigration, and Egypt after 1967 closed its universities to Palestinians from Gaza (Rockwell, 1985).

The necessary creation of the Palestinian state, then, has a paradoxical sig- nificance for women. While the new state may provide basic necessities for Palestinian women and protection from foreign incursion, at the same time the Palestinian state can come into existence only as a member of a world community controlled by and for the benefit of alliances of ruling-class men. The focus of many women's organizations on civil liberties in the new state—the right to inheritance, education, child care, jobs, political participation, travel, however various groups define civil liberties—is critical to their participation in the nationalist struggle. That women's organizations, official and unofficial, are working to create an autonomous economic base for women by providing them with literacy skills for entering the job market and by creating independent cooperatives, is crucial both to their participation in the new state economy and to the attempt to free Palestinians from the exploitation of dependence upon the Israeli economy. In addition, women are forced into poverty when men who cannot find work emigrate and are unable to, or do not continue to, send support back to their family. In this situation, women are often forced into degrading situations, involving at best, less than subsistence wages. They may also suffer from loss of status within their community. The notion that it is immoral for women to work outside the home, that is, to work for other men, is written into the historical documentation of heteropatriarchy. Rewriting that history will not automatically occur with the formation of the new state, a fact that many Palestinian activists recognize and address.

In the conclusion to "Capitalist Development and Subsistence Production: Rural Women in India," Maria Mies argues that given that the exploitation of women's subsistence work is a necessary condition for wage exploitation (illustrated by the case of Gaza under Israeli occupation), this exploitation ". . . cannot be fought unless the sexist reproduction relations, mainly in the family, are revolutionized" (Mies, 1988, p. 45). It might be added that the concept of the nation–state, acting as a kind of surrogate family, must also be revolutionized. In fact, the possibility of stopping the spiral of violence that we are witnessing in Israel–Palestine—that will continue long after "justice" and "peace" have been contrived in these lands—depends upon it.

CONCLUSION

The phrase, "participation of Palestinian women in the intifada," implies that women are attached to a movement that originates and is controlled outside their sphere. But the history, current activities, and politics of Palestinian women indicate that the uprising has been possible because of women's political agenda; and, as important, that the issue of women—women's status, roles, and gender hierarchy—is a central, if unacknowledged, aspect of what the uprising is. It is therefore logical that most analysts designate women's committees as the infrastructure of the new state, and that the political perspectives of Palestinian women are a subject of increasing interest. Much more than has yet been acknowledged, these perspectives will determine the evolution of Palestinian politics.

Israeli women struggled in pre-state Palestine and struggle today, as they work out their politics in the arena of nationalist politics in the modern era. The boundaries of the nation–state become the boundaries of their struggles and of their identities. The incorporation of women into the nationalist agenda is central to the nationalist project.

From this perspective, the work of Palestinian women in organizations organized during and prior to the current stage of nationalist resistance, the intifada, centers on those areas that have been defined by the nation–state as women's sphere. Domestic skills are brought into the arena of nationalist struggle where they are utilized to bring women out of the home in defense of and in support of the possibility of statehood, of an economic infrastructure, a health-care system, and education for citizenship.

Palestinian and Israeli women are linked by the roles assigned them, even as they are polarized by those roles. They are linked by their marginalization, as well as by their importance in upholding the nationalist project of their respective peoples. The ethnic-cultural constructions defining their identities have been created by men to serve the nation–state.

In fact, ethnic-cultural history confirms links between women, rather than divisions. The racial categories of "Ashkenazi" and "Sephardi" conceal the intermingling of Jews from all parts of the world in the Diaspora. "Oriental" is a political term in the Israeli state, utilized to conceal the fact that many Israeli Jewish women are Arab (Davis, 1977). As Israeli scholar Uri Davis points out, 60% of the post-1948 Israeli population from Middle Eastern countries were (and continue to be) divorced from their Arab roots as second-class citizens in a polity ". . . based on the distinction between Jew and Arab" (Davis, 1977, p. 34). Artificially created nationalist boundaries polarize women with historical ties. Palestinian Jewish women whose families were indigenous to Palestine, or whose families emigrated to Palestine before the founding of the state, have been "lost" within Europeanized ethnic-cultural constructions. This critical aspect of nationalist rewriting of history serves to alienate those forces that have supported the many spheres of cross-cultural relations and interpenetration of Jew and Arab. Nationalist ethnic-racial constructions in Israel conceal the historic intermingling of Jewish, Muslim, and Christian women.

It is inaccurate then to talk about two groups of women, Israeli and Palestinian. To do so is to confuse and to conceal issues critical to the current conflict that are directly related to intersections of gender and race exploitation. Furthermore, fusion of European and Semitic peoples through intermarriage, and/or through rape, is concealed by nationalist ethnic-racial categories. A Palestinian woman, Khitam, explains to Robin Morgan the fact that one often sees Palestinians with blue, gray, or green eyes and red hair. "The Crusades," she shrugs. "All those Plantagenets and their troops. Perhaps a few marriages — but mostly rape." Ayisha, the nutritionist who works with her, adds with a bitter smile, "Maybe it's one reason the other Arabs resent us so much — light eyes, light hair. Racism, or racism in reverse, it's all the same. It usually comes down to rape" (Morgan, 1989, p. 260).

It is also clear that some Israeli and Palestinian women's groups have links as they affirm those forces that act to oppress both. Some Orthodox Jewish and fundamentalist Muslim women have taken on the role of transmitters of culture defined by and supporting male hegemony. These women take their power from ascriptive roles elevating women as mother and wife and denigrating her as whore and sinner. In this case, they have made the one choice they feel will support their survival. They have capitulated to the social contract of liberal democracy, which promises protection in exchange for obedience.

On the other hand, within both orthodox movements, some Jewish, Muslim, and Christian women are reformulating religious tenets, re-visioning, and restoring women's place in history, reconstructing the path along which women have shaped spiritual traditions and along which women have been both misinterpreted and murdered.

Other groups working within the current legal and political structure of occupation and modern statehood (liberal democratic) may also serve the goals of national hegemony, although in more subtle ways. For example, The Bridge utilizes the role of woman as citizen and mother to foster coexistence. The effect can be to promote reconciliation on the basis of shared identity as mothers without any significant improvement in the second-class status of Palestinian women as Palestinians (or as women). This is often the case when Arab-Jewish reconciliation groups representing a range of sectors meet. The politics of the Palestinian, assumed as "outsider," is subsumed by that of the Israeli who decides what speech is permissible. This is a tactic familiar to women as women, a factor that in turn has a deep impact on the possibilities and limitations of peace work. The silencing of women in the modern liberal democratic state through the perpetuation of structural and direct forms of violence against her makes a mockery of the notion of free speech.

As long as Zionist women and Palestinian women struggle for national rights—that is, for two separate states each with its legitimate claims to the land—both engage from within a cycle of violence that feeds on itself. The dualistic, hierarchical framework defining the struggle ensures the continuation of a dichotomizing of women worldwide. The freedom of any group of women who attain benefits of modernization, albeit with costs, is won at the expense of another group of women who experience a new wave of exploitation by that same system.

One example, in the case of the Israeli-Palestinian conflict, is that of the Jewish settler woman who acquires a home because her husband is able to obtain an interest-free loan from the Israeli government as incentive to settle in a particular location outside the green line; because of this a Palestinian woman is forced to leave her land, her home, and often her place of birth.

Similarly, population control, a central concern of the nationalist project and national hegemony, often results in deportations for Palestinian women. For example, Palestinian women who cannot read are intentionally given a visitor's visa instead of being permitted to return to their homes after a visit in Jordan or elsewhere. When they attempt to return, they are instead expelled, told that their visa has expired. In this way, and utilizing other bureaucratic procedures, hundreds of women and children are being wrenched from their families, homes, and means of support. Residency laws have been designed to exclude as many Palestinians as possible, a disguise for the transfer policy considered and utilized in the process of founding the Jewish state.

Population control is utilized differently, but also utilized, to control Israeli women. As reproducers of Jewish citizenry in the "race" against Arab "over-population," Israeli Jewish women are given monetary incentives for having children. In 1983, for example, the Law on Families Blessed with Children, gave subsidies to families with more than three children (Yuval-Davis, 1989). Nonetheless, Sephardi women, many of whom comprise the lower classes, are blamed for having too many children, in overcrowded conditions and with little means of support. Again, this argument conceals the goal of European hegemony for which Ashkenazi women are rewarded. Nationalist constructions of race, class, and gender are utilized to divide women who are Jewish as well as to divide Jewish and Palestinian women.

Palestinian women and Jewish women from Arab countries, within and outside the boundaries of Israeli citizenship, struggling with divisive nationalist ethnic-cultural constructions, are called upon to prove that they don't have horns. The bestiality ascribed to both groups as Semites and as women by religious and secular literature throughout the ages, creates a common sex and race class struggle across social class divisions.

While European-born Jewish women benefit in holding positions with more power within Israel — the few that women fill — their struggles within those positions indicate that development and westernization, as measures of women's liberation, have limitations. The liberties of women who benefit from a system which ideologically and practically excludes and denigrates other women, are both limited and fragile.

Furthermore, the benefits of modernization for Israeli women are moot in a society that supports and is supported by the armaments industry. In January and February 1990, more than half a million Israelis lived below the official poverty line, and women's incomes were below this minimum. Twenty-five percent of Israeli children lived below the poverty line ($12,000 a year for a family of four). Ten percent of the work force, 170,000 people, were unemployed, and unemployment continues to rise (*The Other Israel*, 1990, Jan./Feb.) The infant mortality rate of Arab babies was twice that of Israelis, and the life expectancy of Arab citizens was two years less than that of Jews. Israeli women live in a segregated society, as women and as Jews.

Twenty-six percent of Israeli Arabs live in overcrowded conditions, for the most part in all-Arab settlements (Beinin, 1989).

Violence against women and children, intrinsic to policies that siphon off money from poor neighborhoods to support military buildup, increases daily. Women are asked to contribute to this military buildup by serving their country, which in turn promises them protection. This is the protection they are promised. Because military protection of Israeli women is promulgated at the expense of Palestinian women against whom that same protection is utilized to perpetrate violence, women must suspect the logic that inherently sees all women as possible prey. The iron fist policy of Defense Minister Yitzhak Rabin to quell the intifada, to crush Palestinian "vermin," legitimizes rape under a liberal democratic legal system that protects the rapist, as it protects its soldiers.

Control of land is a feminist issue. Control of the earth, exploitation of the earth as an exploitable resource utilized to benefit the goals of development, industrialization in the context of unlimited growth, and male hegemony, or the fraternity of men composing the elite ruling classes, is connected to exploitation of women as women. A movement of Israeli and Palestinian women engaged in analysis of those connections has the potential to formulate a solution to the Israeli-Palestinian conflict transcending the boundaries of nation–state patriarchalism. Such a movement has the potential to move beyond the two-state solution, and to create a form of social organization based on the continuation of life rather than its reduction, objectification, vilification, pollution, and destruction.

Women sewing bandages in the woods. Women sneaking out at night, quietly making their way down a deserted street to meet others. Women in prison forced to defecate in front of their "superiors." Women in refugee camps quietly coming home to their women lovers. Women waiting to survive their husbands who rape them nightly. Women with missing limbs training to be surgeons. Women on strike together, refusing food, resisting humiliation.

These are the everyday survival skills that woman has learned under occupation. The test of her fortitude is incomprehensible in a world that turns its back on her suffering, that assumes her suffering, that condones her suffering, that believes she is made to suffer, whose bible says that woman is ordained to suffer. Because her suffering is "inevitable" she must be a hero. She must be a hero to have survived, and that is where, then, she will be put–up on the pedestal. Brought down, put up; brought up, put down.

The popular uprising dominating the Israeli-Palestinian conflict into 1990 has precipitated an exodus of women from the clutches of phallocratic rules proscribing who they are and how they must live. Through the Medical Relief Committees, Palestinian women who would otherwise not be allowed to leave their homes are now working and learning in a politically volatile context. Women are meeting one another in discussions that range across subjects they might otherwise never have spoken about.

For some Palestinian men, the events of the intifada have radically altered relations with wives, sisters, daughters. From a position of powerlessness, confined by prison walls, men must relinquish control over their women. Some Palestinian women and men assert that from this perspective men are beginning to look differently at women—for example, fathers and brothers who support the participation of daughters and sisters in the resistance.

The uprising has been building for 20 years and during this time, Palestinian women have been engaging in activities critical to their survival: schooling, health care, job training. The Women's Committees have taken on the task of providing state services. Because so many women's energies are focused on political struggle, their energies are being released from the preoccupations of dependency on men. Gender relations are strained. Stateless, the boundaries are shifting. Fixed rules must bend to accommodate the resistance. As they come up against the boundaries of male culture and of women's world, Palestinian identity is shaken: a source of anguish, a source of new possibilities.

Women's associations are a critical aspect of what the uprising is. They can become a vehicle for self-determination. As the Israeli government attempts to destroy the structures of male dominance supporting indigenous culture, those structures begin to break open. The actions of women to end occupation become who they are: their actions and not their roles.

As Palestinian and Israeli women meet on the battlefield, the possibility arises for re-visioning identity; for defrauding the occupier–occupied relationship that conspires to separate them. These meetings are the necessary condition for exposing the antifeminism of nationalism and the underlying paradigms of exploitation of women and of the earth. In order for this to happen, the web of fixed identities must break open.

What can we learn, then, from this war? Can the loosening of boundaries, cracks in the armor of the phallocracy, become a vehicle for self-determination? One part of this process is the unraveling of phallocratic language, of colonialist identity, because the concepts are colonized—"woman," "Jew," "Arab," "self-determination," "culture."

Thus women characterized as the women of colonialist discourse—"European" and "civilized," "non-European" and "backward"—are the women who, crossing over boundaries of colonialist discourse, turn the prison cell into a meeting place, a ground of association, creating the necessary conditions for their survival. These meetings are not frequent, are dangerous, are fraught with complexities and strains of torn allegiances, loyalties, contradictory needs. They have their genesis in work that has been the necessary activity of women in the historical struggle to end occupation. The antecedents for the political activity of Palestinian and Israeli women are the subject of chapter 2.

Chapter Two
Historical Precedents:
Women Supporting Women's Survival

In 1990, in the current stage of the Israeli-Palestinian conflict, women with a range of identifications and political perspectives are demanding change. Utilizing a politics rooted in nationalist ideology creates difficulties in this process. From this vantage point, Israeli and Palestinian women have contradictory goals.

But as groups of women in intercommunal and intracommunal association identify the occupation of women as intrinsic to the occupation of Palestinians, they cross boundaries.

Exploring the androcentric conceptualization of the Israeli-Palestinian conflict, women can re-envision the possibilities for peace. Language is rooted in historical developments and interpretations of those developments. The view that Jew and Arab are eternal enemies is one example, connected to the view that women are natural enemies.

The following exploration of forces supporting intercommunal association among Jew and Arab is not an attempt to idealize the possibilities for cooperation in the present. Historians who represent the historic evolution of relations in the Middle Eastern lands as shaped by enmity between those men and women who become the "Jews" and "Arabs" of the current conflict commit a form of historic genocide against both. Historical researchers and anthropologists who pay attention to women note that women's associations among and between one another are a critical aspect of inter- and intracommunal survival. Women are central to historical developments culminating in the current conflict, both as actors and as a vehicle for solidification of nationalist boundaries.

Women's activities, and the kinds of questions women are raising in the current stage of the conflict, have historical roots. It is necessary to reawaken and retrieve that history because androcentric historiographers conceal information critical to efforts at creating resolutions to the current conflict. To construct a new social organization of Palestinian and Israeli identities and relations that will only perpetuate class exploitation of misogyny and racism is self-defeating. Examining the range of women's experiences brings to the foreground the confluence of forces disrupting interethnic relations and reducing women and the earth to commodities to be mined, exploited, raped. Survival for all peoples depends upon refusing both.

BEHIND THE WALL OF HETERO-PATRIARCHY

> Hetero-reality, the world view that woman exists always in relation to man, has consistently perceived women together as women alone. (Raymond, 1986, p. 3)

> Informal associations . . . although formed for differing purposes, organize groups of women to defend rights and promote the interests of their participants . . . act through credibility of leadership within wider political systems and through effectiveness of communication networks they engender. (March & Taqqu, 1986, p. 81)

Androcentric historiography ignores and trivializes, misinterprets and even romanticizes, women's associations. The significant fact and impact of women's associations, explored, for example, in Janice Raymond's groundbreaking work, *A Passion for Friends: Toward a Philosophy of Female Affection* (1986), across geographic boundaries, is multifaceted, varied in form, structure, and content, and supportive of women's survival.

But a complex system described by Raymond as the world of hetero-relations thwarts and disguises the work that women do to support self-determination. From the perspective of hetero-relational proscriptions the possibility for alternative forms of social organization seems remote:

> Not only heterosexuality, but an extended range of hetero-relations, such as traditional family roles, sexual division of labor, and gender defined childrearing and education, are rationalized as necessary for the continued preservation and maintenance of the human race. (Raymond, 1986, p. 57)

From another vantage point, historian Mervat Hatem maintains that the sexual basis of patriarchal systems is sustained by relations among women and among men as well as between women and men (Hatem, 1986).

It is critical to examine how associations of women have become and can become the ground for liberating social relations, and to examine the ways in which alliances of men as well as compliance and competition among women support patriarchal control. Further, what may look like compliance and competition may not be: ethnocentric or misogynist perspectives can conceal mutuality and bonding.

For example, sex segregated systems, from the vantage point of Western liberalism, foster competition and compliance among women, and represent women's "inequality." But the meanings and uses of sex segregation across geographic boundaries and in different historic periods also reveal woman's ability to create and sustain herself. Hatem gives evidence that sex segregation supported a revolt of lesbians in the Mamluk court of 14th-century Egypt that challenged the gender-class patriarchal structure (Hatem, 1986).

Women's associations—formal and informal networks, acting autonomously or connected to wider political systems—have historically supported intercommunal relations among Jews, Muslims, and Christians in the Arab world. They have also been utilized to support patriarchalism in the form of nationalist wars disrupting those relations. Both aspects of women's political history provide vital information about the possibilities and limitations of what women are doing today.

The history of women's associations in the Arab world begins with the ancient migrations from which early nationalist movements emerged. A gynocentric exploration of that history reveals many traditions supporting women's associations, as well as the fact that disruption of women's associations was a tenet of ideologies supporting a range of nationalist–religious movements.

FROM TRIBE TO KINGDOM: WOMEN IN SOCIAL-SPIRITUAL POLITICS OF THE ANCIENT WORLD

Relations between women who were known as "Arabi" began in pre-biblical times with tribal migrations in the lands of their common origins: the deserts and fertile basins from North Africa, Nile Valley, the Syrian lands and Mesopotamia (modern-day Iraq), Iranian highlands, and Arabian peninsula. Social groups known as clans were internally autonomous but were most often grouped in larger associations known as "tribes" (Hodgson, 1974; O'Leary, 1927). Tribes were organized in loose confederations with loyalty based on kinship groupings and alliances.

In northern Arabia, the birthplace of Islam, Jews and other Arab tribes evolved a way of life based on complementarity between the settled and the nomadic populations. Sedentary populations built agricultural communities around river banks, utilizing systems of irrigation. Bedouins (from Arabic, *badawi,* referring to the steppes and semideserts of Arabia), called themselves Arab, a name that became associated also with the settled tribespeople who lived from the date palms and grain of the oases in addition to engaging in commerce (Hodgson, 1974).

Cooperative systems, developed in response to the challenges of daily life, contributed to peaceful coexistence between tribes. Extensive agriculture, possible in areas such as southern Arabia and Yemen, supported a sedentary way of life over centuries. Tribes of Jews and other Arab tribes had extensive experience in developing irrigation systems for cultivation; the refinement of irrigation systems encouraged development of crafts and, subsequently, commerce in the towns.

From 750 B.C.E. on, invasions by a series of conquering empires—Assyrians, Neo-Babylonians, ancient Persians, Macedonians, Romans—contributed to cooperation and to dissension between tribes, some of which were used as buffers between warring factions.

Spiritual intermingling centered around agriculture. Planets were "givers of the harvest," guiding the growing season. Arabs of the Sinai offered animal sacrifices to three goddesses: al-Uzza, identified with the planet Venus; Al-lat, the Sun Goddess; and Manat, Goddess of Fate. Jews who entered the land of Canaan in the 13th century B.C.E. adopted many of these practices. Pilgrimages to holy places linked religious and economic life, leading to the development of markets for exchange of goods at those sites.

Gynocentric customs appear in the social–spiritual systems of tribal peoples of Egypt, Canaan–Palestine, and North and South Arabia. Historian W. Robertson Smith has shown that Hebrew and Arabic etymologies confirm female kinship; for example, mother kinship is disguised by the change "from female to male eponymns" (person [name] from which a tribe takes its name) (Smith, 1903, p. 34). Throughout the Semitic world, the tent or house belonged to the women. In one type of marriage among the ancient Canaanites, Arameans, and Hebrews, a man went to the woman's tent. The husband was then adopted into the wife's kin and her children remained within her tribe (Smith, 1903).

Information about the conditions and social life of Arabs in the 5th and 6th centuries C.E. comes from poetry. Women were among the outstanding poets and literary critics, recognized as tribal spokespersons and respected for renditions of tribal life (Abbott, 1941; O'Leary, 1927). The women of Arabia were famous for songs and poems reflecting not only details of daily life, but also political circumstances of their times.

Throughout the Middle Eastern lands, women were known as *kahinah*, seers, temple priestesses and prophetesses. Leaders in religious life, linked as it was "with the economic and political development and welfare of the people," these women influenced tribal migrations (Abbott, 1941, p. 260).

Historian Nabia Abbott traces the lineage of Arab queens related to the four Arab kingdoms between the fall of Zenobia and the rise of Muhammad: the Himyars of South Arabia (founded by the Queen of Sheba); the Kindah of central Arabia; the Ghassānids of Syria, and the Lakhmids of Hīrah. Known for her "beauty, learning and valor," Zenobia, for example, ruled her state of Palmyra and most of the east until defeated by the Romans (Abbott, 1941, pp. 13, 14). Those Arab queens who for periods of time ruled in their own right affected ruling-class alliances. As mothers of influential rulers, Arab women were sometimes in a position, though a precarious one, to influence political developments. When Mamaea counseled her son Alexander Severus, who ruled Rome from 222 to 235, to seek peace instead of battle on an expedition, his troops, resenting her influence, engineered a revolt resulting in the murder of both Alexander and Mamaea (Abbott, 1941, p. 11).

Abbott notes that "what a queen does, other women frequently do" (Abbott, 1941, p. 262). It is conceivable that women of the ruling classes were in a position to affect social policies that had bearing on the lives of women in general. Many also suffered violent, brutal deaths. The legendary first Hind of the Kingdom of Kindah was "one of several wives and seems to have had little love for her husband . . . " (Abbott, 1941, p. 16). After she discredited her husband to his enemies, Hind's husband "had her bound between two (wild) horses which tore her to pieces" (Abbott, 1941, p. 16).

The decisions and actions of women such as the queens of Sheba, Zabibi, Samsi, and Iati'e who fought the Assyrians, the empress Julia Domna, Bath Zabbai, Dahya bint Tatit al-Kahina, Jewish priestess of the Berber tribes of North Africa, and others, affected the course of history, as women sought to secure positions of influence. A woman secured a place for herself sometimes through strategies lived out in the realm of politics, sometimes in the spiritual realm, and often in a way that explicitly benefited other women.

Hind, great-granddaughter of the founder of the Kindah, entered a marriage alliance that brought together two opposing houses. She was a Christian, who in the reign of her son 'Amr (554–570) founded a convent, named after her (Abbott, 1941). Another "Hind," probably the great-granddaughter of the first and greater Hind mentioned above, was also associated with a convent. According to one interpretation, she retired to a convent after the murder of her Christian poet husband; according to another, after the death of her father. A third interpretation connects her decision with "the death of a beloved girl friend named Zarqa. She lived in her convent well into Islamic times" (Abbott, 1941, p. 20).

Convent living in the early history of women of the Arab world may have been a way of escaping the proscriptions of hetero-patriarchy, as well as a way of sanctifying women's space. As Janice Raymond puts it: "The male hierarchy was always in conflict with the independent spirit which had drawn many women to convent living initially" (Raymond, 1986, p. 75). In early Christian times nuns living in religious communities carried on the tradition of "loose women" of pre-Christian times; that is, autonomous women who detached themselves from men (Raymond, 1986, pp. 74, 75). Christianity . . . "domesticated the earlier traditions of loose women . . . by gradually regulating the Rule and living conditions of nuns" (Raymond, 1986, p. 75).

Philo (20 B.C.E. to after 40 C.E.) records flourishing associations of women devoted to scriptural study in Alexandria and non-Greek countries (Brooten, 1982). Celibate Jewish women living in a monastery beside an order of celibate men whose prophet was Moses, honored the prophet Miriam. Miriam was an important figure in the cultic life of the community. She was forced to abdicate to Moses but not without a struggle. The monastic life of women associating themselves with her was both an affirmation of women's spirituality and a rejection of male hegemony. Historian Bernadette Brooten notes that a temple founded by a Jerusalem family, the Onaids, and enduring for almost 2½ centuries, may have preserved the cultic role of women:

> Could it be that practices such as allowing women to exercise cultic functions were among the reasons for the rabbis' hesitancy to recognize the sacrifices offered there as valid? (Brooten, 1982, p. 88)

Such disputes among religious men were typical of early Judaism, Christianity, and Islam, in the process of propagating teachings diminishing women's spiritual power. Brooten's example points to evidence that women controlled some of the many sects of Judaism, as they did some sects of Christianity. In spite of accusations of "adultery and whoredom," the school of the first-century prophet and teacher Jezebel, withstanding the influence of John, "continued to be a part of the community at Thyatira" (Fiorenza, 1979, p. 41).

Jewish and Christian patriarchs, and Muhammad as well, were assiduous in their efforts to convince women to join their ranks. Rosemary Reuther notes for example that Paul considers the authority of two women in the community at Philippi "so great that their dissensions might be a serious threat to the existence of this community" (Fiorenza, 1979, p. 34). Women affiliated with the dominant religious movements of their times persuaded others to follow. For example, Priscilla, well-known Jewish-Christian teacher in the early church, probably influenced many women to join her. Bernadette Brooten notes that active leading Jewish women were influential in attracting women who were not Jews to join their community (Brooten, 1982).

Bernadette Brooten's study of tomb inscriptions of Hebrew women from 27 B.C.E. through the 6th century C.E. brings to light evidence of women's important spiritual and communal roles, evidence that has been misconstrued and suppressed by male historians. Androcentric historians have interpreted inscriptions such as "leader," "priest," "mother" of the synagogue, as honorific, that is, assumed through association with husbands. Brooten demonstrates, however, that there is no evidence that women bearing these inscriptions were married. Furthermore, some Jewish women controlled their own property and were sufficiently wealthy to donate money (Brooten, 1982).

Women of means donate money to religious causes within all three traditions, in many cases providing support for women without resources. Associations of women, whether in convents, associated with monasteries, temples, or mosques, were a source of financial support and emotional and spiritual sustenance for women. This tradition has many variations in the lives and survival of women of the Middle Eastern lands.

Women's Friendships Supporting Interethnic Relations

In the Old Testament, ideologies condemning local religious beliefs and cults reflect attempts by an emerging ruling elite to control spiritual life. Disruption of women's associations followed, a process that fed interethnic tensions. Interpretation of the Bible from a gynocentric perspective brings to the surface a hidden history, as women in jeopardy rescue and inspire one another and as they are set against one another.

Jewish historian Savina J. Teubal in her study, *Sarah the Priestess,* traces the story of Sarah (wife to Abram), and Hagar (concubine slave to Abram) in the context of the transition from matrilineage to patrilineage, from respect for women's associations to their disruption and suppression.

Sarah was a priestess with the power of oracle who spent most of her life in Mamre where there was a sacred grove of terebinths (a tree of the Mediterranean region yielding turpentine) associated with the Goddess Asherah. Ur, her birthplace, and Haran, where she traveled, were both centers of moon worship. Sarah and Abram offered sacrifices in Shechem, center of terebinth veneration and ritual observance in the second millenium B.C.E. and "known as the 'Navel of the Land' (Judges 9:37)" (Teubal, 1984, pp. 90–93). Teubal notes:

> The spirit embodied in a fruit or leafy type tree or grove in the ancient Near East was female, the most popular in Canaan being the Goddess Asherah. Asherah was venerated from Babylonia (as Ashratum) to Ugarit, Southern Arabia (Atharath) and Egypt. It is not surprising therefore to find Israelite devotion to the Goddess so strongly entrenched in Hebrew religion that her devotees held fast to her worship throughout the periods of Judges and Kings and well into the sixth century B.C.E. It was not until King Josiah's reign, a hundred years after the invasion of Israel by the Assyrian king Shalmanesser that this ardent Yahwist reformer had the Asherahs hewn down and burnt, in accordance with the Deutoronomic law: You shall not plant for yourself an asherah, any tree, beside the altar of Yahweh your god, which you shall make for yourself. (Teubal, 1984, p. 91)

Abram may have built altars at holy sites to receive oracular direction from Sarah, whose barrenness may have been an indication of her sacred office (Teubal, 1984). Priestesses associated with the Goddess Inanna (the Semitic Ishtar or Astarte) remained childless. Teubal conjectures that the binding of Isaac, borne by Sarah in her old age, was an attempt to comply with a later tradition stating that the child of a priestess was to be "exposed to elements and left to its fate, which was usually death" (Teubal, 1984, p. 82). Sarah's relationship to Hagar is generally interpreted in the context of the relationship of each to Abram. However, they may have been connected as priestesses involved in cultic practices. Their activities echo the roles of priestesses involved in ancient fertility rites, but androcentric historiography acknowledges women only in their relations to men.

It follows then, that the banishment of Hagar and Ishmael (her son by Abram) signifies changing relations between women, with the evolution of monotheisms and concomitant changes in social relations and social organizations. What comes between Sarah and Hagar, who both held sacred offices, is the covenant between God and Abram, and their attempts to raise their sons within a changing context. The Old Testament describes this changing context; the religion of the emerging Hebrew nation supplanted popular cults, including spiritual practices, with which women were associated. It is Sarah's "privilege," then, to be the wife of the patriarch chosen by God as the "father" of the new religion, and Hagar's "misfortune" to be the disavowed "foreigner," the Arab servant—an interpretation that distorts the origins of both women's struggles.

Women's Friendships Affecting the Course of History

Several themes in the Book of Ruth, centered on the association between Naomi of the Israelite nation and Arab Ruth, a Moabite, parallel the story of Sarah and Hagar. Through her association with and love for Naomi, Ruth adopts Naomi's god and through her marriage with Boaz provides Naomi with a "son," from whom the Israelite leader David is descended. Naomi and her family travel to Moab because of a famine in Bethlehem. After the death of her husband and two sons, and upon hearing that conditions have improved, Naomi returns home. Both her daughters-in-law want to return with her. Naomi encourages them to stay among their people. Ophrah acquiesces, while Ruth chooses to stay with Naomi. Upon their return, Ruth seeks food for them, joining gleaners in the field of a wealthy landowner, Boaz, kinsman of Naomi's husband. Boaz protects Ruth from possible mistreatment as a foreigner and as a woman. Naomi encourages the marriage of Ruth and Boaz, consummated after a nearer kinsman relinquishes first rights to Ruth. The women of Bethlehem recognize the son of Ruth and Boaz as ancestor of the Israelite leader, David.

The names "Naomi" and "Ruth" both derive from epithets related to fertility rituals (Staples, 1937). Naomi comes from Bethlehem, center of a nature cult. Historian W. P. Staples notes evidence of the fertility cult theme:

> . . . Passages throughout the story reflect the cult ideas of Tammuz—Adonis-Osiris . . . The "dead" in each case refers to Elimelach, the dead God; . . . the "living" refers to Naomi, the mother-goddess. (Staples, 1937, p. 155)

Staples interprets the story as a midrash, "an interpretation of present history in the light of past experiences, legends, myths, folk-lore, etc." (Staples, 1937, p.148) written to comfort the exiled Israelites after their return home. In his analysis, Ruth is an appendage of Naomi. The son of Naomi becomes the promise of the new Israel. But if Ruth "disappears into Naomi," just as the priestess and sacred rites of women were absorbed into and obliterated by the new image of women evolving in the post-exilic period, the midrash may evoke rituals, legends, and folklore affirming women's associations in the face of their transformation and suppression in the new Israel.

This possibility is affirmed by two themes informing the Book of Ruth. Ruth was a foreigner whose marriage to one of the "great men of the city" was approved by those in authority and by the people at large. The story may then be a "plea for inclusion of foreigners in the 'assembly of Israel'" (The Interpreter's Bible, 1953, p. 831):

> If it is in specific opposition to Nehemiah's attempt to annul all mixed marriages (Neh.13:23–25) it should be dated toward the end of the fifth century. (The Interpreter's Bible, 1953, p. 830)

And it is through the relationship between two women that the plea is made. Foremost the Book of Ruth is:

> . . . a tale of trust and affection between two women . . . a tale of friendship in the true sense and the friends are women. The relation between Boaz and Ruth is subordinated to the relation between Naomi and her daughter-in-law . . . for her daughter-in-law who loved her was . . . better, . . . than seven sons. (The Interpreter's Bible, 1953, p. 831)

The trust between Naomi and Ruth stands as a symbol of the fusion of Hebrew and Arab tribes, over against the increasing pressure of exclusionism and isolationist ideologies that contribute to suppression of women, women's rites, and women's associations, and that contribute to the solidification of ethnic-cultural identity which supports national boundaries. The process of redefining "peoples" on the basis of national boundaries is not gender neutral. Some women resisted exclusionary ideologies as they attempted to define what the new nation would be. The association between Deborah and Jael offers another motif for exploring the role of women's friendships in that process.

Deborah was a prophet of the Israelites, but, as historian Rachel Adler points out, "what is emphasized is her role as a quasi-military leader, uniting, encouraging, and reassuring the tribal armies" (Adler, 1977, p. 246). Deborah is given credit for the defeat of Sisera with the help of the Kenite, Jael. Bernadette Brooten cites evidence of Jael's function "as a priestess at the sacred precincts related to the terebinth of Elon-Bezaanannim" (Brooten, 1982, p. 85). While the story suggests that Jael lured Sisera to her tent with the offer of milk and a place to rest:

> . . . It may be concluded that Sisera fled from the battle to the tent of Jael . . . because of the special exalted position of Jael, and because her dwelling place, Elon Bezaannaim, was recognized as a sanctified spot and a place of refuge where protection was given to an enemy. (Mazar in Brooten, 1982, p. 85)

As a prophet and leader, it would follow that Deborah would have participated in the social and religious movements of her times, displaying authority and courage. Nonetheless, it seems that here, Deborah did not support the separatism of Yahwist ideology. According to the text, while Deborah "restores the Israelite nation to the God they have forsaken," she also "embraces the alien tribe of the Kenites . . . by blessing not only Jael, but her whole tribe" (The Interpreter's Bible, 1953, p. 168).

The priestly functions of women were also connected to economic power; ousted from those roles, women lost the means of obtaining economic security. This fact may have motivated Deborah and Jael in their apparent ruthless attempt to assassinate Sisera. As Rachel Adler points out, Sarah, Rebecca, Rachael, and Leah, all wives of wealthy chieftains, attempted to "secure for their sons the preeminent rights to political power and riches, or, as in the case of Rachael and Leah, struggle(s) to become the more powerful wife by having more sons and hence having access to the political power of these sons in the future," a phenomenon not limited to women of the upper classes (Adler, 1977, pp. 245, 246). Similarly Sarah may have cast out Hagar, attempting to secure access to political and economic power through her son, an example of horizontal violence as women's options are increasingly foreclosed. Yet, divisiveness was countered by the strength of women's associations as those associations continued to support strategies for survival.

The Challenge of Islam

As Muhammad rose to power on the Arabian peninsula, Jewish-Arab tribes, Qurayzah and an-Nadīr, settled the fertile lands in the oasis of Yathrib or Medina. The Jewish-Arab Qaynuqā' were known for their crafts and craft markets. Two dominant Arab clans, Aws and Khazraj, formed confederations with the Jewish tribes of "jiwar": they protected one another as neighbors (Watt, 1974).

Struggles between alliances of tribes dominated life in Medina prior to the Hijra, or migration of Muhammad to Medina in 622 C.E. (year 1 of the Muslim calendar). Muhammad was invited to Medina as arbitrator of intertribal disputes. Abu al-Qasim Muhammad ibn Abd-Allah was born in Mecca, the major trading center of western and central Arabia. During this period, the Meccan economy was in significant transition. An emerging class of merchants claiming trade monopolies became increasingly powerful (Watt, 1974).

Muhammad affirmed his prophethood by placing himself on a continuum with the prophets of Judaism and Christianity, Moses and Jesus. Similarly the Muslim ("one who submits") was asked to give allegiance to one God and doctrine controlling social mores, defining good and evil, prescribing right behavior and punishing wrongdoers. Those who responded were given the historic responsibility to create a social order harmonious with the dictates of that god. Islam evolved next to the Monophysites and Nestorians of the Christian church, and Jewish tribes in Mesopotamia (Iraq), the Syrian highlands, including Palestine, northern and southern Arabia. Judaism became the official religion of the Himyarite kings of the Yemen in the 5th century, until they were superseded by the Ethiopian Christians in 525 C.E. Hanifism, Arabian monotheism, probably influenced Muhammad's vision of unification of Arab tribes under Islam. The prophet Muhammad and his supporters structured the Muslim state on the basis of faith and submission to the authority of Muhammad and to his descendants, the Caliphs, rulers of the empire (Hodgson, 1974; Lewis, 1984; Stillman, 1979).

Like the Jewish community, governed by Halaka, a set of rules prescribing every aspect of daily behavior, the Muslim community was governed by the holy law, Shari'a, developed by jurists from the Qur'an and traditions (Hadith) of the Prophet. This code reflected an ideal pattern of conduct toward which society must strive. According to the Shari'a, the Caliph, or ruler, was elected by God and had ultimate power in military, civil, and religious matters. His charge was to maintain the spiritual and material legacy of the prophet. Support came from the "Ulama"—doctors of divine law, who interpreted and advised (Lewis, 1984).

A struggle for power within Meccan society (as well as in Medina) shaped events leading to the consolidation of Islam. Merchants in Mecca, wealthy from expanded commercial activity in conjunction with war, and claiming rights over land based on wealth, fought Muhammad and his followers. Mecca was the religious and economic center of important trade routes connecting North and South Arabia. It was the site of the sacred shrine, the Ka'ba, and of the important Hajj, or yearly pilgrimage. The harem, sacred circle of stones, within the Ka'ba, housed the three goddesses venerated by Arabs.

Muhammad fled to Medina in the face of animosity from Meccans and assumed his role as arbitrator of intertribal disputes. Two women from Medina were among the first of 75 Medinese converts to Islam in June, 622 (Stern, 1939). Jewish women became allies to Muhammad through their associations with tribes accepting Islam. Other tribes rejected Muhammad as a false Messiah and were duly punished.

With the surrender of Mecca, many tribes requested missionaries to teach them the new faith. The Islamic federation was open to Jews, Christians, Zoroastrians, and other monotheists as protected minorities. Once settlement was made of an annual tribute and poll tax, they could no longer be attacked (Hodgson, 1974; Watt, 1974).

The new constitution announcing the Umma, or community of Islam, solidifed ethnic and nationalist boundaries and disrupted women's associations. The new religious-nationalist identification created alliances between men and competition for control of land, wealth, and women. In the course of ensuing wars, women suffered the ravages of hunger, rape, murder, loss of homes, loss of land, separation from clans, and from women across newly defined boundaries. The imposition of a new hierarchy further transformed women's world: a world of spiritual, political, and economic activity supporting intercommunality. The gradual dissolution of women's spiritual and economic power is symbolized by the replacement of the harem of the goddesses by the harem of the lord or husband.

The revolt of the "harlots" of Hadramaut is an example of bonding as a strategy for survival and for attempting to affect the course of historical events. Historian A. F. L. Beeston discusses a revolt led by women of Hadramaut in Yemen (southern Arabia) after the death of Muhammad (cited in the Kitab al-Muhabbor of Muhammad ibn Habīb al-Bagdādī). The revolt was led by six women of Kindah and Hadramaut. Upon hearing of Muhammad's death they "dyed their hands with henna and played on the tambourine. To them came out the harlots of Hadramaut, and did likewise, so that some twenty-odd women joined the six" (Beeston, 1952, p. 17). Some of the women came from Tin'ah, a center of pagan cult, and Sabwah, the most important religious center of Hadramaut. Among them was the Jewess Hirr, daughter of Ya'min, "from whose name is derived the proverbial expression for adulterousness . . . " (Beeston, 1952, p. 17). Local tribes supported their revolt; but they were routed by emissaries of the first Caliph Abu Bakr who "took the women and cut off their hands; and the women's partisans were killed, and some of the women fled to Kufah" (Beeston, 1952, p. 19).

Beeston demonstrates that the so called harlots were priestesses reasserting their rites in an attempt to encourage revival of the pagan cults. Eight of the women were associated with nobility through class or tribe, including the Jewess Hirr, and therefore could not have been "common prostitutes":

> This attempt was at the outset successful and aided by the discontent aroused by the methods of collecting the zākat-tax . . . they gathered a force of sympathizers among the tribes, so that only the energetic measures of the Caliph crushed the movement and saved South Arabia for Islam. (Beeston, 1952, p. 20)

The severity of punishment makes clear the threat of the priestesses to the authority of the Caliph and the new religion. In the context of the new religion, the temple priestess is the "loose woman" (Raymond, 1989) and defined as "harlot," as criminal:

> . . . The so-called Temple prostitutes were in reality women who reserved for themselves the ancient prerogative to choose their own lovers and bear children who would inherit their property. Kadistu or qadishtu, a word often translated by male scholars as "harlot," literally means "holy woman." (Starhawk, 1987, p. 58)

The presence of a Jew, Hirr, is, according to Beeston, easily accounted for since the Jews would have wanted to counteract the influence of Islam. It is likely, however, that Hirr's presence confirms her association with other Arab women of cultic influence. Theirs, then, was not only a revolt against the new faith, it was also an assertion of a widely accepted tradition of women's intercommunal associations. It is likely that revolt may also have brought together women from a range of social classes other than nobility; a fact obscured by history when defined as the exploits of elite classes.

The period immediately following Muhammad's death was one of apostasy on the part of groups and individuals resisting, for a range of reasons, the new socioeconomic-spiritual system. Women actively protected their rights in many ways, both before and after Muhammad's death. Hind bint Utbah, of an important Arab tribe, wife of the tribal chief and mother of a future Caliph, was a leader in her own right. She is noted to have rebelled against Islam, so that when an uncle of Muhammad antagonistic to the new faith joined the Meccan opposition, he "asked and received her [Hind's] approval of his conduct in the cause of Allāt and al-Uzzā [female goddesses of the Kaba] and in the cause of those who followed them" (Abbott, 1941, p. 271).

In spite of her opposition to Islam, Hind chose to assist Zainab, daughter of Muhammad, in her flight to join her father at Medina " . . . justifying her unexpected action to the suspicious Zainab by a statement to the effect that the affairs of the men did not concern the women" (Abbott, 1941, p. 272). Hind led women in battle in 625, and as their tribe faced the final battle with Muhammad, she continued to press for victory. When it became clear that her cause was lost "she vented her wrath this time on her powerless gods. Shattering her idols to pieces, she cried, 'We have certainly been deceived in you!' " (Abbott, 1941, p. 275). Hind was finally forced to take the oath of allegiance to Muhammad; when she did, she is said to have supported it wholeheartedly (Abbott, 1941, p. 277).

Another woman who led a revolt against Muhammad was not given the same opportunity to embrace Islam. Soldiers of Islam took captive Umm Qirfah Fātimah bint Rabī'ah, along with her daughter Umm Zim Salmā bint Mālik. She was put to a "barbarous execution, tying each foot to a beast which when driven tore her in two," while her daughter, given to Muhammad's wife, Aisha, eventually died on the battlefield, while avenging her mother's death (Abbott, 1941, p. 280).

After Muhammad's death, Umm Sādir Sajāh bint Aws ibn Hiqq, a prophetess, led her tribes in a revolt in her name against the new faith. She is characterized by one school of historiographers as "a weak woman and a false prophetess who eventually saw the true light and died a good Moslem" (Abbott, 1941, p. 281). Another school, however, found that she had many followers as she risked asserting her political and spiritual right to leadership (Abbott, 1941, p. 281). After losing several battles, Umm Sādir Sajāh agreed to a settlement in return for withdrawing her troops. The success of Islam on the battlefield effectively quelled resistance. Yet, "Emerging from an almost complete obscurity, Sajāh, the warrior–prophetess, played a brief but major role on the political stage of Central Arabia and then stepped off that stage into an even more dense obscurity than that out of which she had first emerged" (Abbott, 1941, p. 284).

Some women readily accepted the new faith—for example, women who did not have important religous functions and women who married outside their tribes and went to live with husbands, adopting their faith. Bedouin women who married Medinese converted when their new clan allied with Muhammad. Women with high social standing in tribes allied with Muhammad were among the first converts. The first martyr of the new faith may have been a slave, Sumayyah. (Stern, 1939). Many women with close contact with Jewish and Christian women were already familiar with aspects of the new faith.

Muhammad took as wives two Jewish women captured in battle. Joining the harem relationship they took on the status of "Mothers of the Believers." The term *mother*, noted by Bernadette Brooten and others, is a sign of social authority: in this case Muhammad's wives were to serve as examples of the new Arab woman. Raihānah bint Zaid, of the Banū Nadīr, had married into the Jewish tribe of Banū Quraizah and lost her husband and other male relatives in the massacre of that tribe (Abbott, 1941). According to some accounts, she may have chosen the status of concubine slave rather than becoming a full fledged wife, "a status in which she could retain her old faith and escape the limitations of seclusion" (Abbott, 1941, p. 38). Safiyah bint Huayy, widow of Kinānah, chief of the Jews of Khaibar, accepted Islam. When Muhammad asked his favored wife, Aisha, for her opinion, she responded: "She is but a Jewess" (Abbott, 1942, pp. 39–42). Muhammad coached Safiyah to retort: "How can you be above me when Aaron is my father, Moses is my uncle, and Mohammed is my husband!" (Abbott, 1942, p. 42). Nonetheless, a significant incident challenging their loyalty to Islam illustrates that Muhammad's wives did act in consort as women in a rapidly changing social milieu.

In the Verse of Choice, Muhammad exhorts his wives to choose between a life of wordly pleasures or dedication to Allah and his prophet. Interpretations of the events leading to Muhammad's dissatisfaction and subsequent withdrawal for a month from his wives point to the possibility that they sought "consciously or unconsciously some sort of tangible compensation for the loss of their liberty in the demand for more worldly goods . . . " (Abbott, 1942, p. 49). When Aisha's father attempts to meddle in the affair, one of Muhammad's wives responds and wins the "admiration and gratitude of the rest of the 'sisterhood' " (Abbott, 1942, p. 53). In the end, Aisha leads the way as all of Muhammad's wives reaffirm their commitment to Allah and to his prophet. Subsequent harem regulations may have been instituted to demoralize this active association. Middle East scholar Leila Ahmed asserts that the influence exerted by Aisha and her bold "sisters" on Muhammad in the incident described, is an indication of the strength of women's position in the Jahiliya (the Age of Ignorance, so termed to describe the time before Muhammad's advent in the 7th century) (Ahmed, 1986). When Aisha attempts to extend her political influence after Muhammad's death, she is respected by many who view her as an authority in her own right. Her opponents, on the other hand, are well armed with invectives against a woman assuming public leadership, interpreting the sayings of the prophet to confirm their misogyny.

Conversion of Women into Property

Israelite women lived among the Caananites, North Arabian Midanites, Kenites, Edomites, Nabateans, and Himyarites of South Arabia. Hebrew tribes worshipped alongside other Arab tribes at sacred groves where stone altars represented the Goddess Inanna-Astarte-Asherah. Among the Kenites, circumcision was a male initation rite intended to ward off demons. Spring fertility rites characteristic of Semitic tribes included sacrifice of the first-born animals (Vriezen, 1963).

Thus it stands to reason that the Hebrew god Yahweh was originally:

> . . . a Caananite fertility deity before taken over and transformed by the early Hebrews, or that Aaron was conforming to customary practice when he fashioned a graven image of the divine while Moses was on Mt. Sinai receiving the Ten Commandments. (Oschorn, 1981, p. 135)

Tribes that escaped a protracted stay in Egypt during a period of social repression accepted a new code of laws received from Moses. The Mosaic God, Yahweh, underwent centuries of evolution, shaped by political and economic developments and their reverberations in social life.

Yahweh was the "Lord of all Gods," whose covenant with the Israelites established a hierarchy of duties and responsibilities that gave meaning to the solidification of the Israelites as a people. Yahweh promised to bless his people in exchange for obedience to his code of law. The notion of an indwelling spirit is superseded by the notion of power outside of and over nature. Those who came within the sphere of Yahwism would be controlled by its laws and its God, a God who controlled nature, and therefore feast and famine.

Yahweh replaced Inanna-Astarte as giver of life: his laws conflicted with customary religious practice associated with the harvest. Those associated with the magical rites, sexual rites, and sacrifices connected to the harvest were eliminated or absorbed. Yahwism propagated laws against local cults, mourning customs and sorcery, and instituted laws regulating daily life, as well as the "rights and duties of the king" (Vriezen, 1963, p. 230). A shift in sexual laws, probably representing competition among alliances of men for control of women's sexual and spiritual lives, changed the relationship of women to sacred rites, affecting women's associations within the context of cultic life.

The institutionalization of "chosen-ness," hierarchy, and control over nature represented the institutionalization of the stage of phallocentrism characteristic of the major religious movements affecting social organization and ethnic relations.

Yahweh was not only a "giver of wine, oil and fruit," he was also a warrior god who triumphed over other gods on behalf of his people. He was a national god: the covenant of Abram and the patriarchs signified the establishment and maintenance of his people. Through renewal of the covenant (Moses receiving the Ten Commandments at Sinai), the historical development of monotheism solidified the doctrine of fidelity to a male god and observance of his laws. In return for "purity of heart," . . . "God offers to make of that remnant a new community which shall become the basis of a new nation . . . obedience to the law and purity of heart lead to salvation" (Carella & Sheres, 1988, pp. 238, 239).

The connection between nationalist ideology and control of women and the conviction that violent means were necessary to break women's associations, is evident in the biblical story of Dinah. Dinah, daughter of Leah, is raped by the "pagan" Shechem. When Jacob, her father, finds out, he insists that the men of Shechem's tribe become circumcised. They agree; nonetheless they are slaughtered by Dinah's brothers. Historian Jeffrey K. Salkin offers the following interpretation of the Dinah story:

> There is another explanation that says that Dinah was *lured* outside. Pirke DeRabbi Eliezer 38:4 states that Shechem lured her from her tent with dancing women; these are the Biblical text's "daughters of the land." Dinah, in her curiosity and, perhaps, in her search for companionship, went out to see them and was seduced by Shechem. Hence, she is lured outside by pagan influences. She heard the revelry of the Canaanite women and wanted to be like them. Her desire to sink to the level of pagan women was ultimately her ruin.
>
> In sum, it is all laid at her door. Had she not gone out, an entire city would have been spared the sword. Yet, tragically, Dinah has no chance to defend herself against the rabbinic charges of immodesty and wanton assimilation, for she says nothing in the narrative. Neither does she speak in any of the post-Biblical and rabbinic accounts. If she is mute, then she can only be a symbol of the silence of the Jewish woman in pre-modern history. (Salkin, 1986, pp. 285, 286)

This interpretation of the story, blaming Dinah, indicates the ethnic-class separation of women in the name of protecting the "purity" of the Israelite people. But from Dinah's perspective, she heard the revelry of the Canaanite women and wanted to be like them. Herself a daughter of the land she most likely recognized their dancing and their rituals. Dinah's link with the women of the land, reflecting both the literal and symbolic intermingling of Israelites and their Caananite neighbors, was indeed her downfall.

> As the story is explored and discussed by the Rabbis, Dinah comes to receive the full force of their attitude toward women. Hence, Bereshit Rabbah 45:5 says that she was a gadabout. Elsewhere, she is hidden from the eyes of men. Bereshit Rabbah 76:9 states that when Jacob was bringing his family across the Jabbok River, fleeing from the wrath of his brother, Esau, he put Dinah in a casket so that Esau would not see her and take her. Me'am Loez, the eighteenth century

Ladino commentary by Jacob Culi, reads the Dinah story as a practical lesson for Jewish parents: Keep your daughters inside! (Salkin, 1986, p. 285)

If Dinah is a gadabout, then she is anyone's prey. What makes her a gadabout? That she heard the revelry of the Canaanite women and wanted to be like them. That she was taken by the gadabout Shechem. The full force of the rabbis' attitude toward her is institutionalized by separation of women and of women's space. Jacob, the father, becomes the guardian of her sexuality, which defines her. This reduction of women to their sexual and reproductive capabilities is signified by Dinah's rape. On the basis of Dinah's rape, Shechem asks for official confirmation of his ownership of her. The need to separate and segregate her from other men who may want her is economic; she—her sexuality—is a man's (her father's and then her husband's) property. The proscriptions controlling her and her sexuality are proscriptions against her associations with other women, to whom she is drawn, and with whom she associates in maintaining rites affirming the sacredness of the earth. Here the lesson—keep your daughters inside—resonates as an indictment against women's associations, particularly as they represent and support interethnic co-mingling. Seduction by Shechem deters Dinah from her original goal: association with other women. Put another way, rape must be used to convince her to give up her original goal.

Dinah's story connects silencing of women and disruption of women's associations and of women's relationship to the land to institutions and ideologies that call intermingling of cultures "wanton assimilation." " . . . If she is mute then she can only be a symbol of the 'silenc[ing]' of women in pre-modern history" (Salkin, 1986, p. 286). Her silencing is connected to her relation to the land and to the "daughters of the land." The consequences of her search for companionship are rape and war.

Injunctions narrowing the range of women's associations, a source of their power and survival, parallel early nationalist-patristic religious movements. Nationalist-patristic religious movements redefine social mores: private land ownership is a sacred right of an elite with economic and political control. Control of the fertility of the earth and of women is necessary to this project. "God has the authority of possession and control over Israel that a husband has over a wife" (Setel, 1985, p. 92). Attempting to suppress as well as to utilize Canaanite nature cults, the Yahweh of the Mosaic revolution sets promiscuity in opposition to fertility, identifying women both with the land and with Israel. An Israel that strays from the rule of Yahweh through promiscuity suffers the consequences of famine and plague. A woman who strays from the rule of Yahweh, thus from Israel, suffers humiliation, even death. The purification of Israel from sin is identified with the "washing away of moral filth" of the proud daughters of Zion (Oschorn, 1981, p. 161).

Similarly, centuries later, the Koran compares women to cultivated land, exhorting Islamic men to "come then to your cultivated land as ye wish but send forward something for yourselves and act piously towards Allah, and know that ye are going to meet Him . . . (2:223)" (Wiebke, 1981, p. 112). Just as the success of the Israelite god and nation depended upon a process of incorporation of popular customs, so Muhammad's teachings reframed, and eventually superseded, familiar customs:

> Some accounts depict Muhammad as having been so eager to gain the acceptance of the Meccan leaders that he even conceded that three pagan goddesses, al-Lat, al-Uzza and Manat, were "sacred swans" worthy of veneration. This horrified some of the Muslims. When Muhammad realized the full meaning of what he had done, he emphatically disowned what he had supposed to be a revelation from God, blamed it on Satan, and added:
> What, would you have males and He females?
> That would indeed be an unjust division.
> They are nothing but names you and your fathers have named.
> God has sent down no authority touching them. (Quran, 53:21–23) (Goldschmidt, 1983, p. 31)

The early Israelite experience, solidification of Christian religious and military power, and the period of transition from the Jahiliya (Age of Ignorance before Islam) to consolidation of Islam, share characteristics in the history of appropriation of women and land as the private domain of men. Social organization based on nationalist-religious movements, concentration of wealth by men and by women associated with those men, assimilation of policies promoting war into social organization, all brought significant changes into women's lives. Women's bodies, invaded by figurative and literal armies of men, are the ground of occupation.

For example, in 6th-century Arabia, as men who owned more cattle claimed privileges of land use, others were left landless, with no means of production. Rights over property resulting in surplus produce and increased wealth led to identification of power with wealth, rather than with respect and custom. Historian Montgomery Watt connects this phenomenon with the introduction of Arabic marriages of dominion of male over female. Among the Hebrews and Arameans, the husband becomes the woman's lord or owner. The official position of wife in the house of her husband is that of a captive slave (Smith, 1903). Smith points out that wherever the husband is the wife's *ba'al*, or lord, marriage by purchase becomes the rule. Men seek control of her reproductive capabilities through moral injunctions: definitions of chastity, marriage, and divorce laws. "Woman" is redefined as nature, as fertility, an equation based on mythification and appropriation of women's labor.

Nationalist-militarist movements subsume women and land on the basis of ethno-demographic needs, reducing both to their use value. Both serve the continuation and productivity of the state. Division of the land of Canaan, for example, occurred among adult males of tribes leaving Egypt with Moses. Women were included as wives, mothers, daughters; that is, in relations with

and to men (Oschorn, 1981). In this capacity, women are among the first settlers in the transition to the family-based land ownership fueling intertribal
warfare. Women were also the first to suffer "when urban centers drained off
the productivity of the land to support the monarchy and the military" (Meyers,
1978, p. 107).

Social controls dictating manners, speech, customs, and dress prescribed
a woman's status as property of the male state. The custom of veiling women
predated Islam throughout the Middle East. Historian Emile Marmorstein traces
the maintenance of sex-class status by dress code. Borders of gold and silver
on the dresses of middle-class Jewish and Christian women prior to the rise
of Islam indicated their prosperity (Marmorstein, 1954). Urban Jewish women
wore the veil in Palestine in the 3rd century C.E. (Marmorstein 1954, p. 5).
Marmorstein's analysis shows:

> . . . the similarity which existed in respect of the deportment of women within
> the pattern of Jewish social life in Palestine, in the third century C.E. and that
> of the social life of Islamic society through the centuries up to the present day.
> There was then, as there is now, a contrast between the simple, unveiled women
> of the villages, working in the fields and herding cattle and playing their full
> part in the intricate pattern of village economy, and the veiled women of the
> towns, almost confined to their homes and certainly to the company of women,
> watched and protected at the same time against the less reputable of their own
> inclinations and the wiles and intrigues of the passionate and dissolute inhabi-
> tants of cities. (Marmorstein, 1954, p. 6)

From an androcentric perspective, confinement to the company of women
is a punishment for what women do to men—entice men to rape. Further,
confinement with the "right" women is "protection" from the "wrong" women.
In fact, women sought one another for protection from what men did to
women. So that enforced seclusion in the home and sex-class separation on
the basis of the social-class status of the men with whom they associated set
limits on women's freedom to associate with one another. Men concealed
their utilization of women as servants of the phallocracy by distinguishing
"reputable" women associated with them as wives from "disreputable" women
who survived on the streets.

Marmorstein traces seclusion of "high-born" women to the consolidation
of the United Monarchy (10th century B.C.E.), when the rule of kings was firmly
established:

> One begins to notice a greater degree of seclusion of high-born women, now
> confined to their quarters and guarded by eunuchs. A fashionable female soci-
> ety emerged in the capital, refined and pampered, revelling in details of cos-
> tume, perfumes, adornment and luxury, which provoked the prophetic wrath
> of Isaiah. (Marmorstein, 1954, p. 10)

He traces use of the veil, to "protect" respectable married women, to the Assyrian code. By the Middle Assyrian period (Middle Assyrian Laws date from

the 15th to the 11th centuries B.C.E.), when a father protected his daughter's virginity as one of his assets, the state had firm control of female sexuality. Rules about veiling reflect that control. A married woman had to wear a veil, symbolizing her domestication. Slave women and prostitutes went unveiled, marking their vulnerability as game for any man. Punishment prescribed for a woman who did not comply included flogging and cutting off her ears. Men who were seen with women who did not comply were also punished. Lerner notes that sex-class regulation of women undergirds state power (Lerner, 1986). Marmorstein comments on similarities in strategies for instituting sex-class status: "The distinction between chaperones in the West and veils and seclusion in less temperate zones appears to be one of degree rather than of principle" (Marmorstein, 1954, p. 11).

The ingenuity of women in transforming discriminatory conditions applies both to acts of resistance and to collective strategies for survival. Women engaging in acts of resistance utilize the veil to conceal their identities. In "seclusion" women plot to protect their rights. As Leila Ahmed notes:

> Mohammad's contemporaries, were not themselves molded by the ordinances and practices of Islam though adhering to them consciously no doubt; those that had molded them were the attitudes and practices of the Jahilia society that Islam was transforming, a society in which women had been remarkably active and independent. (Ahmed, 1986, p. 691)

Women's Associations between Caliphate and Ottoman Rule

The emergence and expansion of Islam in the 7th century and consolidation of the Islamic state had restructered social organizations and relations between women. Under the Islamic state, Jews and Christians were *dhimmi* (People of the Book) worthy of privileges, but second-class citizens. In exchange for protection by and service to the state, their lives were circumscribed by a set of conditions or laws. Where wealth and power are accumulated at the top of a hierarchical system, the notion of inevitability—that some are naturally more deserving than others—serves unjust distribution of decision-making and resources.

The actual situation of dhimmi varied geographically and depended upon political developments and individual rulers. Peasants in particular were burdened by the imposition of the *jizya* or poll tax. Traveling dhimmi carried papers confirming payment of the tax and had to return periodically to their place of residence to renew that paper. The state sporadically enforced restrictions on what clothes could be worn; prohibitions against owning certain animals and against bearing arms; limits on buildings and uses of places of worship. Nonetheless, Jews reported the benefits of dhimmi life, encouraging others to emigrate to the Islamic lands to escape persecutions in Christian Europe. Many Jews suffering persecution from the Western Christian church emigrated to Palestine–Syria, Egypt, and surrounding areas. Jews and certain Christians (Nestorian and Monophysites suffering from oppression in Byzantium) viewed the Muslim Arabs as liberators. The persecutions of Heraclius (610–641) after the recapture of Palestine from the Persians in 629 had severely disrupted Jewish life. The legal, material, and spiritual restrictions suffered by Jewish and Christian communities of the Near East were less onerous under Islam. Payment of the poll tax was an obligation that kept intact a system from which benefits were derived: the promise of protection of life, religious freedom, and economic viability.

Under Islam, Jews and Christians maintained legal jurisdiction over intracommunal affairs. Many dhimmi became important members of the Muslim autocracy. For example, a Jewish convert to Islam administered the newly founded Fatimid Empire of the East, with the help of a Christian finance director in charge of Egypt and a Jew in charge of Syria. Under pressure, the Caliph eventually removed both, but these kinds of assignments nonetheless persisted. Those Jews who acquired power within the state system were sometimes able to assist poorer Jews by interceding for them. The Islamic state benefited economically from allowing its conquered subjects to keep their communities intact and by utilizing their skills in exchange for privileges. This system supported cultural reciprocity among Arabic speaking peoples. An efflorescence of Arabic-Judaic culture in literature, philosophy, and science, particularly in Muslim Spain, attests to the value of tolerance and of support for continuing integration.

How did women fare in a society that ascribed second-class citizenship to men and women who did not subscribe to the proper faith? Within a range of interpretations, religious tenets of Islam informed state policy. A nationalist-militarist movement, Islam prescribed the place of women intracommunally, but within villages, towns, cities, and classes, how the laws of Islam were interpreted and lived out, varied. The Islamic state gave dhimmi men jurisdictional control over "their women" in exchange for service to the state. Intercommunal relations continued, supported by Jewish, Muslim, and Christian women. Associations between women were important to the maintenance of their communities, and intercommunally, to the state. They also could provide support to women deprived of civil liberties available to men. On rare occasions, their associations acted to overturn male-state hegemony.

Historian S. D. Goitein analyzed documents, called Geniza, discovered in the vault of the synagogue of Fustat, or Old Cairo, to ascertain the quality of life and of intercommunal relations under Fatimid and Ayyubid Caliphates (10th through 13th centuries). The term *Geniza* means storeroom, most often of a synagogue. Jews collected documents and letters bearing the word "God" in the vault of the synagogue since, by law, they could not be destroyed. The documents detail the world of Muslims, Jews, and Christians living and traveling in areas spanning Spain and Morocco, Aden and India. Goitein's analysis pays some attention to the particular situation of women.

Within communal organizations, men continued to utilize religious and legal prescriptions delimiting women's access to decision making, resources, and liberties. Islamic hegemony placed further restrictions on Jewish and Christian women as minorities. Women's access to resources within their communities and restrictions on their lives varied geographically as well as according to rank or social class.

Despite restrictions against this, women appeared in court as witnesses for themselves, and women used courts to secure resources due them when the state refused to grant these resources. Some women owned businesses and rental properties. Business partnerships between Jewish, Muslim, and Christian women supported intercommunal relations. Women of all classes possessed immovables through gifts, dowry, or inheritance. Women with property took active control, buying and selling, renting or leasing: houses, stores, workshops, flour mills, and "other types of urban real estate . . . " and also maintained these properties, often in conjunction with and to benefit women friends or relations (Goitein, 1978, p. 326). While, according to Goitein's findings, daughters of rich and influential Jews who emigrated from Iraq and Iran to Syria–Palestine, Egypt, and Tunisia, were more independent (Goitein, 1978), it is likely that independent women in all social strata were women who responded to the opportunities available, given their economic situations.

In a brief historical survey of the status of women in the ancient Middle East, Goitein notes that " . . . the women of ancient Israel reacted against the antifeminism of the national religion by turning to foreign gods . . . They baked cakes and offered libations and incense to the sweet 'Queen of Heaven' . . . " (Goitein, 1978, p. 321). Goitein refers to this tradition of rejecting the national religion in his analysis of women's names. His findings affirm the "chasm between the popular local subculture of women and the worldwide [Hebrew] book culture of the men" (Goitein, 1978, p. 315).

In the world of the Geniza documents, female names were "living words" (Goitein, 1978, p. 314). The name a woman chose for her daughter reflected her aspirations for her daughter and for herself. Women chose to exclude Biblical and Hebrew names and names from classical Arabic. The chosen names contained no reference to God or to religious concepts. Furthermore, Goitein notes that chastity and fertility, "regarded by men as the most praiseworthy attributes of a woman," don't appear in women's vocabulary of naming (Goitein, 1978, p. 317).

Names were infused with a sense of power, ruling, overcoming, and victory. The title *Sitt* (mistress or female ruler) was used with an abstract noun — "the idea of eminence is found throughout"; Glory, Praise, Fame, Leadership, Excellence, Overcoming (Goitein, 1978, p. 316). Names included: "Female Ruler," "She Who Rules over the Turbans" (namely, the men), "Mistress of Her

Time" (Goitein, 1978, p. 316). Names such as "Wishes Fulfilled," "The One Hoped for," "Good Luck," and "Cherished Gift" may have indicated protest against the male prejudice toward birth of a girl (Goitein, 1978, p. 318). Goitein notes:

> . . . the longevity of some names, even rare ones, is remarkable. Umm al-Khayr, "Possessor (literally 'Mother') of Goodness," found thus far only once in a Jewish document, dated 1029, appears again as the name of a Muslim noble woman, married in Aswan three hundred years later, in 1334. And some female names from the Geniza, especially those composed with Sitt have lived well into the second half of the twentieth century, at least in the Karaite community of Cairo . . . (Goitein, 1978, p. 319)

The longevity of the name may also be evidence of a powerful, if unrecognized, tradition of common strategies among Muslim, Jewish, and Christian women.

The range of women's intercommunal relations is expressed in interpersonal as well as economic realms. For example, a Muslim collection of legal opinions questioning whether or not a Jewish ritual slaughterer must be employed in a Muslim household employing a Jewish wet nurse, allowing the nurse to eat with the rest of the family (Goitein, 1978), indicates concern for the well-being of the nurse. Goitein notes a case in the 13th century of a Jewish woman who died after nursing a Muslim boy. She leaves a child of her own. "It was impossible to establish which was the Jewish boy and which the Muslim" (Goitein, 1978, p. 127).

A Muslim woman receives monthly rent for a drugstore from a Jewish pharmacist. Another Muslim woman sells a workshop of clothes dyeing to a Jewish dyer. Three Christian women sell the remaining share of a house belonging to them to a Jew who had acquired the other shares (Goitein, 1978). Goitein recounts in detail the story of an "independent woman"—officially unattached to a man, who nonetheless had children—a shrewd businesswoman, who made an impression on her contemporaries:

> Al-Wuhsha dealt with other women, and by no means only in small matters. Part of her gold, as stated in her will, was deposited with "Lady Choice," under what circumstances is not said. In an enormous document, of which, unfortunately, mostly the legal verbiage is preserved, al-Wuhsha releases a "Lady Beauty" from all obligations she might have incurred while making transactions on her behalf. A gift was also involved, probably of real estate, for al-Wuhsha, her son Abū Sa'd and her other heirs are obliged to defend Lady Beauty's rights, if any claim is made against her. (Goitein, 1978, p. 350)

Finally, the synagogue expelled al-Wuhsha, ostensibly because of her illicit, well-known love affair, demonstrating that " . . . even a rich woman may not permit herself to violate accepted rules of behavior" (Goitein, 1978, p. 351).

As a result of experience in the commercial world, women were sometimes appointed as guardians of their children and as executors of estates.

Many women left wills specifying that their daughters have formal education. Goitein notes one such case of a woman whose mother and grandmother were formally educated, and were considered spiritual leaders (Goitein, 1978).

On the other hand, most evidence of the Geniza points to a pervasive lack of opportunity for women to acquire literacy skills, limiting their ability to support themselves and to relate to the outside world. Most upper-class women did not have free access to the marketplace. Female brokers acted as intermediaries, assisting women in commercial transactions. Most female brokers and agents were poor. In general, women were not " . . . in the mainstream of the economy—the large scale production and exchange of goods. Moreover a married woman, so far as she did not possess means outside the common pool of the nuclear family, depended entirely on her husband and, in this absence, on his male relatives, even her own sons, or his business partners or friends" (Goitein, 1978, p. 332). Her share in economic life was, as Goitein points out, derivative, and for the most part insignificant. Women married in their teens, and moved to their husbands' domicile. Marriages were class alliances. Within that system, some women had access to resources and to derivative power. But, like all dhimmi, their subordinate position meant that whatever gains they made were precarious and often acquired through humiliating and even dangerous circumstances. Furthermore, while women inherited and utilized property, and could and did engage in many spheres:

> . . . there is no doubt that their special position in these cases ensured further existence of their patrilineage and of its property. Instead of breaking down the patrilineal system of descent and inheritance they acted as a secure measure for its smooth working even in extreme situations in which patriliny was threatened . . . (Grosz, 1989, p. 180)

Goitein applauds the integration of men and women in Geniza society, citing examples of women on their own and in need for a range of reasons, who interact with men as they make use of social services. But interaction with men does not mean equal access to power. In this case, interaction with men is the result of humiliating dependence on men for survival (whether individual husbands or the communal organization). It is then especially significant that women made use of intercommunal associations to secure what means they did have.

Access to courts was one way women were able to make use of their assets. Jewish women applied to Muslim courts when Muslim jurisprudence worked in their favor. Muslim women appeared in Jewish courts when to do so would provide benefits not available through their own court system. Titles such as, "The Ruler," "The Mistress Over the Kingdom" belong to women of importance in the 11th-century Fatimid courts. Mallāl, also known as al-Sayyida, "The Mistress" or "The Ruler" held the post of regent (d. 1023). The first Fatimid Caliph married a Christian woman who obtained appointments for her sons as patriarchs of the Melchite Church. Her daughter, Sayyidat al-Mulk, "The Mistress Over the Kingdom," may have engineered the murder of her brother, the notoriously cruel ruler, al-Hākim. She ruled the country for 4 years after his death. The Sudanese mother of Caliph al-Mustansir (1036–1094) held power while her son was a minor. She had been a slave in the possession of a Jew (Goitein, 1878, p. 357). Again, while women with access to official power within the court of state bureaucracy could be influential, their power was dependent upon the approval and good will of men.

The Caliphate ruled by incorporating, synthesizing, and utilizing religious, legal, economic, and social practices of conquered populations. Muslims of Jewish descent influenced the evolution of the Hadith (sayings transmitted in Muhammad's name) through which Islam absorbed Jewish, Christian, and Zoroastrian teachings and legal concepts (Baron, 1943). While conquering Arabs formed an elite class, they allowed conquered populations to maintain administration of their communities. In this way they acquired support for the new regime, while focusing on expansion.

Rules and customs controlling women's lives supported smooth functioning of Muslim, Christian, and Jewish court systems. Economic partnerships among women segregated by class served maintenance of patriarchal communal organization. Women could utilize flexibility between court systems to benefit themselves, their children, and specifically, women friends. But many of the privileges of upper-class women were tied to the role of lower-class women, assigned subsistence production roles in the home. The husband provided the family domicile and the domestics to do the drudge work, freeing his wife to take charge of economic transactions protecting his properties and to enjoy leisurely activities. "Concubinage with slave girls was the most dreaded source of marital conflict . . . " and an additional source of horizontal antagonism between women (Goitein, 1978, p. 317). Class segregation of women, as well as the class status of women as women, is thus instituted to maintain a system of male dominion: " . . . The woman was . . . the drudge, who, by definition, did not enjoy the privilege of liberty and leisure required for learning" (Goitein, 1978, p. 355).

Some lower-class women developed skills denied to most upper-class women. This included female brokers and other poor women who were more likely to have literacy skills than were middle- or upper-class women. Teaching was open to women; however, husbands could prohibit them from teaching. Goitein cites a case of a woman without means who made a living running a school. Absent for long periods of time, her husband refused to support her and their two children. Nonetheless, he had the right to prohibit her from teaching if she stayed with him. To be free of him, she was forced to forfeit her marriage gift. Once divorced, however, she was free to teach (Goitein, 1978). In addition: "In the poorer sections of the population there was the mwallima, the female Bible teacher, usually a relative of the teacher who owned the school" (Goitein, 1978, p. 355). Here, a woman with property utilizes her assets to assist a poorer relative. In general, however, professions open to women brought little income (Goitein, 1978).

According to Goitein, the Geniza documents do not record any literary achievements of women. Says Goitein: "One may argue that a woman's voice was not to be heard in the synagogue. Thus, there was no 'seat in life,' no incentive for the creation of a religious poem by a woman" (Goitein, 1978, p. 358). On the other hand, Goitein does mention that a Jewish woman writing Arabic poetry in Spain is known through Muslim sources. Given the tradition of women poets and literary critics in the Arabic-speaking world, this is not surprising. Furthermore, the Geniza documents are stored because they contain reference to God. When Goitein asks a Yemenite girl whether or not her mother prays, she replies, "Yes, but she prays to God what *she* wants . . ." (Goitein, 1978, p. 355). Many women, no doubt, not only said what they wanted, but said it in their own way, whether or not their creations were recognized by the "book learning of men."

Associations between women in the period documented by the Cairo Geniza enhance and sometimes support women's survival. In this sense they are strategies for resistance to women's invisibility and exploitation. Those that appear through Goitein's analysis of the Genizas do not explicitly challenge the structure of patriarchal dominion. Yet, women defy restrictions, traveling, for example, under hazardous conditions to "visit a female relative in another town who was either expecting a baby, recuperating after delivery, ill, or suffering by being in an unaccustomed or unfriendly environment" (Goitein, 1978, p. 337). They go on religious pilgrimages together, in spite of proscriptions that a woman should not travel without a husband, brother, or other male companion. They meet in bathhouses, in the marketplace, in the courts. While their second class status is maintained by the world of "Warriors, courtiers, men of religion, scholars, physicians, merchants, and craftsmen . . . brothers to one another, and like brothers, often [fighting] among themselves . . . " (Goitein, 1978, p. 313), women belong to the world they create for themselves. This belonging is active, alive with conflict as well as compassion, negotiated as it was within and against the parameters of patriarchal dominion.

Protected Status in the Ottoman Domains

Carrying her goods on her back, Ester Kira was a well-known figure in the harems of the sultans of Turkey. An itinerant tradeswoman and a Jew, she was one of many dhimmi who made a living purchasing goods for upper-class Muslim women, a common practice in 16th-century Turkey. Eventually, Ester Kira became a Muslim, changing her name to Fatma (Davis, 1986).

The tradeswoman and her Muslim employer often became friends, providing services for one another beyond the roles stipulated by Ottoman society. A Muslim woman of the sultan's harem could not be seen trading in the marketplace. Lower-class women made a living providing services necessary to the status of upper-class women. The job of Kira, institutionalized, also provided a site for support of women by women across the boundaries of the sex-class system. It provided opportunities for women to influence and even subvert state politics. Jewish, Greek, Armenian, and eventually French women sold their wares—jewels, handiwork, clothing, perfumes, in a special room set aside for them in the harem:

> Being as they were, one of the few links between the sequestered woman and the outside world, they were often the agents of intrigue of one sort or another. Because of their entry into many harems they often acted as gorücü [a seer; also a woman sent to find a prospective bride]. They were also thought to possess medical knowledge and were in demand for that reason also. (Davis, 1986, p. 144)

The Kira and her patron formed associations that could benefit both. In repayment for purchasing goods for the upper-class woman of the harem, Ester Kira and her heirs were granted immunity from certain taxes. But the women of the harem could not save her from the final vulnerability of her dhimmi status. Soldiers whose pay was reduced by the Ottoman state because of debasement of the currency blamed Jews, and murdered Ester Kira.

Intercommunal relations remained stable during the early period of Ottoman rule. The Turkish-Muslim Empire, consolidated with the conquest of Constantinople, renamed Istanbul in 1453, included Syria–Palestine, Iraq, and Egypt, as well as all the territories encompassing Islam, eastern Judaism, and the eastern Christian communities. The Ottoman rulers encouraged settlement of Iberian Jews (exiled from Spain and Portugal, 1492–1493) and encouraged them, along with indigenous Jews and Christians, to occupy important positions in developing the economic life of the empire. The Ottoman state retained the social organization established by their Muslim-Arab predecessors. Jewish and Christian men had control of their respective religio-ethnic communities, organized into distinct corporate bodies known as *millets*.

Jewish men were influential advisors in the Ottoman court; they held important tax farms (jurisdiction over tax collection in specified areas); they were bankers and court physicians, and they negotiated commercial exchanges between foreign traders and local merchants. Ottoman sarrafs and Jewish merchants cooperated to the benefit of both. *Sarrafs* were government agents who distributed and recalled coinage. They served as agents for tax farmers, collecting fees for their service. Jewish customs and dock employees had knowledge of day-to-day affairs necessary to the sarrafs, who had knowledge of economic fluctuations critical to the Jewish merchants. The successful functioning of both groups depended upon keeping abreast of political and eco-

nomic developments within the government and the empire. Their successful operations assured the treasury of income and assured funds to support
officials whose salaries were derived from tax farm concessions (Braude &
Lewis, 1982; Epstein, 1980; Lewis, 1984).

Yet, Jewish tax farmers important to the government were a small percentage of the population. Local shopkeepers, peddlers, and artisans maintained
a level of vitality necessary to the success of the more privileged. They distributed goods and developed client–patron relations with local potentates.
Jewish peddlers were protected by local patrons in exchange for their services. An attack on a Jewish trader was considered an attack on his patron.
In areas where these relations were less fixed, Jewish traders were able to
maintain a relative degree of freedom by playing off one potentate against
another (Deshen & Zenner, 1982).

Under what circumstances did discrimination and persecution occur?
Dhimmi suffered during periods characterized by a resurgence of religious
orthodoxy and messianic fervor promoting religious purity. Restraining measures were sometimes enforced when Muslims perceived dhimmi as over-
stepping bounds, as too rich or too powerful. Imposition of restrictions also
occurred during periods of military buildup due to social unrest or weakening of power abroad.

During such periods, Jewish, Christian, and Muslim women suffered. Religious orthodoxy promoted the image of the obedient woman, keeper of the
hearth and of the purity of her community. Conformity kept the state intact
when threatened by outside forces or by internal rebellion. The state procured
the loyalty of dhimmi men and women in exchange for measured rights, access to resources, and support of the state. Intracommunally, men procured
the loyalty of women in exchange for protection, limited access to resources,
and conformity to prescribed roles in support of the smooth functioning of
the millet. In periods and areas where institutionalized discrimination was
enforced, it was more difficult for women to overstep bounds intercommunally
and for women to cross sex-class boundaries intracommunally.

In areas remote from the state bureaucracy, Jews, Muslims, and Christians
continued to share indigenous culture. They sought protection and interces-
sion of women saints and healers. Intermingling was necessary and assumed
in the lives of rural peasant women. Where and when institutionalized discrimination was not enforced, women benefited from close relations with one
another and from their ability to utilize the court system of their neighbors.

The Jewish millet was at times forced to adopt Muslim customary practices enforced by Muslim courts. For example, Muslim women inherited waqf
property—property endowed for religious purposes. In order to take advantage of more beneficial inheritance laws, Jewish women could go to Muslim
courts. To prevent this, the custom of inheriting waqf property was instituted
for Jewish women.

The male state, through legal and customary presciption, separated the world of women and of men, keeping women confined to domestic roles associated with maintenance of male hegemony. Historian Ian Dengler argues that Ottoman society provided considerable incentive for women to accept confinement to the role of wife and mother. A woman could be confident of her daily maintenance and acceptance by her extended kin groupings, family, and friends (Dengler, 1978). However, while acceptance into the world of hetero-relations was critical to her survival within that world, some women utilized its rewards to subvert male hegemony.

Social-class status, as it shaped sex class, prescribed a woman's possibilities and limitations. The ways in which women were able to take advantage of their positions in society varied accordingly.

In public transport, women traveled in separate compartments that were often cramped and poorly maintained. Although in most instances they had to be accompanied by men, Jewish, Muslim, and Christian women of all classes traveled on their own and in the company of women, to visit family and on pilgrimages. Employment for women in commerce and industry was, until the 19th century, confined to health care, nursing, and midwifery, and to some areas of textile manufacture, much of which could be done in the home. Sale and distribution of fabrics was generally handled by intermediaries, most often Jewish and Armenian women. Marriage, as in earlier periods, gave some women control over property. If a woman of the upper classes outlived her husband, she could acquire considerable power and wealth as guardian of the family estate (Dengler, 1978).

Limited training in Arabic and Persian restricted women further in terms of vocation. But music and dance, vocations closed to men, were the domain of women. Guilds of female entertainers made their own rules for recruitment and training (Dengler, 1978). The state rationalized this digression from the social order by claiming that they were " . . . not Muslims, but variously Jews, Armenians and other Christians, or gypsies . . . " (Dengler,1978, p. 233). Unmarried women and prostitutes had the status of chattel in Ottoman society. They were not considered fit for acceptance into the legal code. The Ottoman government considered prostitutes " . . . errant married women whose husbands were either unwilling or unable to control them . . . " (Dengler, 1978, p. 233), and charged them with adultery. However, while unmarried women without legal status were not legally "women," they could utilize this nonstatus to interact in society in ways prohibited to married women.

Women in 17th-century Bursa acted as independent artisans, producing items in their homes and selling them in the streets. When a silk merchants' guild challenged a group of eight artisans, producers of silk cords, the artisans sued and won their case on the basis of "an old Sultanic order attesting that by tradition they enjoyed the privilege of roaming unmolested in the city and selling their wares in whichever market they wished" (Gerber, 1980,

p. 237). A large number of silk-spinning tools were owned by women who worked in their homes for merchant-financiers. According to Gerber, most women engaged in silk spinning were involved in a piecework production system. He cites documentation showing that women most likely supported one another even when working in their homes. Women requested reduction of the tax on silk-spinning implements in the city on the basis that "most workers in the occupation were 'poor women'" (Gerber, 1980, p. 237).

Jewish and Christian women of the upper classes held important positions as tax farmers and entrepreneurs, negotiating commercial exchanges between foreign traders and local merchants. Similarly, Muslim women of the elite and ruling classes engaged in commerce and trade as partners with husbands or as backers of commercial ventures.

Women of the servant class, many of whom were brought to Turkey as slaves, cooked, cleaned, washed, and raised children for elite women who were then free to engage in the world of commerce and politics. The ruling elite were "surrounded by a vast hierarchy of governesses, teachers, bath attendants, personal servants, bed makers, scullery women, pipe cleaners" (Dengler, 1978, p. 236). A slave, however, who bore a child of a sultan (or any head of household) became eligible for the benefits of a wife. This may account for the literature of the upper classes referred to by Dengler, discussing the " . . . suitability of women of different nationalities for the future stability of the household" (Dengler, 1978, p. 234).

The state benefited from a large domestic industry fulfilling the material needs of women of the elite and ruling classes (Dengler, 1978). As consumers of goods such as clothes, perfumes, and furniture, all indicative of their status, they fulfilled their hetero-relational roles, earning the legal right to be women as defined by the patriarchal state. An important aspect of this role was the hierarchical subordination of women. The hetero-relational world of women was characterized by separation of women by nationality, association with men, and sex-class division of labor.

CONCLUSION

Associations between women, as old as recorded history, have supported intercommunal relations. They have also been utilized to support nationalist boundaries severing ties of intercommunal relations sustaining daily life. Associations between women politicize women. They also can cement bonds of patriarchalism.

Early nationalist movements were a site for negotiation of relations between groups of men and, to a lesser degree, between men and women. Exploitation of women—that is, expropriation of women's labor—was critical to the success of nationalist-patristic movements. Monotheism solidified male hegemony, slowly eradicating ideologies and practices supporting the sacredness of the earth. Control of the earth and of women was enforced through regulation of a sex-class system separating women by social class and by ethnic-racial identification. Control of women's sexuality is a critical aspect of what class is.

The male state institutionalizes and protects sexualized power over women. The success of patriarchy is dependent upon the formation of social-sexual-political alliances among men (Hatem, 1986). Central to that system is sexual control of women, bought and sold to profit and cement alliances among men.

Alliances between women, when acknowledged at all, have been reinterpreted to look like feuds. The misogynist notion that women are natural enemies, and that Jew and Arab are natural enemies, is propagated by androcentric historiography. Nonetheless, women's associations surface and resurface as central to movements defying ideologies and practices that exploit the earth, that rupture intercommunal relations, that exploit, suppress, and murder women.

Anthropologist Yael Katzir and historian Mervat Hatem note examples of how women's associations have overcome barriers solidifying patriarchal dominion. Muslim-Jewish relations in Yemen were far more stratified than those detailed in the Cairo Geniza documents. As elsewhere, under various rulers, relations were looser or more segregated. Shi'a Muslim rule, beginning in the 7th century, confined dhimmi to official restrictions, leaving them impoverished and vulnerable. Limited in their choice of occupation, forced to walk on the section of the road for transport animals, prohibited from building houses taller than Muslim houses, Yemini Jews were the prototypical dhimmi.

Relations intracommunally also reflected a pattern of subordination, this time of women, the dhimmi of patriarchy. Women were:

> . . . regarded as property of the patrilineage and a resource in which female labor power, sexual services and childbearing power were transferred to the husband's lineage in exchange for bride-wealth upon marriage. Women were excluded from formal control of any form of the economic, political and religious resources of the patrilineage . . . (Katzir, 1982, p. 271)

While Muslim Yemini women could inherit property, Jewish Yemini women could not: they had ". . . no independent source of income or property" (Katzir, 1982, p. 272).

But Katzir notes that despite the marginality of women, institutionalized restrictions segregating Muslim and Jew did not affect relations between Muslim and Jewish women. Women mingled in the marketplace; they exchanged customary practices and shared daily struggles:

> Women, who were marginal to the perpetuation of religious and vocational traditions and who did not carry the daily burden of keeping and guarding the

formal features of Jewish ethnicity, were far more free than men to absorb the local non-Jewish cultural elements. Women thus often served as the cultural mediators within the sociocultural environment. (Katzir, 1982, p. 277)

Noting the commonality of folksong and dance of Muslim and Jewish women, Katzir leaves us with an image reminiscent of Dinah and the dancing women who inspired her to break out of her segregation.

According to Mervat Hatem, lesbianism challenged the political use of heterosexuality to control women in the Mamluk harems of 14th-century Egypt (Hatem, 1986). Hatem is concerned with tracing historical changes in systems of male alliances and sexual control. The Mamluks, a military caste (former slaves of the Ayyubid sultans who eventually overthrew the Ayyubids in Egypt and conquered as well parts of Libya, Syria, Palestine, and western Arabia [Stillman, 1979]), classed women according to association with men, and according to race. Sexual relations determined their possibilities for moving up in a hierarchy that carefully regulated relations between women:

> Thus age, sexual status (as wife or concubine), as well as race (Turco-Circassian or Ethiopian), served to segment the female household (the harem), and these divisions among the female members of the household explain the relatively uncontested power of the patriarchs. (Hatem, 1986, pp. 258, 259)

Lesbianism was one response to the social segregation of women who, in spite of class divisions, relied upon each other for emotional and social support. In the 14th-century Mamluk harems, lesbians engaged in activities (hunting, games, riding horses) generally confined to men. In addition, they refused to use male intermediaries with the sultan, and were apparently able, with his cooperation, to accumulate wealth and land, thus weakening the power of the military aristocracy (Hatem, 1986). Hatem also notes that lesbians would have interfered with another aspect of hetero-relational control: sexual traffic in women. Mamluks freed slaves, selling them into marriage with members of the Egyptian middle class as a way of solidifying alliances. "Lesbianism challenged this political use of female sexuality for patriarchal solidarity and was therefore dangerous" (Hatem, 1986, pp. 259, 260). Furthermore, historian David Ayalon notes that the " . . . abuse of sacred Mamluk rules penetrated down the social ladder." On pilgrimage to Mecca, wives of Mamluk officials gave their camel drivers and water carriers robes of honor to wear (Ayalon, 1979, p. 287).

Practices of the Islamic state supported continuation of customs and practices of conquered populations, as well as encouraging the continuing integration of Jewish, Muslim, and Christian peoples. Among the lower classes, forms of integration most often had to do with exchange of services necessary for daily survival. Within the state bureaucracy, Jews and Christians could hold positions of power as long as they supported state policies. Jews and Christians had autonomous systems of social organization with jurisdiction over their own affairs in most areas. Women participated in those communal organizations (millets) as second class, with varying access to power, determined by social-class status through association with men. Women utilized access to resources to develop autonomous means of supporting themselves and to benefit other women. The term *dhimmi* takes on additional signficance when looked at from a gynocentric perspective. Men and women who were considered less enlightened because they had not yet received the teachings of Islam were confined to a status that afforded protection in exchange for limitations on their civil liberties. The meaning of civil liberties for women, constructed as it has been, in the male image, is lived out in the context of the ethnic-racial social construction of second-class dhimmi status.

Mervat Hatem points to structural contradictions underpinning maintenance of patriarchy—a social system that propagates hetero-relations as the ideal, and at the same time contradicts that ideal through maintenance of women's second-class status, degradation, and humiliation. On the boundary of that contradiction, women struggle for self-determination. In this process, women utilize state policy, attempt to alter state policy within a general framework of support for the state, and/or rebel against and in rare instances supersede the state, replacing its services with associations supporting women's survival and inimical to a sex-class system. Examples of this range of strategies surface within the world of the Cairo Geniza documents and, in exploring Mamluk society, through individual acts of courage, as well as associations between women. The system of male alliances across ethnic-racial-religous boundaries, of dhimmi, and of Muslim elites, for example, helped to keep women in their "proper" place. But women were also able to utilize their dhimmi status to cross boundaries in the village market, and in some instances, in the wider world market of commercial enterprise. During the early Ottoman period (15th–17th centuries), examples of both continued to be significant.

Support for acts of resistance to social-sexual utilization of women, and examination of structural contradictions underpinning historical manifestations of patriarchal control, are critical to women's survival. In the period of Turkish-Muslim rule of the Ottoman Empire and with the emergence of the modern nation–state, women continued to be at the center of ideological debate and practical policies. Historical changes in the system of male alliances and sexual control disrupted traditional avenues for association between women. But women continue to utilize the power of collectivity to resist increasingly severe forms of brutalization accompanying those changes.

Chapter Three

In the Modern Era: Women's Rights and Interethnic Relations

In the late 19th and early 20th centuries, social organization structuring interethnic relations in the Ottoman domains underwent major changes. The Ottoman government, seeking unification of all members of the empire under a single nation–state, initiated a series of reforms that eliminated the millet system. Discussion of interethnic relations, and of the role of women, took on a new vocabulary: the language of civil liberties.

Jewish and Christian women, as members of millets, experienced a change in status that at first seemed promising. Eradication of dhimmi status in favor of citizenship meant an end to restrictions and vulnerability. However, citizenship did not eradicate interethnic tensions. Instead, it introduced a new set of conflicts related to the imposition of a new class structure by the state and resulting from imperial intervention of the British and French.

Transition to the modern nation–state was both complex and violent. Options debated for national identification shaped interethnic relations. A central focus of debate was the social construction of "woman." Nationalist movements utilized women to press for control of social organization. Their varying perspectives tell us about the ways in which male hegemony has been instituted in the modern nation–state. Women's emancipation, variously defined by groups of men vying for power and by groups of women connected to, and influencing male-dominated movements, was a key theme of nationalist revolution. The terms of the discussion reflected the meaning of modernization. Kumari Jayawardena, a political scientist, puts it this way:

> . . . To foreign and local capitalists and landowners women were the cheapest source of labour for plantations, agriculture and industry. To colonial authorities and missionaries, local women had to be educated to be good (preferably Christian) wives and mothers to the professional and white-collar personnel who were being trained to man the colonial economy. To male reformers of the local bourgeosie, women needed to be adequately westernized and educated in order to enhance the modern and 'civilized' image of their country and of themselves, and to be a good influence on the next generation; the

demand grew for 'civilized housewives' . . . traditions and practices which restricted women's mobility or enforced their seclusion were thus detrimental to
capitalism in its search for cheap 'free labor.' (Jayawardena, 1986, p. 8)

Nationalism became the carrier of modernization, defined as the imposition of a legal code and of a military initiative expanding the material base
of capitalist–patriarchy. Modernization for women has been a contradictory
multifaceted experience. Allowing new forms of association among women
and new kinds of political involvement, modernization has also brought new
forms of violence against women and precipitates new forms of divisiveness
between women.

The benefits of modernization for men as members of minority groups have
also been contradictory. While many have profited, others have found themselves targets of a new style of race hatred from imperialists. But the options
for dhimmi men were far broader than those for dhimmi women, who have
continued to be admitted into society on the basis of their associations with
and uses by, alliances of men.

Class divisions among Muslim, Jewish, and Christian women have taken
on new forms and significance in the modern era, both within communities
and intercommunally. Nationalist identification is itself a class division, forcing women to take sides and ally themselves with movements whose goals
appear to be mutually exclusive.

In chapter 3, I examine the consequences of modernization for interethnic relations and for women. I examine Arab nationalist movements and Zionism as carriers of modernization, demonstrating how the current state of
relations between Jew and Arab is connected to misogynist ideology and practices of both.

Misogyny is institutionalized by alliances of men across ethnic-religious
identification, even when those men act as rivals. Appropriation of women's
bodies, labor, and associations holds those alliances in place, just as subjugation of colonized men in a hierarchical system of race and class exploitation holds those alliances in place. From this perspective, the question of
whether or not barriers in the 20th century between Jews and Arabs are un-
bridgeable takes on a new dimension.

THE LAND BASE:
WOMEN AND TERRITORIAL RIGHTS

Industrial advances in the 17th and 18th centuries escalated rivalry between
the growing nation–states of Europe for control of land and resources. Great
Britain and France negotiated a series of economic arrangements with the
Ottoman Empire granting them easy access to trade and immunity from taxes.
The so-called great powers pursued control of material resources in the Arab

lands. They utilized more technically efficient tools of warfare and legal systems, " . . . enforc(ing) capital accumulation on a world-wide scale . . . " (Von Werlholf, 1988, pp. 24, 25)

Men have always admitted women into society through domestication. The dhimmi, both men and women, defined as second-class citizens, were admitted into society through their relationship to capital: control of means of production, property, ownership of goods. Just as the capitalist allows the wage worker a mini-monopoly over a ("his") woman, the state allowed each millet legal, moral, and economic jurisdiction over "its" women. Those women who functioned as revenue-producing elements of the Ottoman state knew how to function in those roles, not because of having escaped domestication, but because of how well they were domesticated.

Domestication of the women of the Arabs lands was central to the imperialist project; domestication, that is, in Western, or modern terms. Women's roles had to fit the needs of the newly emerging nation–state as unpaid labor within the home, cheap labor in the marketplace, and as markers of national-ethnic boundaries. Similarly, Europeans promulgated domestication of the Arab, particularly poor Jewish Arabs and Muslims. The Ottoman government, seeking its "rightful" place within the new world order, initiated economic policies, as well as a series of reforms, designed to centralize power. These policies were part of, and stimulated, debate by Arab men and women about the proper terms for domestication of women of the Arab world in the modern era. Those who benefited from the new policies—for the most part Christians, favored by the European governments, but some Muslims and Jews as well—formed new classes tied to and promoting European interests.

OTTOMAN REFORMS

The Ottoman reforms brought about changes in interethnic relations that affected how women were able to access resources and power. This period proved critical for the way in which relations between Jews, Muslims, and Christians took shape, as well as for relations between European powers and the Ottoman government. Under the banner of Ottomanism, the reforms attempted, but failed, to stem the tide of nationalist revolts in the Ottoman domains. Western capitalism depended upon trade acccess to routes in the eastern provinces of the Ottoman Empire. Reforms in the Tanzimat period, which involved dissolution of the millet, new class alliances, and economic agreements, helped to solidify new alliances abetting this process. Zionist expansionism in Palestine in the late 19th century exacerbated and took advantage of social-class, race-class, and sex-class tensions stimulated during this period.

Reorganization of the Brotherhood

The Tanzimat, or regulations instituted by Abdulmejid (1839–1861), utilized European standards of law administration and "civil liberties." They enabled the Ottoman empire to reorganize itself creating a military conscription and a more efficient tax system. They granted "equality of status" to the dhimmi, including freedom of worship, equality in administration of justice, and abolition of the poll tax and the prohibition against carrying arms (Ma'oz, 1968).

By stripping the millets of administrative autonomy, the government took direct responsibility for ensuring "civic" rights and freedoms. Those rights and freedoms, newly defined, were no longer the affair of the millets, which were transformed into "simple confessional groups," dealing strictly with religious matters (Karpat, 1982, p. 164).

With reform of the millet, religious differences became a focus for persecution. Competition became the basis for relations between diverse groups struggling "equally" for economic and political power. Membership in the millet had determined customary modes of economic interaction and viability and customary forms of mutuality supporting daily survival. Class tensions escalated as those practices became irrelevant. In many instances, power passed from the religious patriarch to the wealthy, who represented state interests. In addition, European governments established relationships with and control over confessional groups to gain their loyalty (Ma'oz, 1968).

Historian Deniz Kandiyoti maintains that:

> Beneath Tanzimat liberalism were powerful undercurrents which had a strong material basis. The Tanzimat reforms had failed to stem the tide of nationalism in the Christian Balkan provinces and had essentially strengthened the hand of local Christian merchants who were the preferred trading partners of European powers in Ottoman lands. (Kandiyoti, 1989, p. 133)

Liberal reforms strengthened class alliances on the basis of relationship to capital. Christian, Jewish, and Muslim men who carried on the new commerce as bankers, financial advisors, or moneylenders, often at the expense of the indigenous poor, supported the growing infrastructure of European technology and business practices. Called protégés, agents of the European governments challenged the prestige, power, and wealth of the traditional elites. As the demands and fluctuations of the world market affected economic stability, peasants and craftsmen became dependent upon urban creditors who in turn depended upon European subsidiaries (Owen, 1981).

In response to the growing demand of European governments for raw materials and agricultural commodities, the Ottoman government encouraged introduction of cash crop farming and introduced commercial reforms that proved harmful to local commerce (Ma'oz, 1968). Imports of British cotton manufactured goods to Turkey, Egypt, and Syria–Palestine and cheap European fabrics protected by minimal tariffs harmed many indigenous spinners, weavers, and dyers: the first two occupations were largely occupied by women (Owen, 1981).

The Ottoman government revised revenue collection systems and borrowed from European creditors to finance modernization of its army by building new factories and importing European advisors. New financial institutions in Europe supported foreign investment. European-controlled banks established in the Ottoman domains accrued large profits under the aegis of "economic development of the region." Local men and women, however, did not benefit. By 1875, the Ottoman government, bankrupt, increased revenues to meet interest payments on the state debt. The increased burden was most devastating to the peasantry. While capitulation agreements protected Europeans and their protégés from taxation, in rural areas peasants had no protections against abuses of the tax system by local representatives of the government.

Implications for Women

Dissolution of the millets had contrary consequences for women. Women utilized the court apparatus to demand rights within the boundaries of their religio-ethnic communities. When possible, women also utilized court systems intercommunally. On the other hand, religious law restricted their access to rights, through a carefully delineated set of rules defining "woman." At times women could make use of the state to acquire rights not given them through customary practices. The Tanzimat reforms, for example, introduced a 1856 (land) law granting equal inheritance rights to daughters and supported ratification of a treaty abolishing slavery and concubinage (Kandiyoti, 1989).

Women suffered in interethnic clashes in reaction to economic competition stimulated by a changing class structure. Riots erupted in Aleppo and Damascus between 1850 and 1860 in which 5,000 Christians died and in the Mosul region where 8,000 Jews were killed (Issawi, 1982). As traditional occupations of minorities were no longer viable, or as minorities displaced one another, they were forced to find new occupations. Jewish women and children, for example, began working in the tobacco factories of Istanbul and Salonika, and in Izmir as laundresses, servants, nurses, and lacemakers (Drumont, 1982). Displacement of women from traditional occupations, whether in crafts or trade, increased their dependency, both in relation to family and to the state.

TITLE TO LAND: REFORM OR EXPROPRIATION?

The title to agriculturally productive land, or *miri* (conquered) land, in the Ottoman domains belonged to the state. Tenants enjoyed rights derived from working the land. Men and women had a variety of ways to establish rights over land. For example, in southern Syria, communal systems of land use assured regular distribution of land among the local population (Owen, 1981).

The government assigned to *siphahi,* or cavalrymen, administrative control of land as payment for services. As the usefulness of the siphahi declined with the development of more sophisticated weaponry, the state farmed out tax collecting. Peasants suffered from unfair practices because tax farmers kept the difference between what they collected from the peasantry and what they owed to the government. Absentee landlords who depended upon local shaykhs to control peasant production, increasingly controlled land.

Land Law of 1858

The Ottoman government, plagued by inefficient tax collection in the struggle for land, wealth, and power, and needing to increase tax revenues for military buildup and to encourage agricultural production, instituted a new system of land control. The Land Law of 1858 required registration of land, granted title deeds, and forbid communal ownership. The government hoped to control tax revenues by creating a class of small cultivators with clear title to land.

Fear of tax demands discouraged peasants from registering their land. Registration meant vulnerability to manipulation by those seeking control of land. Titles were given to those who had political power, rather than to cultivators (Owen, 1981). Furthermore, the Law of 1867 granted foreigners rights to own land in the Ottoman Empire and ensured foreigners' privileges, making it impossible for local courts to enforce land laws (Owen, 1981). Control of property rights by Europeans and their protégés signified fundamental changes in the land tenure system. Increasingly, outsiders provided working capital and employed a system of sharecropping: in return for half the produce, they provided seed and equipment. The state created rural cooperative banks, supplying cheap credit to farmers, but terms of the loans prohibited poorer farmers from participating. To control return of tax revenues to the state, the government incorporated landowners and merchants into local administration. Policies to assist the local population benefited only the upper classes, who used their new authority to exact peasant labor (Owen, 1981). Customary laws, reduced to a single standard, described and validated the new international law.

Effects on Women

Increased taxation, conscription, and forced labor had devastating effects upon peasant women, who were often left alone, or were themselves conscripted. Women lost positions as tax farmers. Women from all classes were affected by foreign competition in trade and agriculture. Those few who were merchants lost economic advantages. The fact that agricultural produce was subject to outside controls increased the demands on peasant women who worked the land.

Land laws and interventionist policies benefiting European imperials restricted women's ability to assert customary rights over land, moveable properties, and various forms of social production. Families no longer able to control their land were not able to transmit it to successive generations in ways that previously had sometimes benefited women. For example, Islamic law gave women a set portion of inheritable rights. A woman could buy and sell property acquired as part of her bridal gift and could acquire property through inheritance or through participation in and support of the family as an economic unit. While officially excluded from access to miri land (state land), women of upper classes could obtain rights through holding tax farms. Furthermore, it could be critical to a woman's family to protect her customary rights because of her economic contribution through dowry, debts owed her, her work, and her moveable property (Tucker, 1985). Women acquired property as beneficiaries, founders, or administrators of waqf property, property endowed for religious purposes. The benefits of establishing waqf property were twofold: it was a religious act, and once endowed, the land or other property could not be sold or subject to certain taxes (Tucker, 1985). Judith Tucker cites the case of a woman who utilized her wealth in buildings, palm trees, fishing grounds, and land to promote a limited form of matrilineal inheritance: " . . . the income of the waqf she founded was to accrue to her daughter's children through the generations and then, upon the extinction of the daughter's line, to the women of the ashrāf, the descendants of the Prophet" (Tucker, 1985, p. 95). In addition:

> Many founders of waqfs, both male and female, appear to have used the institution, in part, to provide specifically for female heirs whose claims on the inheritance would normally be weaker than those of men. (Tucker, 1985, pp. 95, 96)

Women utilized access to land to strengthen their position and to strengthen bonds with other women. Economic associations between sisters were common in 19th-century Egypt (Tucker, 1985). Given that patrifocal marriage (in which the woman becomes part of her husband's kinship grouping):

> . . . inhibited the development of economic relations with her household of birth . . . in league with their sisters, women could pool small amounts of capital and purchase property without depending on a husband, who might be absent, or male relatives, who might ride roughshod over female rights. (Tucker, 1985, p. 98)

On the other hand, men granted women access to control of land in order to create new family alliances. Transactions designed to solidify family bonds also solidifed women's domestication. Men instituted control over women through control of their access to land. The Ottoman land reforms strengthened the hand of the state in that role. Furthermore, although women could benefit from legislation, for example, the 1856 Land Law granting equal inheritance to daughters, benefits were obfuscated by class struggle for control of land that robbed peasants, in general, of access to land.

RACE AND SEX: THE 'CIVILIZING' DIVISIONS

British and French colonizers pursued a "civilizing mission" among the indigenous peoples of the Ottoman domains, recruited in the process of carrying out policies of land expropriation and expropriation of women's labor. One aspect of this civilizing mission involved forming alliances with men within the state bureaucracy, who were granted favors and benefits in exchange for services. British and French nationals replaced local potentates by introducing a new legal system in conjunction with the Ottoman government.

While making use of their services, European imperials characterized Jew and Muslim alike as "backward," "primitive," "unruly," "untrustworthy." Among the institutions of domestication of the "violent" Arab were missionary and European-style schools supporting Europeanization. Such schools prepared students for their roles in the new world order. Among those organizations, for example, were the schools of the Alliance Israelite Universelle, created in the 1860s throughout the Ottoman domains. The Alliance set itself the task of correcting the "bad habits" of the impoverished and "backward" Jews of the Islamic lands; one such bad habit was speaking Arabic. Learning English and French, Jews studied a European curriculum, with the promise of cultural enrichment and better employment opportunities (Laskier, 1983).

The Alliance sought to improve the Jewish self-image, by ensuring the disappearance of the Jewish Arab from Jews' historic experience and daily lives. The acceptable Jewish image was that of the upper-class, "cultured," western-European, Jewish male.

Knowledge of English, French, and Spanish proved a great asset for Jews acting as commercial intermediaries. The Alliance created a new Jewish male elite to fill the roles of clerk, interpreter, and diplomat, skilled to meet the demands of the economic and political challenges of the late 19th century. In urban areas, graduates were placed in banking institutions, post offices, commerical houses. However, many graduates complained of lack of access to top bureaucratic mangerial positions, and joined a growing emigration movement. Thus, graduates of the new schools were often geographically, as well as culturally, alienated from their communities (Laskier, 1983).

Alliance schools provided vocational training for women preparing them for low-paying service work to which women were confined in the newly industrializing work force. Gender segregation in the labor market dictated courses open to women. British and French schools stressed homemaking as the natural role of women. Missionary schools provided training in becoming a modern housekeeper and wife, or in performing specialized services such as seamstresses and hairdressers.

British and French colonials, ruling for a period in Egypt and North Africa, and instituting economic and political controls in the Arab provinces of the Ottoman Empire, drew a sharp distinction between the world of men and the world of women. Under the guise of liberating women from backward gender roles of the East, they instituted new forms of segregation. Associations of women emerged, based on new class associations.

Sociologist Barbara Rogers notes the homosocial base of institution building under colonial rule:

> Male hierarchies were used for direct or indirect forms of colonial rule, while female hierarchies atrophied or were actively suppressed . . . The new institutions, including army, police, civil service, political parties, trade unions, churches, schools and universities, banks, local affiliates of multinational companies and in fact all key development institutions are built up mainly or exclusively by male nationals. (Rogers, 1980, p. 36)

Civil liberties for women were necessary to solidify women's role in building the modern state. Control of woman's labor—as wife, mother, worker—could be brought about only by controlling her admittance into the new society. This process disrupted customary associations among women and provided new platforms for resistance to traditional forms of exploitation. Women took their new skills into the streets to advocate for equality.

European imperialists opposed an idealized image of the educated free woman of the West—"self-reliant," "independent," and "efficient"—to an image of a "confined," "ignorant," and "dependent" woman of the East. The "civilized" West represented "progress," as opposed to the "stagnant" societies of the East, labeled "underdeveloped"—a rationale for exploitation under the guise of development. Similarly, impersonal legal status was instituted by the Europeans under the guise of freedom, thus concealing the utilization of women's sexual services to cement alliances among men, and also concealing expansion of the base of capital accumulation that impersonal legal status allowed.

Bifurcation of the African-Eurasian land mass into a "West" and an "East" conceals interconnected developments, as well as distorting the social and material life of the Islamic world. For example, Jewish, Christian, and Muslim men participated in social, economic, and political movements that redefined "Jew" and "Arab" in modern terms. Changing modes of interrelation between European governments and the Ottoman Empire, beginning in the 15th century, accompanied transformation in modes of procuring land and women. Superior weaponry and new legal systems aided expansion of the commercial base in Europe into a global market. Reordering of life in the Islamic lands disrupted traditional forms of economic complementarity between

Jew and Muslim, man and woman. The Jew came to be regarded as having shifted allegiance to the Christian world. These and other changes came about as a result of the activities and the range of responses of Jews, Muslims, and Christians, men and women, who created and resisted a new world order. They came about because of how Europe viewed Arabs (whether Jewish, Christian, Muslim, or other) in this process, and because of how Jews, Muslims, and Christians viewed one another. Historian Peter Gran points out that given the importance of trade to both the Europeans and the Ottomans, the " . . . type of market which the industrial market required would not have come into existence without transformations in the countries of the third world—the creation of new social classes and the mutation of old ones . . . ," and that without those indigenous changes, " . . . Forces that opposed the industrial revolution from within Europe might well have gained the upper hand" (Gran, 1941, p. xii). The industrial revolution was a global event:

> . . . non-western regions collaborating in the larger social transformation of the late nineteenth century had indigenous roots for their own modern capitalist cultures, formed through processes of indigenous struggle and in some form of struggle with the European part of the system. (Gran, 1941, p. xii)

Collaboration of West and East in social transformations of the late 19th century focused on subsuming women under the banner of modernization. In the Arab world and in Europe the debate over women's rights was waged as men sought control over resources critical to capitalist–patriarchy in the modern era. Opposing women of the West to women of the East was part of the male-class struggle. Power is what class is: conditioning of various segments of the populace to take their places in support of the new system. An ongoing process of technical specialization, including impersonal legal status under the guise of progress, subsumed women and land as the domain of men. Sociologist Claudia Von Werlhof puts it this way:

> The diverse forms of patriarchal control over women seen in preceding systems, such as exchange and theft of women, marriage regulations and kinship systems, never attained the intensity, extremes and absoluteness of those operating at present, leaving aside for a moment its global extension—a fact unaltered by any seeming "emancipation." (Von Werlhof, 1988, p. 103)

Women of the Islamic lands experienced the ambiguous consequence of modernization in ways similar to the dhimmi: punished by the colonizer if they defied his imperial rule, punished intracommunally if they strayed from or defied indigenous prescriptions.

Women's admittance into the new world order through modern definitions and forms of domestication is both compulsory and voluntary, and in both cases is a violent process. In reference to that process in Egypt, historian Leila Ahmed cites the Arab historian Al-Jabarti (1745–1825) who:

> . . . laments the "pernicious innovation" and the corruption of women that the French occupation brought about, and he records that the daughter of one of the greatest religious notables, Shaykh al-Bakri, was killed after the French departed because she had mingled with them and dressed like a French woman. (Ahmed, 1984, p. 111)

Women walked a thin line between Western colonial patriarchies and indigenous patriarchal imperatives. Utilization of women as the measure of cultural integrity is not new; Shaykh al-Bakri's daughter may have been the modern Dinah, punished for her predilection for "pagan" influences.

Horizontal hostility between women claiming access to goods, bearing the distinctions of their sex-class status, and fighting for survival supported the rivalry among men necessary to the new world order. In their new roles, women solidified nationalist boundaries. At the same time, horizontal hostility was offset by bonding between those women resisting change. But female networks were a part of the work of instituting the new world order. They aided as well as disrupted it. Small associations of women traders, for instance, resisted state control and provided protections not afforded by the state. Muslim and Jewish women attending Alliance schools had a common experience, learning French and English and acquiring skills suited to their new vocations. Rural women formed networks to cope with increased workloads in the absence of men who migrated seeking employment.

Describing the impact of capitalist development on women in Morocco in the 19th and 20th centuries, Fatima Mernissi points out that the emergence of a new class of women fulfilling the needs of the modern nation–state (civil servants, professional women with diplomas and salaries) marked the:

> . . . emergence of a relationship of dominance and exploitation which this group maintains with the rest of the masses of women, incarnated in the relationship with the housemaid. This dichotomization of the female world constitutes one of the most influential facts in the perception of women's productive potential since independence . . . (Mernissi, 1982, p. 96)

A new "elite woman" tied to capital through acquiring credentials that define her limitations and possibilities, represents what technology, as progress, can offer: a life free from the rigors of manual labor. Education and progress, opposed to illiteracy and manual labor, legitimize the modern technocratic state. Women benefit from and make use of admittance into the ranks of professionals and from changes in how they are perceived by some sectors of society. But the dichotomizations of capitalist–patriarchy ensure that their success is linked to degradation of the women living in poverty and confined to the despised realm of manual labor (Mernissi, 1982). Contempt for manual labor becomes contempt for "woman"—she who works with her hands. In this way women are utilized to institute the new class system necessary to the modern industrial revolution. Colonizing divisions between women upheld the new class system. Hence:

... Through a contradictory effect, the educated women, because of their small number, constitute in relation to the female masses, where poverty and illiteracy are rife, an "exception" which proves the rule and reaffirms the attitudes of domination, exploitation, and contempt toward the poor masses. (Mernissi, 1982, p. 99)

Dualistic and hierarchical separation of manual labor from professionalism, of educated from illiterate, of country from city, all characterize capitalist-patriarchal expansion in the 19th and 20th centuries. Women in the Arab world — Jewish, Muslim, Christian, and others — compete within the new regime for a place in the hierarchy as they align themselves with modern nationalist movements. In the late 19th century, pre-state Zionist women, competing with Arab women for work, became agents of expropriation of land and labor within the Zionist framework. On the other hand, one reason why Zionist men resist and in most cases refuse women access to labor, and hence to land, is the potential for association, alliance, and support between (European) Jewish and Arab women, which does in fact occur. Sustaining colonizing divisions between groups of women is a function of the modern nationalist project.

In the nineteenth and twentieth centuries capitalist–patriarchy's colonizing divisions of race and sex have contributed to a crisis of relations between the Jews, Muslims, and Christians of the Middle East. That crisis finds its "resolution" in the bifurcation of Arab and Jew, two nationalities, fighting for equal access to the promises of the modern era. Land and women are the battleground and the trophies.

NATIONALIST MOVEMENTS AND WOMEN'S LOYALTIES

Three interrelated factors informed the course of nationalism in the Ottoman domains. Dissatisfaction with Ottoman reforms and the repressive measures of Abdulhamid II culminated in the Young Turk Revolution, an attempt to redefine Ottomanism. Second, nationalism penetrated the Ottoman domains through missionary schools, colonial intervention, and an emerging Western-educated elite class of men. Third, in the post-World War I period, nationalism became the primary vehicle for resistance to the West; or more precisely, a vehicle for confrontation of upper and lower classes of men vying for control as old power structures gave way to and accommodated the new. The language of ethnic-cultural survival predominated as a vehicle for that process.

As early as 1917, and with inexorable certainty by 1948, a language sharply dividing "Arab" and "Jew" in terms of cultural and historic description dominated official diplomacy and, to a growing extent, popular consciousness. A dramatic indication is the disappearance of reference to the Palestinian Jew, now subsumed under European, from discussion of events in

Palestine. Nationalism contains the ideological underpinnings that foster those divisions, whether on the basis of imperialist designs to control Jew and Arab or on the basis of choice by Jews and Arabs to define themselves by the tenets of nationalist ideology.

A COMMON SECULAR GROUND: THE CONSTITUTIONAL EXPERIMENT

Nationalist movements subsume women under the seemingly gender-neutral concept of "human beings," or "peoples." They restructure and redefine relations between ruling classes intercommunally, on the basis of "territorial rights," a concept that conceals the power of those classes to determine uses of land and resources, as well as concealing means of obtaining them. "Rights" are privileges, a fact concealed by liberal humanism:

> Rights are inherent only for the group in power. To be powerless means to be granted only those rights which do not conflict with the interests and goals of the powerful. Rights, then, stem from powerful self-interest. They are derived from the system of beliefs and the ideology of the dominant group; the ideology which in turn defines values and attitudes as it determines behavior. (Barry, 1979, p. 217)

Nationalism grants rights to patriots. Central to the question of women and nationalism is the question of women and patriotism. Again, Kathleen Barry:

> Patriotism is loyalty to the fatherland for the rights and privileges it guarantees its citizens . . . Above all, loyalty is patriarchal—it is the granting and protecting of rights and privileges to men, by men, for men. It is the bonding of the brotherhood.
> Consider the question of female loyalty in the brotherhood of patriarchy, for that is where all women live. (Barry, 1979, p. 158)

On what basis did men form workable units in the 19th and 20th centuries? How was patriotism defined by opposing alliances of men vying for power? How did those men view women in this process? How did women view themselves?

Throughout the Ottoman domains in the 19th century, response to Ottoman reforms and European intervention precipitated political movements that focused on the relation of Islam to Ottomanism and to westernization. In Egypt a nationalist organization, al-hizab al-watani, the Party of the Fatherland, claimed that Egyptian Muhammedans, Christians, and Jews, were " . . . all brothers in this land and must have equal political rights" (Kohn, 1962, p. 83). Muslims, Christians, and Jews welcomed the 1876 constitution of Abdulhamid II (1876–1909) which promised representative government through parliamentary rule. But Abdulhamid claimed national rebellions in the Balkans and threats from Russia as the reason for suspending the constitution, dissolving the parliament, and exiling liberal reformists. He promulgated pan-Islamism, instigating massacres of Armenians who were accused of forming allegiances with Russia. Women, men, and children were starved to death, shot, thrown down wells, forced to turn against one another.

Abdulhamid suppressed the Young Ottomans, who interpreted the Koran and Hadith as supportive of modern reform. One hadith, for example, was cited to corroborate that " . . . love of one's native place is a part of faith" (Hodgson, 1974, p. 252). Advocating and promising modern reform, military officers ended Abdulhamid's reign, restoring the constitution in the Young Turk Rebellion of 1908. The Ottoman Committee of Union and Progress (the Young Turks) ruled for the next 10 years " . . . under the guise of constitutional monarchy" (Kohn, 1962, p. 106). Many Jews, Muslims, and Christians held high hopes for the Committee of Union and Progress (CUP), which promised to subordinate religious and ethnic differences, shifting from the Islamic civilization of the past and accommodating Europeanized elements of Ottoman society. Women, some of whom had supported Abdulhamid, and others of whom had rallied against him, carried messages for the Young Turks during the 1908 revolution. Police agents were not allowed to search them, but, " . . . these agents could, nonetheless, make life very difficult for the women they suspected of indulging in illicit political activity" (Davis, 1986, p. 182).

However, as it became increasingly clear to the CUP that Ottomanism, uniting Muslim and non-Muslim, had not solved the problem of nationalist movements within the Ottoman domains, it turned to pan-Turanism which aspired to the racial and cultural unity of all populations speaking the Turkish language and which looked upon Turkestan in Central Asia as a common home (Kandiyoti 1989; Kohn, 1962). The CUP defined Ottoman to mean Turkish, instituting Turkish as the official language and ensuring Turkish domination in Parliament. Responding to pressures of European imperialism and Balkan nationalism, the Young Turk government assumed the character of a dictatorship, suppressing minority rights.

While the actions of the CUP were considered contrary to its stated goals, the modern institutions it adopted, of parliamentary rule and minority rights, institutionalized power in the hands of men who controlled them. Their "superior right" was confirmed through control and suppression of minorities— women and men who deviated from the proscriptions and norms of the state. Their superior right was confirmed through strategic admittance of women and minority men into the state apparatus.

As a range of brotherhoods sprang up, vying for power in the name of social justice, the question of what nationalism to adopt—that is, on what basis to assert national hegemony—precipitated divided loyalties. For example, were Jews Arabs, Ottomans, or first and foremost, followers of the Jewish faith? (Hodgson, 1974). As noted, many Jews supported unification under Ottomanism. And many supported unification under the Committee of Union and Progress with its "progressive" platform. Jewish, Muslim, and Christian men embraced various nationalisms as vehicles for economic and political power. Ethnic-religious survival increasingly depended upon allegiances to and inclusion in those classes and government policies associated with European expansionist policies. But those policies were not inimical to processes of class formation already taking hold in the Ottoman domains. They were not inimical to the institutionalized violence against and control of women by alliances of men dominating political-economic-social-spiritual life.

In order to meet the demands of the new economy, the CUP attempted to create a middle class of Turkish-Muslim entrepreneurs, utilizing Turkish as the language of correspondence with foreign firms. They instituted vocational classes in commerce and banking, with special business classes for women (Kandiyoti, 1989). As men were conscripted in the wake of nationalist rebellions, women were needed to support the economy.

The Ottoman Arab Brotherhood, founded in Constantinople in 1880, and the Ottoman Decentralization Party, formed in 1912 by Syrians in Cairo, promoted greater local autonomy to counteract the centralizing policies of the government. The threat of Pan-Turanism brought together Muslim and Christian Arab with a platform calling for local general councils with budgetary control, the right to legislate domestic affairs in the Arab provinces, and the institutionalization of Arabic as the official language along with Turkish (Mandel, 1976). A secret society of mostly young Muslim Arabs, calling itself al-Fatat, convened the first Arab congress in Paris in 1913, demanding equal rights and cultural autonomy for Arabs. The aim of a secret society of Arab officers, al-Ahd (covenant), was to create an Arab-Turkish style monarchy.

Women utilized the language of modern nationalism to advocate for the right to education, supporting the notion that women must be educated " . . . for the sake of progress and the advancement of the nation" (Ahmed, 1984, p. 116). *Al-Fatat*, a journal founded by a Lebanese woman, appeared as early as 1892. By 1913, Muslim, Copt (native Egyptians who believe in the singular divine nature of Jesus Christ), Christian, and Jewish women founded as many as fifteen women's journals, addressing their readers as wives and mothers while advocating education and careers (Phillip, 1978). Education and career were identity cards required for entry into the modern economic sector.

The background assumption of male hegemony structured the debates about constitutional reform and the place of women in the state. As debates went on, war raged in the background, the assumed right of men to ravage the earth, rationalized as necessity. The nation must be "secured," as women must be "secured"—protected from their wanton ways, as well as from other men who would claim them as their territory.

A central theme within the arena of Arab nationalisms was that Islam and women must be secured from the threat of the polluting influence of the West.

Advocates of this position attributed weakening of Ottoman power to straying from the path of righteousness. "Pollution" resulted from allowing women to stray from the path of righteous living. Nationalists identified themselves on the basis of control of women's bodies. Modernists claimed that women could further the cause of Islam by adopting modern garb—dress, manners, and values. Educated women were needed to raise patriots. On both ends of the debate hung the woman as wife and mother in service of the state. The incipient stages of modern nationalism brought into the foreground the antifeminism of nationalist ideology. Control of women's bodies and territorial rights structured nationalist identity. Loyalty to the state was conditioned by identity. Identity assumed a kind of biological determinism, structuring social relations and social organization.

Class interests structured the nationalist debate on the position and role of women in the new state. For example, a new class of elite European-educated men rallied against arranged marriages. Class interests also structured the terms of debate for women. The traditional family offered protection, if at the expense of self-determination. Deniz Kandiyoti addresses the reluctance of many women to embrace "emancipation" "in a society which offered women no shelter outside the traditional family . . . " (Kandiyoti, 1989, p. 133). Nonetheless, women expected to benefit from the overthrow of Abdulhamid and from the promise of liberty and equality of the 1908 revolution. Kandiyoti notes their disillusionment: "A woman's periodical, on the occasion of the fifth anniversary of the Constitution proclaimed that it was 'men's National Celebration Day' (Taskiran, 1973:38)" (Kandiyoti, 1989, p. 135).

A proliferation of women's associations in this period accompanied new educational and employment opportunities for women. Employment of women increased with a 1915 Ottoman trade law instituting mandatory employment (Kandiyoti, 1989). World War I precipitated involvement of women as nurses and workers at the front, as well as in areas vacated by men, as had national rebellions in the Ottoman domains. The Islamic Association for the Employment of Ottoman Women underscored the reproductive role of the woman worker:

> The Association used newspaper columns for matchmaking, provided girls with a trousseau and staged well appointed wedding ceremonies. Those who passed the marriage age limit or did not accept the matrimonial candidates proposed by the Association had 15 per cent of their salary withheld and were excluded from membership. Conversely, marriage was rewarded by a 20 per cent salary increase and similar increases for the birth of each child (Z. Toprak 1982:317–318, 412). (Kandiyoti, 1989, p. 136)

The 1917 Ottoman Family Code Law gave the secular state, as opposed to religious authorities, control over some aspects of personal status by legislating contractual marriages for all religious groups in the Empire, and introducing a conciliation divorce procedure (Kandiyoti, 1989). Polygyny was "legalized," but required the consent of the first wife. While there was resistance from religious minorities resenting loss of authority, state control of legislation affecting women's possibilities and limitations gave women from religious-ethnic communities a common arena for negotiation.

Debates polarizing Islam and westernization could conceal parallels in how women were utilized by Islamicists opposing westernization and by modernists upholding westernization. As guardians of tradition, as keepers of the history, as mothers training the young, as domestics, as professionals, as revolutionaries, women in service of the state were domesticated women. Islam would protect women learning and working among Western nationals from degenerating into sexual objects and from exposing themselves to the disease of Western feminism. By adhering to a strict interpretation of Islam as guardian of women's purity, women would lead men away from the corruptions of capitalist greed. A modernized Islam would do away with family law and regulations, giving women freedom of consent. A monopoly of one man over one woman suited the needs of the new economics, and affirmed the liberal principles of individualism and "equality." In both cases, women's liberation was reduced to a political platform for groups of men vying for and negotiating state power. Women were encouraged to be independent and self-reliant in so far as their independence and self-reliance served the goal of maximum efficiency and technicalization. Their liberation was characterized in terms that suited the transformations of class structure, legal structure and values that supported capitalist–patriarchy in the 20th century. Some women resisted these changes insofar as they eroded customary practices supporting women's survival, including associations of women. Women also became "agents for change," absorbing and supporting Western mores, as associations of women utilized new opportunities provided by education and job training to advocate for women's rights.

The dismemberment of the Ottoman Empire after World War I mobilized women supporting independence from foreign rule. Syrian women had joined secret societies in 1914, opposing Turkish dominance; women would lose their lives resisting foreign occupation in Cairo, Jerusalem, and Damascus in 1919. In the violent upheaval accompanying imperial expansion and the attendant class transformations shaping intercommunal relations, women seized opportunities to shape the course of historical developments.

ARAB NATIONALISM AND ZIONISM: POLAR OPPOSITES?

Arab nationalism in the 19th century emerged in response to, and as a vehicle for, three interconnected historical developments. In the face of Turkish hegemony, politicized Arabists sought Arab rights within the framework of the Ottoman Empire (Muslih, 1987). Second, embroiled in arguments about the validity of Islamic legacy in meeting demands of modernization, Arab nationalist movements were a vehicle for negotiation between West and East. This debate stimulated structural changes in gender relations necessary to the new economics. In what mode would control of women's bodies be instituted? Third, by the end of World War I, the focus of Arab nationalisms shifted, as European imperialists utilized nationalist movements to achieve imperial goals. Arab nationalists advocated pan-Arabism in an attempt to unite the provinces of Greater Syria, including Lebanon and Palestine. Britain and France attempted to control nationalist movements through coercion, persuasion, force, and control of women, so that those advocating independence would create institutions supporting the goals of European governments. In the post-war period, Palestinians active in the movement for political autonomy of a Greater Syria increasingly confronted an issue that stimulated the development of a separate and local Palestinian movement. That issue was Zionism; specifically, Zionist expropriation of land in the districts of Palestine.

In Palestine, urban notables connected with a rural elite claiming legal rights to land supported Ottomanism—a nationalism inclusive of Muslims, Christians, and indigenous Jews. Although they faced increasing opposition from the younger Arab nationalists advocating autonomy for the Arab provinces of the Ottoman Empire, both recognized the emergence of a specifically Palestinian issue. Arab nationalists became fragmented as local issues defined the form nationalism would take. But in Syria and Iraq, the fight for independence from Britain and France predominated. In Palestine, Ottomanists and Arab nationalists confronted the issue of land acquisition by an emerging nationalist movement of Jews from Europe.

SHIFTING ALLIANCES:
ARAB NATIONALISM, ZIONIST LAND
SETTLEMENT, AND OTTOMAN POLICIES

In the late 19th and early 20th centuries, shifting alliances between indigenous men and between indigenous men and Europeans competing for control of the region would have a critical impact on interethnic relations and on women's survival. Those shifting alliances surfaced in the course of disagreements within both the Zionist and Arab nationalist movements regarding relations between the two and regarding relations with Europe.

Four factors influenced Ottoman policy toward Jewish immigration into Palestine in the 1880s: (1) loss of territories in the Balkans as a result of nationalist uprisings, (2) issues of great power control of Jerusalem raised by the Crimean war, (3) intrusion of British, French, Americans, and Russians into the Ottoman domains through the capitulations, missionary schools, and advanced communications systems, and (4) internal power struggles as a result of changing class formations and ethnic-national identifications. Local craftsmen and merchants feared economic competition from foreign Jews whose population between 1882 and 1890 rose from 24,000 to 47,000 (Mandel, 1976, p. 20). In instances where influential Arabs attempted to stop the sale of land to Jews, European heads of state persuaded the Porte (central authorities) to grant concessions: administrative regulations were overlooked or lifted, and Jews continued to conduct business and to purchase land. By the time of the first Zionist Congress in 1897, there were 18 new settlements and 50,000 Jews in Palestine, swelling the indigenous population (Mandel, 1976).

Diplomatic maneuvers between the Ottoman government and European governments exacerbated tensions between Arab notables and the Porte. Absentee landlords sold land they had alienated from peasant farmers. Tensions between rural Arabs and newly arrived Jews erupted as early as 1886. Land reforms requiring registration of miri (state) land utilized European definitions of land use, property rights, and ownership. Settlers violated customary grazing and crop sharing practices on land peasants had lost by default to money-lenders and absentee landlords.

In the period following the Young Turk revolution of 1908, Muslim, Christian, and Jewish Arabs founded a joint branch of the CUP and a literary political club, the Jerusalem patriotic party. Fellahin (peasants) and Jewish settlers formed a society to promote their own interests (Mandel, 1976). Jews in Salonika, where Jews and members of a Judeo-Islamic syncretist sect, Donmes, were a majority of the population, organized opposition against Zionist land purchase. Members of the Alliance Israelite Universelle opposed Zionist goals as contradictory to the Alliance's aim of improving Jewish life in the Diaspora. A Jewish society, the Club des Intimes, opposed Zionism and supported Ottomanism (Flapan, 1979).

But joint activities of Muslims, Christians, and Jews were overwhelmed by Zionists of the Second Aliyah (1904–1914), parading the Zionist flag in Jaffa and insisting on the election of Zionist deputies to the Ottoman parliament to promote their claims to Palestine. Disillusioned Arab nationalists criticized the CUP's economic motivations for support of Zionism. Arab notables loyal to the CUP decried dangers of Zionism to the state. They associated Zionists with administrative corruption in that Zionists received special rights in association with foreign powers ("Palestine," 1947; Mandel, 1976). Another movement including the formation of the Patriotic Ottoman party in 1913, encouraged Arabs to resist land purchase by Jews and to buy goods produced by Arabs. They encouraged wealthy Arabs to promote local commerce and industry and fellahin (peasants) to learn modern techniques used by Jews (Porath, 1974).

Some British and French promoted anti-Zionist activity, asserting that Zionism was a front for German influence in the Empire. Competing for control of the Middle Eastern lands, the British government alternately related to Zionists as allies and as adversaries. Furthermore, the threat to the Triple Entente (Great Britain, France, Russia) of the Triple Alliance (Germany, Austro-Hungary, Italy) dominated diplomacy with the Arabs. Competing alliances of heads of state dominated the push for control of the resources and land base of the Middle Eastern lands, critical to control of industrial expansion.

The need for capital motivated the CUP's Central Committee in 1913 to propose a Muslim-Jewish alliance. Some Arabs involved in movements calling for reform within the Empire—the Ottoman Arab Brotherhood, Beirut Reform Society, and Decentralization party—also suggested an alliance between Arabs and Zionists (Mandel, 1976). Decentralists, impressed by Jewish achievements in Palestine, believed that Jewish capital and knowledge could contribute to the party's goal of Arab self-rule. For the most part, these nationalists, who were not from Palestine, viewed Zionism from a pan-Arab perspective; that is, affecting the Arab provinces as a whole (Mandel, 1976).

The Christian Public Charity Society for Ladies, formed in 1911 by women in Haifa, was one of several women's charitable associations formed throughout the Arab provinces addressing nationalist concerns. The Arab Union of Haifa, consisting of Muslims and Christians, acted as liaison among women's organizations throughout Palestine (Mogannam, 1937). Active as members of secret societies and in associations of women whose service work supported their communities, women were minimally involved in nationalist activity at this stage, and they functioned on the periphery of male-controlled power structures.

The First Arab Congress met in June 1913, enlisting support for Arab demands for reform within the Empire. The chairperson, Al-Zahrawi, made a statement proposing alliance with Jews to "bring about the triumph of our common cause for the material and moral rehabilitation of our common land" (Mandel, 1976, p. 162). Nonetheless Zionist officials continued to discourage agreements with Arab nationalists and to influence the Ottoman government to relax restrictions on settlement and purchase of land. Allying with the Ottoman government was important because in order to aquire financial support from European Jews they had to ensure the ability of those Jews to settle in Palestine. Furthermore, once the Arab Congress had negotiated an agreement with the CUP, its efforts toward agreement with Zionists waned (Mandel, 1976).

Editors of the newspaper, *Falastin,* asserted that "Zionist" was not synonymous with "Jew," and that the wave of immigrants (second Aliyah) sought national autonomy, lived separately, and discouraged Jews from mixing with Muslims and Christians. Some Arab officials encouraged Zionists to integrate by becoming Ottoman subjects and to work with the local population by creating joint economic ventures and integrated schools (Mandel, 1976).

Some Muslims encouraged alliance with Zionists on the basis that Christian Arabs wanted the great powers to occupy Palestine, which was not in the interest of either Jews or Muslims. They encouraged Jews and Muslims to work together to defeat the Turks. Others encouraged an alliance of Christian, Muslim, and Jew against the Ottoman government. In July, 1914, Nahum Sokolow and Dr. Victor Jacobson, Zionist representatives in Constantinople, forwarded proposals to the Decentralist party similar to those of Al-Zahrawi at the First Arab Congress, affirming that Arabs and Jews " . . . are from one stock" (Mandel, 1976, p. 198); and that they must pool their resources. In response, the Decentralist party insisted that the Zionists meet first with Arabs in Palestine and then with Arab nationalists from all groups, since the Zionist question concerned first of all the local population in Palestine and secondly the Arab question in general. In the meantime, Zionists in Palestine were negotiating a meeting with Palestinians, a meeting that was delayed in the face of opposition by both Arab notables and Zionists in Palestine who felt that the meeting was unnecessary, and that the other was acting in accord with orders from the Ottoman government. The aim of Zionists who were wary of the outcome of the proposed meeting was to avoid a confrontation with the Arabs at this time. The eruption of World War I in August 1914 halted all further negotiations toward a possible Arab nationalist-Zionist alliance (Mandel, 1976).

LAND, LABOR, WOMEN'S BODIES: THE MYTHOS OF RECLAMATION

Zionist ideology describes Jewish history as exile. Jewish sects promoting return to Zion, Jerusalem, site of the first Temple, have always existed. Some believed in a messianic return; others advocated political strategies. In the 20th century, Zionism became the ideological framework for a coalescing of European bourgeois men who had a range of relationships to Judaism and who supported modern reforms by advocating territorial rights for world Jewry. Some of these men were Jews, others Christians.

Anti-Jewish politics in Europe had a long history revolving around struggle for hegemony between the Christian church and the state. Both utilized Jew hatred to solidify wealth and defuse social unrest. Violent massacres, banishment, and discriminatory social policies threatened the religious, economic, and political survival of Jews. The intensity of that violence varied by geographic and historic context, as did the groups most affected within the Jewish community. In reaction, some Jews responding to social movements in the 19th and 20th centuries envisioned a new society based on egalitarian principles ensuring all citizens economic, cultural, and religious survival. Resettlement of the Jews in "Zion" was supported by the Protestant Reformation revival of the Old Testament emphasizing that the second coming depended upon return of the Hebrew people to Zion, where they would become Christians again. In addition, the view of some British imperialists who supported settlement of Jews in Palestine is characterized by the Earl of Shaftesbury who, in 1876, asserted that England must get hold of Syria before her rivals did. England, he said, must therefore foster the nationality of the Jews:

> England is the great trading and maritime power of the world. To England, then naturally belongs the role of favoring the settlement of the Jews in Palestine. The nationality of the Jews exists: the spirit is there and has been there for 3,000 years, but the external form, the crowning bond of union is still wanting. A nation must have a country. The old land, the old people. This is not an artificial experiment: it is nature, it is history. ("Palestine," 1947, p. 5)

If fostering the nationality of the Jews was nature, so too was anti-Semitism nature, according to Zionist leader Theodore Herzl. Anti-Semitism was the "propelling force" that, like the "wave of the future," would bring Jews into the new society, the promised land (Arendt, 1978, p. 174). The Zionist conceptualization of history reduced all historical experience and variations of class and gender to one unchanging fact: anti-Semitism set all non-Jews against all Jews. Herzl's solution was the modern solution of self-rule on the basis of a territorially defined identity. Protected by the nation–state, Jews would be unavailable as political scapegoats. Leo Pinsker, elected president of the Hovevei Zion (Lovers of Zion) movement in Russia in 1984, asserting that Jewish survival was dependent upon the Jews alone, began to raise funds for settlements in Palestine.

Zionism provided a context in which Jews would be assured entrance into, and a place in, the modern era. Marxist Zionists promoted the rights of Jews as workers. Ber Borochov (1881–1917) believed that the exclusion of Jews from "the most important, most influential and most stable branches of production" was at the root of their problem ("Palestine," 1947, p. 25). Modern capitalism — large-scale industrialization and monopoly — exacerbated this problem, setting Jewish capitalist against Jewish worker and increasing competition between the "native" worker and the "alien" Jewish worker. Asher Ginzberg (Achad Ha'am), a cultural Zionist, wrote in 1913 that the object of Zionism was the reconstruction of Jewish spiritual life through a national revival of Hebrew literature and thought in Palestine. At the Fifth Zionist Congress in 1901, Ha'am formed the Democratic Zionist Faction to call attention to the mandates of his cultural perspective ("Palestine," 1947). In 1902, he had published *Altneuland,* in which he detailed his vision of a society without race laws and based on economic justice and equality for women, where the Arab would live side by side with the Jew (Patai, 1974; Ruppin, 1934). At meetings of the Zionist Congress, Theodore Herzl argued for obtaining a legally secured home for the Jewish people in Palestine. Vladimir Jabotinsky (1880–1940) led the Revisionists, advocating military force and demanding a Jewish state within its historic boundaries, created by a mass evacuation of Jews from Europe. "Practical" Zionists argued that Jews should begin the work of reconstituting the Jewish nation in Palestine without waiting for diplomatic approval (Halpern, 1969). Bernard Lazare's Zionism led him to the conclusion that Weizmann's diplomacy was condescension toward the masses. Philosopher and Zionist Hannah Arendt notes that Lazare believed that a nationalist movement could only succeed as constituted by, of, and for, the people (Arendt, 1978). Lazare identified Zionism with the struggle of all minorities for cultural autonomy and civil rights. Zionist party officials forced Lazare to resign in 1889 because of his opposition to great power diplomacy to secure national goals. By negotiating with heads of governments, Zionist leaders affirmed the continuity of their goals with imperialism.

The Social-Democratic Poalei Zion party, along with other labor Zionists, identified their interests with the supposed interests of the local Palestinian population, now "Arabs" and "Jews." The cultural Zionists stressed the common Semitic origins of Arab and Jew and the necessity to maintain the heritage, traditions, and language of Palestinians. These Zionists provided a background for the binationalists in the 1940s.

Practical Zionists worked for good relations with Arabs to make their task of Jewish colonization easier. In 1899, Herzl wrote to Arab leaders stating that Zionists did not intend to expropriate Palestine (Ro'i, 1982). In general, the "Arab problem" was not considered important until two new Arab nationalist groups formed in the winter of 1912–1913, the Decentralization party and the Beirut Reform Committee. In 1913, Zionist Radler-Feldman advocated for fusion of the two national movements as a necessary objective (Ro'i, 1982).

But from whatever perspective the Zionist question was debated, all discussion pivoted around the key concepts: land and labor. Land and labor signified redemption. Those Jews emigrating to Palestine to redeem the land through their labor envisioned a transformation of the rootless Jew, plagued by discrimination and denied access to the basic means of production. By redeeming the land, they would redeem themselves; the present would be transformed into the past.

Zionist leaders were aware of the existence of indigenous Jews who protested their exploits and of the need to convince or force indigenous peasants to move over. Expropriation of land in the wake of imperialist expansion and internal reforms had already shaken the roots of subsistence existence tied to the land. The Zionist project continued this process.

The mythos of land and labor hid the goal of capitalization of land and labor necessary to the success of the Zionist project. As Zionists sanctified the land and the laborer, the hidden contempt behind sanctification was exposed. Zionism is based on religious justification for return to the "holy" land. The right of return is a religious concept, based in the biblical affirmation of the special mission of the Jewish people. The land is the pulpit from which

the word of God is spread. Devastation of war and use of the land as an endlessly exploitable resource tell another story.

The land then, is like a woman, the "sacred virgin" who must be protected,
the "natural resource" to be exploited. Woman is laborer. In labor she
"reproduces" the nation, and in labor she serves the men who are the state.
While Zionists extol the virtues of labor, they institutionalize a system of social organization in which the labor of some is denigrated. Zionists utilized
indigenous class structure, including denigration of women, to build a modern economic system in which women function as unpaid laborers and as
a base for the expression of male power and control, and in which "minorities" do the low-paid manual labor supporting the professional classes.

In the early stages of Zionist settlement of Palestine, Jews utilized a range
of ideologies to support control of the basic means of production, land and
labor. Socialist Zionists rejected the social inequities of capitalism, decrying
the exploitation of the worker. In the final analysis, however, and from the
vantage point of women, Socialist Zionists and mainstream Zionists supporting capitalization of land and labor were not in conflict. At the practical level,
sexualized race discrimination and violence against women infected both positions from the inception of the Zionist project: the antifeminism of
nationalism.

In 1911, Zionist workers formed a collective at Umm-Juni (later Degania),
the Hadera Commune. It was the first independent workers farm (Maimon,
1962). They were 16 men and one woman, Sarah Malchin. Ada Maimon,
a founder of the Zionist women's movement, explains why Sarah left the
collective:

> It goes without saying that she was utterly devoted to the group and eager
> to do whatever she could to lighten the burdens of the young men working
> in that hot, unhealthy locale. Yet she had some revolutionary ideas of her own
> and she fought for them. She believed that the farm ought to grow its own vegeta-
> bles and raise poultry. Thus work would have been provided for at least one
> other girl, and it would have been possible to introduce shifts in the kitchen.
> Her suggestion met with no response.
>
> When the first cow was bought, Sarah rebelled. She demanded the right to
> milk the cow, but the men were afraid that she would not know how to get
> the maximum amount of milk from it. The "dairy" was entrusted to one of the
> men, and Sarah was given no opportunity to learn the new skills . . . (Maimon,
> 1962, p. 27)

For Zionist women of the Second Aliya, 1904–1913, emigrating to Palestine was a step in their liberation as women: Zionism meant an end to the
feminine occupations of "kitchen work, housekeeping and various services"
(Maimon, 1962, p. 18). Contrary to their expectations, however, Zionist
women found no outlet for their aspirations to become agricultural workers
and build the new state. Disillusioned, they turned to one another for support, forming the Working Women's Movement as a vehicle for obtaining the

benefits of equality and justice promulgated by Socialist Zionists. The Working Women's Movement provided a vehicle for women who hoped for and expected inclusion by male workers in " . . . bringing about the great revolution in modern Jewish history: the return of the Jewish people to its land and to physical labor; the attainment of economic and cultural emancipation; and the establishment of an independent political regime in Palestine" (Maimon, 1962, p. 17). Zionism was the doorway for women into the modern era: "In the life of Jews in exile there was no place for the question of women in the modern sense" (Maimon, 1962, p. 17).

Workers' collectives were organized by pioneers of the Second Aliyah who objected to practices of Jews of the first wave of immigration, which began in 1881. Farmers utilized a wage labor structure and were reluctant to hire Jewish workers when they could pay Arab workers less. Many eastern European women of the Second Aliyah had been active in political movements before they became Zionists. They emigrated to Palestine expecting to create a new society based on socialist principles. Manya Shochat was a Russian Jew born in 1880 into a wealthy bourgeois class, who risked her life fighting for a workers' revolution and then specifically for improved conditions for Jewish workers and ultimately for a Jewish state. She organized the Jewish Independent Labor party and worked with Bundists and Zionists to form self-defense groups. At her brother's request, Manya visited Palestine in 1904, becoming one of the first of the radicalized Russian immigrants of the Second Aliyah. She describes her motivation to visit Palestine as a need to " . . . find out what it was that the country meant for me, as an individual" (Katznelson-Shazar, 1975, p. 21).

In Palestine, Manya made a careful study of existing Jewish colonies, collecting statistics, particularly on details of income and employment of Arab workers. Criticizing the methods of Jewish farmers, she resolved that the agricultural collective and the creation of a Jewish agricultural proletariat was the solution to the intolerable conditions of life in Russia. After several years of study and travel, Manya returned to Palestine and persuaded the Jewish Colonization Association to allow her to form a collective at their farm at Sedjera (in the Galilee) run by the agronomist, Eliyahu Krause.

> At Sedjera, I worked half days on the books and the other half day in the cowbarn. I told Krause that he ought to admit women to the work, and the first three women workers there were the sisters Shturman, Sarah (Krigser), Shifra (Betzer) and Esther (Becker). They were all very young and they followed the plough like real peasants. (Katznelson-Shazar, 1975, p. 25)

Operating for a year and a half with 18 members, the Sedjera Collective became the first self-sufficient agricultural collective where women were not confined to the kitchen and laundry.

> It ended its work successfully, paid the farm its fifth of the harvest, re-
> turned in full the money that had been advanced, and demonstrated once
> for all that a collective economy was a possibility. (Katznelson-Shazar, 1975,
> p. 26)

In spite of this, her contract was not renewed. "Krause's superiors in Paris informed him that he could no longer have Manya at Sejera because she was
a socialist" (Reinharz, 1984, p. 286). Furthermore, the Sejera experiment was
rejected when it was decided that building a Jewish defense force was more
important work. In 1908 Manya had married Israel Shochat, leader of the Labor party, Poalei Zion, and of a secret society for training Jewish workers in
self-defense, Bar Giora. She and Shochat were among the founders of
Hashomer Self-Defense Organization. Israel Shochat was anxious to use the
collective site for a training ground, so that Manya spent the better part of
her career utilizing a skill she had assiduously trained in—smuggling arms.
Apparently, her socialism did not prevent her recruitment into the Jewish Defense Force where she was preoccupied with aiding a military buildup rather
than with improving the situation of Zionist women.

In 1909 there were 165 Jews organized in collectives, or *kvutzot*, in the
Galilee, of whom 11 were women (Izraeli, 1981, p. 93). From the beginning,
Zionist women found themselves condemned to struggle for equality and justice, defined by, in the image of, and for the profit of men. Wandering from
one colony to the next, women seeking agricultural work were ridiculed,
turned away, and forced instead to work in kitchens or to sew shirts, do laundry and work as domestics in farmers' houses (Maimon, 1962). Farmers espoused the biological determinism of sexist economics: they would lose
money; women's honor would be in jeopardy working in an orange grove
full of Arabs or alongside Jewish boys " . . . in groves that are far away from
the village. It would be indecent!" (Maimon, 1962, p. 22). Sarah Malchin,
who did not give up her ambition of working the land, was happy when she
was hired with several Arab women to pull up weeds in a field, until 3 days
later, when a child of a settler died unexpectedly. "The general verdict on
the reason for the tragic loss was that it was a visitation for the sinfulness of
the young woman who had gone to work with men in a field outside the
village" (Sisters of Exile, 1973, p. 91).

Within the confines of women's domain, women suffered helplessness and
humiliation. Conditions in the kitchens were difficult. Fire smoked up small
rooms; provisions were meager, utensils scarce. Many women from bourgeois
families who hired domestics did not have cooking experience. When meals
turned out badly, men would " . . . stop eating and arrange the full plates in
a long row, to be returned to the kitchen." This practice, called the "railroad,"
continued into the period of the Third Aliyah (1919) (Maimon, 1962, p. 25).
Many of the male workers treated women with indifference and scorn. They

left them limited, if any, options for survival. Continually seeking seasonal work, women went hungry, became ill, and died.

Confronting the indifference and the hostility of male workers and of the Palestine Colonization Association in charge of land settlement, Zionist women chose to create alternative structures that under the separate but equal clause would provide for the training, job opportunities and sense of community critical to their survival. [At the first meeting of working women in Kinneret in April 1911, women decided to fight for their right to conduct their own vegetable gardening, dairy work, and poultry raising (Maimon, 1962).] In 1908, Hannah Meisel had begun negotiations for the first training farm for girls. Her plan was to provide instruction in vegetable growing, poultry raising, dairying, cooking and household management. Thus "girls" would command the respect of the men and "work relations between the sexes would improve" (Maimon, 1962, p. 29). Unable to convince the Palestine Office of the Zionist Executive to support her project, she approached a private landowner who would agree to the farm only if they could assure him they would not have a deficit after the first year. Knowing that a training farm could not be expected to balance its budget in the first few years, Meisel negotiated an agreement to set up the farm beside a workers' settlement at Kineret (renamed from the Arabic Daleiga). She was finally able to obtain a subsidy from the Women's Organization for Cultural Work in Palestine, a German-Jewish Zionist organization, to subsidize the monthly wages of the twelve women who came to the farm. Nonetheless, with no inventory or property, it took 18 months and the dissolution of the workers' settlement before they began to function independently.

By 1912, there were 500 Jewish workers organized in kvutzot in Judea, of whom 30 were women (Izraeli, 1981). At the outbreak of World War I in 1914, there were 200 women in Palestine, an increase to over 13% of the 1,500 Jewish workers. Two-thirds were in Judea and the remainder in the Galilee. Conditions for women varied from one colony to another, and those women who graduated from training centers were sometimes able, as a group, to negotiate improved working conditions. When women in one colony sold their vegetables to Arab merchants, their prestige rose (Maimon, 1962). But the war years brought continuing hardship for women. Public works initiated by the Ottoman government were not open to women (Bernstein, 1987). Foreign markets closed, causing a crisis in the citrus fruit industry (Maimon, 1962). Women, whose wage scale was lower than that of men, and many of whom were near starvation, were the first to lose work. The Palestine Office did not consider it unjust when women were dismissed from work. Rather, such dismissals represented how justice was defined: women were expendable, men were not.

In 1914, 30 delegates representing 200 workers, 7 from Judea and 23 from Galilean villages, convened and formed an executive committee to: " . . . keep in touch with working women throughout the country and cooperate with the Agricultural Center in attempting to improve their situation" (Maimon, 1962, p. 38). This was the first of four women's conferences during the war-time period.

Small gains from concerted efforts among women were temporary. Women were not only relegated to "shadow work" but were shadow workers. The Palestine Office did not mention them in annual contracts and did not mention them in their work plans. Men asserted that this was because the women were working for them and not for the Palestine Office. Sarah T'hon, wife of a director of the Palestine Office, in an open letter to women agricultural workers, admonished them to stop trying to be like men and keep in their mind their main task, " . . . to be good 'housewives,' diligent workers and natural human beings, whose behavior is guided by complete harmony, and to weave the future of our people here" (Bernstein, 1987, p. 20). Complaints by Orthodox Jews helped close training centers for women. They complained that women were the cause of economic losses and that women were utilizing resources (land) that belonged to men. Many women, although struggling for recognition, resigned themselves to the so-called natural division of labor according to sex and blamed themselves and each other for their passivity.

Nonetheless, at their Fifth Congress in July 1918 working women stressed that:

> There are so few fields open to women that one has the feeling of being fenced in and practically forced into the kitchen of workers' groups or into kvutzot of women workers. Even girls looking for employment think they have no other alternatives. We must go on fighting to expand women's work opportunities everywhere. (Maimon, 1962, pp. 52, 53)

The Working Women's Committee was formed because Zionist women recognized the need to address the problems facing them as women; problems that were not addressed by the Labor movement at large. For all Zionists, including socialists, Judaism was the overriding particularity calling for political action. That they were Jews first of all, brought Zionist women to Palestine. Nationalist identification bonded Zionist women and men, many of whom sought a socialist solution to the Jewish problem. The experience of Zionist women in Palestine, however, exposed the ideal vision of land and labor underlying Zionist ideology as intrinsically misogynist. Men controlled women's labor, excluding women from highly valued agricultural work, while devaluing labor defined as women's work.

The solution proposed by the Working Women's Committee was self-transformation (Izraeli, 1981; Maimon, 1962). Women advocated for separate living and working collectives to acquire new skills and to divest themselves of historically conditioned passivity and dependence.

> Once the halutza [pioneer woman] proved her skill, not only would she be accepted as a full member in the kvutza, but men would seek her out. . . . An ideology oriented toward self-transformation rather than toward changing men and social institutions helped to legitimate the creation of a separate women's movement within Labor Zionism in that it avoided direct conflict with the male-dominated ideology and with the male pioneers. (Izraeli, 1981, p. 97)

Articulating their goals within the framework of the Zionist labor movement, the Working Women's Movement relied upon the existing structure—the two labor parties (Hapoel Hatzair and Poalei Zion, which eventually became Achdut Haavoda), and two unions of agricultural workers in the Galilee and Judea—to support their goals. Leaders of the Working Women's Committees, organized to coordinate activities between conferences, were connected to Palestine's emerging elites (Izraeli, 1981). The struggle to maintain autonomy and affirm their loyalty to men and to the Zionist vision led to splits within the Working Women's Movement. Ada Maimon and Yael Gordon were among those feminists who continually supported autonomous structures, not with the goal of self-transformation, but because they were necessary to maintain the grass-roots character of the movement. For other women, loyalty to the male-dominated party structure superseded the goals of either self-transformation through autonomous structures, or the maintenance of a grass-roots constituency. This choice in fact encouraged disassociation from the grass-roots movement in favor of absorption into the male-dominated labor movement and centralized control from above.

Splits in the Working Women's Movement were precipitated and fed by strategies employed by men vying for control of the labor movement. After World War I, the Zionist leadership centralized control of the labor movement by creating the Histadrut, the Jewish Federation of Labor. Trade unions, sick funds, labor exchanges, the immigration office, the public works and building office, schools and workers' public kitchens created by political parties, as well as all resource-generating institutions of the labor movement, became part of the new organization (Izraeli, 1981). Viewing its goals as cutting across party differences, women did not submit a separate list of delgates to the first convention of the Histadrut (Izraeli, 1981). Two leading members of Hapoel Hatzair party, Ada Fishman-Maimon, who was also leader of the struggle for women's suffrage in all institutions of the Yishuv (Jewish community), and Yael Gordan attended the first convention of the Histadrut as guests. Strongly objecting to the invisibility of women and women's issues, Maimon threatened to submit an independent electoral list declaring that women delegates must be chosen by the women themselves, and not by the parties. In the ensuing debate, Achdut Haavoda, threatened by the consolidation of women's groups in agricultural villages and urban centers and the creation of the Association of Hebrew Women for Equal Rights in Eretz Yisrael in 1920, insisted that separate interest groups would weaken the Histadrut and waste resources. The 1921 conference established the Women Workers' Council as the organizational arm of the women's movement within the Histadrut (Izraeli, 1981).

To obviate the problem of separation of the worker from the national leadership, women proposed forming women's committees within the local labor councils of the Histadrut. A second debate ensued about how to elect women to the women's committees. If elected by the labor councils in conjunction with the Women Workers' Council, rather than by the women themselves, women would lose all chance of defining their own goals and forms of action (Bernstein, 1987, p. 91). The Histadrut leadership, mainly Achdut Haavoda, supported incorporation of the women's committees into the local councils while Hapoel Hatzair favored independently elected committees (Izraeli, 1981). The struggle for party control of the Histadrut, rather than what might benefit women or support women's goals, determined how the issue would be decided. Women voted along party lines. The majority delegation of the Achdut Haavoda party at the third convention of the Histadrut Executive Council in 1927, approved the proposal for appointment, rather than election by local women workers.

The Women Workers' Council had nominal power within the Histadrut, which controlled election of women to the council. By 1927 all appointments to the Women Workers' Council were internal, reinforcing cooptation, control and the dependence of the Women Workers' Movement on the male-dominated labor movement. Ada Maimon was ousted twice from important decision making positions because she " . . . fought for 50% representation for women among those allocated immigration permits to Palestine" (Izraeli, 1981, p. 109). Maimon was replaced as secretary of the Council by Golda Meir, whose views were in line with the male establishment. A man took Maimon's place on the immigration committee of the Labor party, Hapoi Hatzair.

The existence of the Women Workers' Council did not preclude discrimination against women in Histadrut policies. The Histadrut sanctioned lower wages for women, so that a Histadrut contract gave women with 4 years of experience on a job lower wages than a man beginning the same job (Bernstein, 1987). It supported employment for men in times of crisis, so that between 1926 and 1930, a period of economic hardship, the percentage of women in the work force dropped from 34.7% to 27% (Bernstein, 1987, p. 74). Women had fewer sick-fund rights and no right to use convalescent and recreation homes of the Histadrut. Women were included in union elections only to vote for their husbands' parties (Bernstein, 1987).

The Women Workers' Council was allocated responsibility for women's welfare in lieu of a commitment to women's liberation from the Histadrut as a whole. The woman whose welfare the council concerned itself with was the wife and mother. The male leadership of the Histadrut finally shaped the concept of "woman" that would be acceptable in the new state. If the opportunity had existed for women to create a new model of liberation and self-determination in the "new world," it quickly disintegrated under the impact of the male power structure.

> The WWC . . . sponsored child day-care centers to free women to enter the labor market. Its occupational training prepared girls primarily for traditionally feminine roles as hairdressers, dressmakers, nursemaids, and the like. It turned its attention more and more to looking after welfare needs of mothers and children in the urban centers, leaving the political decisions, the trade union activities, and economic policy in the hands of the male establishment. In addition it served ancillary political functions, the most important of which was mobilizing female support for the party at elections. (Izraeli, 1981, p. 113)

WOMEN/ARAB/WORKER: ALLIES OR ADVERSARIES?

Women of the Second Aliyah connected their plight to that of Arab workers. For example, one woman observed: "The discrepancy between the wages of women and men in the Jewish labor movement is comparable to the discrepancy between the wages of Arab workers and Jewish workers" (Maimon, 1962, p. 76). Manya Shochat early on conceived of her collective as a Jewish-Arab collective. In 1908, visiting the United States, she met with two prominent binationalists and advocates of Arab rights—Judah Magnes and Henrietta Szold. In 1921, she helped form the League for Arab–Jewish Friendship. Women factory workers in Acre protesting intolerable working conditions saw themselves as allies of Arab workers:

> The working conditions in the factory were ghastly. Many of the women received between five and ten piastres (twenty-five to fifty cents) a day. Sanitary conditions were unspeakable. There were no Jewish doctors. We could not make use of the Kupat Cholim, the labor sick fund, because the bosses did not recognize the labor organization. Among the Arabs were children of six and eight who were employed in the most dangerous part of the work. (Katznelson-Shazar, 1975, p. 121)

Women organized a strike on February 16, 1927, that lasted four months and 12 days and included 60 Jewish and 40 Arab workers, many of whom were severely beaten and thrown into prison (Katznelson-Shazar, 1975).

The Zionist infrastructure, however, thwarted all attempts at solidarity between Arab and Jewish workers, fostering horizontal hostility among women. Jews from Arab countries were imported as a cheap labor source, competing with European Jewish women for low-paying skilled jobs. Jewish Arab women suffered longer workdays, lower pay, and more virulent harassment than that directed against Ashkenazi women. When Jewish women workers in Zichron Jakob declared a strike against the Palestine Jewish Colonization Association for reducing their pay, the PJCA sent in Arab women as strikebreakers. Working as domestics, many women from Arab countries did the shadow work of the shadow workers. Struggling under the double yoke—job and family—

one Zionist woman employing another as a domestic nonetheless objected to this "solution," saying " . . . of course we rebel against the intolerable yoke which such a woman carries. And is nothing left but that my comrade, whom I take into the house, shall assume the burden of the family which I myself am not willing to bear?" (Katznelson-Shazar, 1975, p. 181). Jewish Arab women from other Middle East countries competed with Palestinian women for low-paying domestic work, just as Jewish women working in the orchards usurped the domain of Palestinian women who " . . . prevented them from going near the trees" (Katznelson-Shazar, 1975, p. 22).

DIPLOMACY—BETWEEN WARS

The Ottoman government entered World War I in alliance with the Germans, hoping to reconquer Egypt from the British and use German resources to hold together what was left of the Empire (Goldschmidt, 1983). In response to the Turco-German invasion of Sinai in 1914, Britain contacted Sharif Husayn Emir of Mecca, Arab leader of the Hijaz (western Arabia), who had long contended with the Ottoman sultan. The sharif and his son Abdallah opposed the centralizing policies of the CUP. Abdallah's ties with Arab nationalist societies in Syria had prompted him to seek support from the British consul-general, Lord Kitchener, in early 1914. A British/Arab alliance against the Ottoman Empire could prove useful to both (Antonious, 1946; Goldschmidt 1983; Hourani, 1946).

Representing the British, Sir Henry McMahon offered Husayn an assurance of independence in exchange for collaboration in defeating the Turks. Husayn hesitated to make a commitment to Great Britain until the fate of Syria and Palestine was clear. But increased repression by the Ottoman regime put pressure on Husayn to move. In the summer of 1916, the Ottoman governor of Syria, Jemal, accused Muslim and Christian Arab nationalists of treason (trying to establish Syria, Iraq, and Palestine as independent from the Ottoman Sultanate) and executed them (Antonious, 1946; Hourani, 1946).

Two factors affected negotiations between Britain and Arab nationalists. The first was that in May 1916, Sir Mark Sykes, representing Britain, and M. Georges Picot, representing France, concluded an agreement protecting the interests of France, Britain, and Russia in the Ottoman territories. The Sykes-Picot Agreement divided the fertile lands from the southeast coast of the Mediterranean around the Syrian desert north of the Arabian peninsula to the Persian Gulf known as the Fertile Crescent into zones. The second factor was publication of the Balfour Declaration in 1917.

British supporters of the Balfour Declaration hoped that a Zionist-British alliance would further Britain's strategic goals in the Middle East: to secure control in Egypt and to secure trade routes with the Far East (Antonious, 1946). The British were concerned that negotiations between Zionists and the CUP for a Turkish Balfour Declaration would threaten their goals. They hoped to give Jews a reason to support the Allied cause. With much discussion of wording, the Balfour Declaration was issued on November 2, 1917:

> His majesty's Government view with favor the establishment in Palestine of a national home for the Jewish people and will use their best endeavors to facilitate the achievement of this object, it being clearly understood that nothing shall be done which may prejudice the civil and religious rights of existing non-Jewish communities in Palestine, or the rights and political status enjoyed by Jews in any other country. (Antonious, 1946, p. 266)

However, with reassurances from the British, Americans, and French, and in the face of repression of Arab nationalists, Sharif Husayn and his sons joined the Allies against the Turks. At the end of the war, with women, children, and men suffering from hunger, plagues, corruption, and devastation, Turkish troops were routed from the Hijaz. Britain and France set up provisional governments, leaving the cities of Aleppo, Homs, Hama, Damascus, as well as Transjordan, to Amir Faisal, son of Husayn (Antonious, 1946; Hourani, 1946).

The British and French, preparing to decide the fate of the Ottoman territories at the San Remo Conference, proposed French and British mandates and Britain reasserted its obligation to carry out the Balfour Declaration. In southern Syria, in the province of Palestine, the mandate was given full administrative control with a provision for the promise of the Balfour Declaration to help in the construction of a Jewish national home in the British area west of the River Jordan. The region east of the Jordan, referred to as Transjordan and administered by Faisal's government from 1918 to 1920, was given to his brother Abdallah, subject to mandatory control (Antonious, 1946; Hourani, 1946; "Palestine," 1947).

Geographic boundaries between Iraq, Palestine, and Transjordan designated by Anglo-French agreements in 1920 and 1922, arbitrarily divided indigenous communities. In the new "states"—British-mandated Palestine, French Lebanon, and British-controlled Iraq—the British and French instituted their own administrative systems, languages, currencies, and economic systems. The French systematically encouraged regional loyalties and discouraged alliances between Christians, Jews, and Muslims (Antonious, 1946).

Rivalry between European nation–states and creation of the mandate facilitated expropriation of strategic geographic areas by the French and British. For a time, Zionists benefited from the mandate system by acquiring a legitimized foothold in Palestine. But many Ottoman Jews were interested in maintaining traditional ties supported by indigenous systems of social organization (Porath, 1974). Some Orthodox Jews who opposed Zionism formed alliances with anti-Zionist Arabs. For all these Jews, dissolution of communal organization threatened positions of power. Alliances in defense of and against Zionism were further complicated by the policies of the British during the period of the mandate, officially 1920 to 1948. The British played the uneasy role of reassuring two opposed groups of their loyalty, loyalty that had always proven questionable, based as it was on self-serving interests.

WOMEN UNDER BRITISH MANDATE: UNDER THE WAR NET

Between 1918 and 1920 the British military administration controlled Palestine. In the spring of 1920, the British instituted a civil administration run by a High Commissioner.

Zionist women suffered disappointment on several counts as the British assumed control of Palestine. They were frustrated in their attempts to join the Jewish Legion and fight with the British for liberation of the Galilee and other parts of the country (Maimon, 1962). Initially an influx of capital brought by British troops and officials aided the economy. But war conditions closed down markets and exacerbated the plight of women. Women's vegetable collectives collapsed under competition from British imports. The Settlement Department of the Zionist movement discontinued its minimal support of women's farm collectives (Izraeli, 1981). Furthermore, although the Balfour Declaration encouraged the third wave of immigration (1919–1923), the British refused immigration certificates to women unless they came as the " . . . fiancées, wives or sisters of halutzim [pioneers], or as domestic servants attached to Jewish immigrant families" (Maimon, 1962, p. 86).

Women of the First and Second Aliyot concentrated their efforts on attaining economic viability. In the pre-state period beginning in 1918, women were forced to turn their attention to the contested issue of voting rights when they were excluded from electing members of the Jewish council of Jaffa. Adamantly opposed by Orthodox Jews and conservative parties, and co-opted as an issue by liberal parties, women's suffrage was a major controversy in the formative stages of the Yishuv (Jewish community).

Local councils elected delegates to a central body, the Constituent Assembly. In Jaffa in 1918, voting eligibility was granted every Jewish male of age (Maimon, 1962). Opposition forced a new policy, but rabbis, Orthodox Jews, and other antifeminists rebelled, wanting to maintain the status quo, and issued bans against granting suffrage to women. They plastered walls of buildings with quotes of Maimonides forbidding women's participation in government and hired a Yemenite woman to walk through the streets on election day shouting: "It is forbidden to elect women—there is a cablegram from London" (Maimon, 1962, pp. 233, 234). Agricultural colonies feared that women's voting would bring about their ruin. Two women finally elected to the council in Rishon Lezion were blamed when the council disbanded " . . . due to internal strife" (Maimon, 1962, p. 233). In Safed, women were allowed to vote only when their husbands were dead or away from the city (Maimon, 1962).

The 1919 Tel Aviv meeting of the national convention decided to adopt full suffrage after a delay of a year and a half. When elections for the Constituent Assembly took place, special concessions were given to appease and persuade the Orthodox constituency, who insisted that no woman be elected to the National Council, to help " . . . in laying the foundations of the Jewish polity in Palestine" (Maimon, 1962, p. 238). One woman was elected to the Council as vice-chairperson " . . . on the understanding that her office would be purely nominal, on paper only. So it was that the Va'ad Leumi, the National Council of Palestine's Jews came into being" (Maimon, 1962, p. 239). While the constitution of the Jewish community extended suffrage to men and women alike, women delegates to the Assembly could not elect members of the Rabbinical Council, which was in control of domestic relations and laws of personal status (Maimon, 1962). Furthermore, when in 1926 the British instituted municipal self-government, " . . . electoral law . . . restricted suffrage to men twenty years of age or older who paid a minimum of one pound annually in other municipal taxes and the right to be elected to men of thirty and over who paid a minimum of one pound in property taxes or two pounds in other taxes" (Maimon, 1962, p. 242).

The League of Nations sanctioned the imposition of a modern bureaucratic system in Palestine. The British assumed, imposed, and instituted political authority. All recommendations or requests from Palestinians regarding the new state system (mandate) were processed in London. Decisions were made on the basis of the impact of those requests for British international goals.

Under Ottoman rule, Palestine had been divided into three major districts or *sanjaks,* administered by a representative of the Ottoman government and a representative legislative council. Each sanjak was divided into districts headed by local sheikhs, whose power was maintained through traditional custom and enforced by the military at their disposal. Ottoman administrative reforms in the second half of the 19th century weakened the power of sheikhs by putting tax collection into the hands of the newly created class of urban notables, a'yans. Sheikhs were brought within the framework of the Ottoman administration and appointed as mukhtars of villages (Porath, 1974).

The new administrative system gave power over local populations to bureaucrats accountable to the High Commissioner. In rural areas, British utilized mukhtars to control villages. The effect was to divide the Palestinian population in new ways. Mukhtars, villagers, and Palestinian bureaucrats competed for control as customary modes of social organization no longer ensured social, economic, and political benefits. A predominance of Christian Arabs filled positions in a hierarchical system of personnel assigned to various districts and accountable to central offices. In response to demands from Muslims to maintain control over their own religious affairs, and for equal representation, the British created the Supreme Muslim Council in 1921. Muslim elites appointed by the British controlled the Council, another tool for maintaining sectarian, class, and sex-role divisions within Palestinian society (Lesch, 1980; Miller, 1985; Porath, 1974).

As for the critical function of tax collection, the British maintained that the "backward" Arab population was not ready for complete self-government. In other words, the British needed time to condition and prepare the indigenous population (through co-optation and dependence) for participation in modern self-rule; that is, incorporation into the international industrial world complex.

Education continued to be a vehicle for that process. Within Arab society, literacy (for men) was highly valued and was bound up with religious education. Under British control the standard course of study for *fellahin* (peasant) boys was only 4 years, discouraging learning of anything more than basic skills (Miller, 1985). Although by 1926 a large segment of the Muslim population advocated education for both sexes, by July 1934, there were only 10 government schools for women in the villages of Palestine. The government's response to the request for women's schools was the following:

> If female education is to have any direct effect upon the future of the country, girls must be brought up to understand the value of a good home where cleanliness, sanitation and above all care of children are to be regarded as the aim of every woman . . . The excellent work already accomplished by various missionary and other bodies, local and foreign, cannot be overrated. They are the pioneers of female education in Palestine and for what they have done and are doing deserve every commendation. But the tendency in schools under their direction has been, if a word of criticism may be allowed, to cultivate too much the literacy side of education and to neglect almost entirely what may be termed the domestic side. (Miller, 1985, p. 103)

The British administration justified the lack of schools for women by saying that there were not enough women teachers and that schools for women were not accepted in villages. However, there were a large number of women attending foreign or communal schools in Palestine in lieu of government institutions (Mogannam, 1937).

The Zionist movement utilized education as a tool to mobilize young Jews and to promote land and labor as the basis for creating autonomous socioeconomic institutions. Expropriation of land created a class of landless workers who, because of the Zionist boycott of Arab labor, were cut off from alternative sources of income (Sayigh, 1979). Neither Zionists nor the British developed agricultural programs to support the needs of Arab peasants. Furthermore, land ordinances of 1920 and 1929, although instituted to ensure compensation to peasants who gave up rights to land they cultivated, were not enforced. Policies of separation in regard to land and labor reinforced estrangement. Violence that erupted in 1920, 1921, and in the 1936 to 1939 Arab Revolt was symptomatic of horizontal hostility as Zionists and Arab nationalists sought concessions from the British. Riots in 1920 and 1921 in Jaffa and in the Tul-Karm-Hadera region caused dissolution of partnerships and commercial relations between Jews and Arabs. As a result of the 1929 riots provoked by controversy over Muslim versus Jewish rights to the Wailing Wall, Jewish communities left Arab towns in which their families had lived for centuries. After 1936 it was dangerous to continue daily contacts in economic relations and even physical proximity in "mixed" towns (Flapan, 1979).

The concept of 100% Jewish labor was reinforced by the creation of Mapai (unification of the labor parties, Hapoel Hatzair and Achdut Haavoda) in 1930. Control of labor was, however, in the hands of the more conservative Histadrut (Jewish Federation of Workers Union). In 1933, the Histadrut initiated a campaign to remove Arab workers from construction sites and other Jewish enterprises in the cities. They also organized a nationwide campaign to picket citrus groves employing Arab labor, arguing that the mandatory government might assert that Arab labor in the Jewish sector could compensate for labor shortages, giving them an excuse to limit Jewish immigration. Histadrut policies obviated effects of spontaneous joint activities of workers, such as the strike of drivers in November 1931, which demanded reduction of costs of driving licenses, fuel, and tires. Arab workers finally formed a separate Arab trade union movement, the Palestine Arab Workers Society, controlled by Arab national parties (Flapan, 1979).

In reaction to fighting in May 1921, Churchill issued the White Paper on Palestine limiting Jewish immigration to the economic absorptive capacity of the country. Herbert Samuel tried to assure the Arab movement that the British government would not allow all of Palestine to become a Jewish national home ("Palestine," 1947). Successive restrictions on land purchase and immigration followed each serious outbreak of violence. However, the Passfield White Paper of October 1930, recommending restriction of Jewish immigration and settlement because of shortage of land for Arab peasants, was annulled by the McDonald letter of February 1931. As the British mandate moved to restrict immigration in order to appease the Arab movement, Zionists further circumvented restrictions.

The riots of 1929 precipitated a new level of involvement of Arab women in the nationalist struggle. Responding to the killings, the imprisonment of hundreds of men, the destruction of homes and the plight of orphaned children, women organized the first Arab Women's Congress of Palestine. Over 200 Muslim and Christian delegates called for the abrogation of the Balfour Declaration; the establishment of a national government responsible to a council in which the population would be represented in proportion to numerical strength; and national industries and economics. The Congress pledged to support the Arab Executive Committee in all its decisions (Mogannam, 1937).

Women's societies were established in Jerusalem, Acre, Nazareth, Haifa, Jaffa, Ramallah, Tul Karm, Safed, and other major centers to support the resolution of the Congress (Mogannam, 1937). At this stage of the nationalist movement, the most visible women's movement emerged among the elite classes of educated women, connected to leaders of the male-dominated nationalist movement. Matiel Mogannam, who chronicles this aspect of the women's movement during the period of the British Mandate, attributes the focus on the social and charitable work of women's associations to the fact that under British administration women could not pass legislation to better their situation as women. The British Administration, for example, replaced the Ottoman penal code with a draft of a criminal code that stipulated the minimum marriage age for women to be 14. The code was not enforced, as the British were " . . . reluctant to deal with matters which may arouse any objection on the part of any religious authority" (Mogannam, 1937, p. 54). Women recognized the need for autonomous legislative bodies to introduce reforms that would allow women to enter the modern era.

In 1919, Christian and Muslim women had formed the Arab Ladies Association to assist the Arab woman and the poor and distressed. A society in Jaffa provided for the education of girls, and an infant welfare center opened in 1931, distributing food, as well as teaching principles of infant care and providing trained nurses. The goal and approach of women involved in these and other similar societies, to help their less fortunate sisters, reflected their class biases. At the same time, these associations provided services the state did not. Acting as the state, the British administration created conditions that exacerbated class tensions and hurt the poor. The Arab Women's Executive Committee recognized these issues in the 1930s. They called for agricultural assistance for the *fellah* (peasant) in the form of credit opportunities and protection of rights to land. They criticized the administration for refusing to appoint Arabs to important positions within the administration, pointing out that the only Arabs appointed (to land settlement) were from elite families. The policy of appointing elites, they protested, was a form of co-optation as well as a way of silencing them. Furthermore, this policy created family schisms, and "revealed an inclination on the part of the present High Commissioner to arouse family jealousies which have long been forgotten" (Mogannam, 1937, p. 89). Furthermore, they noted that in the Secretariat, the central authority in control of the government, two Jewish senior offices were appointed, and only one was Arab (Mogannam, 1937).

Political participation often necessitated changes in traditional social structure and customs. For example, The First Palestine Arab Woman's Congress of 1929 decided to present its resolutions to the administration in person. They asked to see Lady Chancellor, as it would have contradicted traditional custom for Muslim members to appear before the High Commissioner. When they were refused this request, the 10 members of the Executive Committee " . . . had no other alternative but to ignore all traditional restrictions" (Mogannam, 1937, p. 74). A historic demonstration of Arab women, organized by the Congress, presented the resolutions at the various consulates.

The Executive Committee was responsible for a concerted, but unsuccessful effort to save Arab prisoners sentenced to execution in the wake of the 1929 riots. They wrote:

> ... There is sufficient sorrow, lamentation and racial hatred in the country. It would be a wise step indeed if a curtain is dropped on these cases and thus avoid fresh causes which might lead to the increase of racial hatred. (Mogannam, 1937, p. 79)

In March of 1932 a general conference of Arabs of Palestine at Jaffa adopted a resolution of non-cooperation with the government. Arab women protested the visit of Lord Allenby, one of two British statesmen who visited Palestine to dedicate a new building of the Y.M.C.A. Lord Allenby had betrayed Arab nationalists after having promised independence in exchange for support in the war of 1916 against the Turks. Women organized a boycott of the building and a march to the Mosque of Omar, where for the first time a Christian woman delivered a political speech from the pulpit of a mosque (Mogannam, 1937).

The efforts of Arab women to support the nationalist agenda were thwarted by lack of funds and lack of diplomatic avenues, since there was no way to make complaints directly to London, where all policy decisions were initiated and finalized. Furthermore women's efforts to gain entry into the modern legal system became visible within the framework of the male-dominated movement, where the nationalist agenda defined women's agenda.

In March 1930, the Women's Executive Committee created at the Arab Women's Congress held in October 1929 warned the mandatory administration that Jews were importing firearms for defense:

> The Executive Committee believes that certain Jews have been, and are still, engaged in smuggling firearms to Palestine with a view to the arming of Jewish youth and forming semi-military organizations. (Mogannam, 1937, p. 80)

The discovery of arms at the Jaffa port in October 1935 was one of the events leading to the disturbances of 1936. At the same time disintegration of village society and urban unemployment created the basis for the emergence of an organized armed movement among Arabs. In April 1935 members of the secret organization Ikhwan al-Qassam held up cars, robbing Arab travelers and killing two Jews. Jews retaliated, killing Arabs and holding a mass funeral in Tel Aviv. Politicians in Nablus and Jaffa responded by calling a general strike ("Palestine," 1947).

In spite of enormous hardship, the strike had a broad base of support. Shaykh 'Izz al-Din al-Qassam, martyred militant Islamic preacher, had built a strong base of support among Arab peasants and workers to oust the British. Ruqayya Huri, daughter of a Muslim *shaykh* (a leader, often a learned Muslim), joined an underground women's organization started by Shaykh 'Izz al-Din al-Qassam (Swedenburg, 1989). Matiel Mogannam dedicates her book,

The Arab Woman and the Palestine Problem, to " . . . the memory of all the innocent Arab women who met their death during the disturbances of 1936 as a result of unjust policy" (Mogannam, 1937).

Middle East historian Ted Swedenburg has documented the extent and importance of women's participation in the 1936 revolt (Swedenburg, 1989). Women from the bourgeois classes who comprised the Arab Women's Committee had been involved in anti-British demonstrations. They had also protested by letter and initiated negotiations with the British on behalf of prisoners, in the face of harassment of the Palestinian population, including house demolitions, deportations, lootings, administrative detentions, and torture of prisoners. The 1936 disturbances challenged the Arab Executive Committee to a new level of political activity. In Jerusalem the Arab Women's Committee, replacing the Arab Women's Executive, issued and widely circulated appeals to British women and an Appeal for Peace to the Peace Congress at Brussels (Mogannam, 1937). The Committee raised money and donated jewelry for the revolt, administered funds collected for victims of hostilities and aided families of prisoners (Swedenburg, 1989). Swedenburg notes, as does Middle East scholar Rosemary Sayigh, that the women's movement, although comprised of their wives and sisters, was unaffected by political squabbles among male heads of opposing factions (Sayigh, 1979; Swedenburg, 1989).

Women were arrested when they forced shopkeepers in the Haifa market to observe strikes. Najib Nassar, a professional journalist involved in welfare work with the Arab Women's Committees, who organized and participated in street demonstrations and strike enforcement, was put under administrative detention for nine months. The President of the International Alliance of Women for Suffrage and Equal Citizenship, Margaret Ashby, protested in a letter to the colonial secretary (Swedenburg, 1989).

Rural peasant women supported the nationalist struggle, carrying food to fighters, smuggling weapons, collecting money, and hiding fighters from the British. The flexibility of peasant women, unveiled and accustomed to freedom of movement working in the fields or selling goods in urban markets, was particularly important in rural areas where most of the fighting took place. Possession of weapons or ammunition was a crime punishable by execution. Women transported weapons in clothing or baskets, " . . . since the British either did not suspect them or did not have enough policewomen officers to conduct body searches" (Swedenburg, 1989, p. 7). Women were able to save many rebels from capture by the British: "The wife of one local band commander (qa'id fasil) related that her husband sometimes hid as many as 40–50 men in their house. While they slept with their shoes on, cradling their guns, she went around at night collecting food from her neighbors to feed them" (Swedenburg, 1989, pp. 6, 7).

In January 1938, women advocated for the men of Mujaydal arrested by the British after the Iraq Petroleum Company pipeline was cut. They demonstrated outside the district offices in Nazareth until the government released most of the jailed men. Toward the end of the revolt, women were jailed more frequently; a 25-year-old married woman from Beersheva was given the longest sentence, 10 years, for possession of a revolver and ammunition (Swedenburg, 1989). The British tried to break the spirit of the rebellion by separating the men from the women and forcing them to work all day on roads without food or water. They ransacked houses, throwing together foodstuffs and ruining provisions of self-sufficient households (Swedenburg, 1989).

Peasants utilized the 1936 Arab revolt against the British Mandate and Zionism to confront the power of the elites. One example noted by Ted Swedenburg was the order given by rebel leaders in the summer of 1938 that urban men don the peasant *keffiyah* (Palestinian head scarf) so that rebels could circulate in the cities undetected (Swedenburg, 1989). At the same time women's bodies became once again the symbolic locus of nationalist rebellion. Women wearing Western-style clothes and traveling without male escorts were harassed and criticized for having loose morals and spreading Western corruptions. Women were ordered to veil. Peasant women were fined if they sold their vegetables in the market, as was their custom. Village men complied by bringing the vegetables themselves. A reactionary current in the mosques, perpetrated by the British, contributed to the weakening of women's participation in the struggle (Swedenburg, 1989).

While citrus growers, merchants, Arab workers, and peasants dependent upon the Jewish market went hungry, the strike stimulated Jewish investment and aided the Zionist goal of separation of Arab and Jewish labor. Agricultural collectives replaced seasonal Arab laborers with Zionist women who, destitute, were eager for work (Bernstein, 1987). However, as a result of examination of British policy by the Peel Commission in the autumn of 1936, a final White Paper was issued, prohibiting land transfer to Jews in most of Palestine and making the limit of immigration dependent upon Arab consent. Finally, Zionist officials were faced with the decision whether or not to continue the policy of economic separation or to return Arab workers to the Jewish sector, resume trade, and normalize economic relations (Flapan, 1979).

Some Jews and Arabs supported the latter course. Partnership between Arab and Jewish businessmen stimulated the growth of the Arab urban sector and the growth in Arab citriculture from 20,000 dunam in 1922 to 147,000 dunam in 1935 (Smelansky, 1972). Arab merchants marketed industrial products manufactured by Jewish firms.

Martin Buber, Judah Magnes, and Dr. Nissim Malul were influential members of the binationalist party who in 1936 led the effort to reach a modus vivendi with the Palestinian Arabs. Cooperation with the Arab nationalist movement was the basis of the Brith Shalom (Covenant of Peace) movement in the twenties and of the Ihud (Unity) Association in the forties. Martin Buber maintained that a binational state must be aimed at:

... a social structure based on the reality of two peoples living together. The foundations of this structure cannot be the traditional ones of majority and minority, but must be different . . . . (Buber, 1927, p. 10)

A group of Jewish businessmen and civil leaders known as "The Five" worked with Musa Alami, crown counsel and an associate of the Mufti, to create a proposal including political parity (equality of representation regardless of numbers in population), an immigration limit of 30,000 a year for 10 years, and restrictions on Jewish purchase of land (Flapan, 1979).

The Zionist leadership decided in 1937 to mobilize all efforts to achieve complete economic separation in the form of a Jewish state through "partition."

This decision was not inconsistent with the direction taken by the Zionist leadership when in 1927 they withdrew support from all new economic projects except those initiated by private capital and encouraged private enterprise. This meant that outside investment in support of a Jewish economic base would determine economic policy. This trend hurt women, whose projects were dependent upon the support of the World Zionist Organization and the British Mandate, as well as upon the Histadrut, all of whom initiated policies that excluded, rather than supported, women's participation in the labor force. In 1925, there were no women on the 15-member committee negotiating the first collective agreement between the Histadrut and employers, an agreement that institutionalized lower wages for unskilled women factory workers (Izraeli, 1981). By 1930 the proportion of women in nontraditional jobs dropped to 0.4% in construction and public works. Forty-six percent of women workers were employed in private homes (Izraeli, 1981).

Separation of the Arab sector and utilization of Arab men and women as cheap labor paralleled separation of women; exploitation of Jewish women from Arab countries separated them from Ashkenazi women. Women from Arab countries (33% Yemeni, 9% Sephardi) comprised 42% of housemaids at a time when they were only 10% of all working women (Bernstein, 1987). Five women, newly arrived in the city, were sent by the pimp, the middleman between employer and housemaid, to homes to find work:

> ... They exchange notes: all are totally exhausted—but that is not the main problem. What is worse is the way they are treated. Such gross exploitation! They are all ready to quit. But will this be the solution? Maybe we will get used to it. After one week's work, one of the five is fired: "She" (the employer) wants a "black" (i.e., Oriental Jewish woman). It is not that she does not like the woman, but that she'd rather have a "black," because a "black" is content with one and a half PP per month, and on top of that is willing to sleep in at the employer's. (Bernstein, 1987, p. 83)

Furthermore, housemaids were subject to sexual harassment, including rape, by male employers and harassment by female employers who resented their presence in the household. Class separation of women of the East and of the West was exemplified in the relationship between the head of household, and her maid. In 1926 women were 34.7% of the work force; by 1930,

27% (Bernstein, 1987, p. 94). By 1937, 37% of all working women in the Yishuv were in domestic service (Bernstein, 1987).

Arab men whose interests were in line with or who found ways to utilize the Zionist economic infrastructure benefited from Zionist policies. The policy of the British Mandate of subsuming indigenous Arab structures in order to control them was similar to the policy of incorporation of the Women Workers' Movement into the Histadrut. The survival of both groups depended upon their willingness to cooperate and give allegiance to the governing body of European (Jewish and non-Jewish) men. In both situations intracommunal power struggles intensified between those who sought to create and preserve autonomous structures and those who supported the dominant structure. The British Mandate selected Arabs who would represent their interests to head Arab organizations: the Histadrut selected women to head the executive council and various departments connected to the Women Workers' Council who represented women, but whose loyalty to the party was primary. The attitude of David Ben-Gurion, then leader of Achdut Haavoda, toward the role of the Women Workers' Council, previsages the policy instituted in the early years of the state, to deal with the Arab minority:

> Ben Gurion's interpretation of the role of the WWC (Women Workers' Council) discounts the importance of the movement in the ideology and activity of national rebirth. Instead of being depicted as a creator of a new cultural image for women in the emerging socialist society, it was ascribed the role of watchdog guarding the interests of a "minority" group. (Izraeli, 1981, p. 107)

Women able to attain leadership positions in the Executive Committee of the Women Workers' Council, affiliated with and approved by the male establishment, had less contact with the masses of working women they represented. Many Arab leaders within organizations of the British Mandate, and later the state, lost connection with their constituency. Similarly, the views of women in leadership positions within the Histadrut often diverged from those of women in their daily struggles. One of the purposes of co-optation and centralization was to put into positions of relative power those who voiced the dominant ideology, rather than the sentiments of the masses.

Palestinian women, the elite of the Arab Women's Committee, and the peasant women who hid weapons during the 1936 revolt, lost ground in the face of British military and political power. They lost their lives facing the onslaught of imperialist occupation of the post-war period. It was not the first time. Zionist women lost their lives as they struggled to gain a foothold in the Zionist project. Facing one another on opposite sides of a divide created by alliances of men seeking hegemony through economic and political policies thwarting women, Palestinian and Zionist women subsumed their struggles as women under the banner of nationalist movements promising liberation. Of the 50,000 members of the Haganah, the Jewish Defense Force, 10,000 were

Zionist women, for the most part from the workers' villages. They participated in defense of settlements through the 1929 riots, and during the 3 years of the 1936 revolt, they stood guard along roads (*Sisters of Exile,* 1973). During the British Mandate, Zionist women ran underground radio broadcasts and taught women and children how to defend themselves, while Palestinian women petitioned the British Administration and demonstrated in the streets. Nationalism was the available ideological ground of social struggle. Intrinsically misogynist, nationalism held women tightly in its net, as Palestinian and Zionist women were pulled into the new Israel.

In May 1936, a Royal Commission was appointed to evaluate events in Palestine. They concluded that the British Mandate was no longer workable and recommended partition. The plan proposed the transfer of 296,000 Arabs out of the area to be designated as the Jewish state. Many Jews, Zionists, and others resisted. Members of a Jewish agency representing non-Zionist groups, stated: "We can't say that we want to live with the Arabs and at the same time transfer them to Transjordan" (Flapan, 1979, p. 260). In July 1937, the Jewish Agency rejected a proposal for an independent Palestinian state that would provide for a Jewish national home but not a state (Flapan, 1979).

The activities of the Irgun, a liaison of the Revisionist party led by Jabotinsky, escalated. In 1938, the Irgun placed bombs in Arab markets in Haifa, Jerusalem, and Jaffa; in 1940, their aim was to eliminate British rule. The Mufti's decision to ally with the Nazis in the hope of defeating British rule fed the militarist revisionist mentality.

After the 1939 White Paper, Zionists shifted hopes for political support to the United States. Zionists adopted the Biltmore Program, demanding a Jewish state in Palestine, in New York City in 1942, demanding fulfillment of the "original purpose" of the Balfour Declaration and rejecting the British White Paper. The conference called for support of the Allied war effort by Jews and demands of a post-war settlement assuring "peace, justice and equality" (Flapan, 1979).

Groups of Arabs and Jews in Palestine in favor of a binational solution continued to search for a political settlement. Liberal parties such as Hashomer Hatzair, Poalei Zion, and the Ihud Association met with villagers and students and organized lectures and debates. Arabs and Jews signed an agreement calling for common action and publication of an Arab magazine promoting cooperation. Iraq and Transjordan proposed various forms of federations in the Fertile Crescent with autonomy for Jews. In 1943, Arab notables proposed free immigration up to numerical parity and possible compromise after that point (Flapan, 1979).

Zionist Hannah Arendt's vision of a revolutionary movement of Jews stood in sharp contrast to that of the official Zionist party. A member of the Ihud Association, Arendt criticized the elitism of Herzl and Weizmann, warning that if they allied themselves with the great powers to achieve statehood the Jewish nationalists would become representative of imperial interests. She asserted that the territorial question was secondary and that the primary aim of Jewish nationalism should be emancipation. Arendt insisted that the demand for a Jewish state in Palestine ignored the fact of the Palestinian majority and ignored the realities of the Middle East (Arendt, 1978a). Giving the Arabs the choice of emigration or minority status should be unacceptable to a people involved in their own liberation struggles. Arendt called upon Jewish and Arab movements to give up their nationalist-chauvinistic perspectives. She criticized Zionist officials for instituting a capitalist economic system involving the importation of workers and leaving the native population " . . . a potential proletariat with no prospect of employment as free laborers" (Arendt, 1950/1978c, p. 202). Jewish-Arab cooperation had to be the major objective of Zionist policy: " . . . the only permanent reality in the whole constellation was the presence of Arabs in Palestine, a reality no decision could alter— except, perhaps the decision of a totalitarian state, implemented by its particular brand of ruthless force" (Arendt, 1948/1978b, p. 185). Her proposal for saving the Jewish homeland from becoming a military state employing terrorism and supporting imperial interests included the following criteria:

1. The real goal of the Jews in Palestine is the building up of a Jewish homeland. This goal must never be sacrificed to the pseudo-sovereignty of a Jewish state.
2. The independence of Palestine can be achieved only on a solid basis of Jewish-Arab cooperation. As long as Jewish and Arab leaders both claim that there is "no bridge" between Jews and Arabs . . . the territory cannot be left to the political wisdom of its own inhabitants.
3. Elimination of all terrorist groups (and not agreements with them) and swift punishment of all terrorist deeds (and not merely protests against them) will be the only valid proof that the Jewish people in Palestine has recovered its sense of political reality and that Zionist leadership is again responsible enough to be trusted with the destinies of the Yishuv.
4. Immigration to Palestine, limited in numbers and in time, is the only "irreducible minimum" in Jewish politics.
5. Local self government and mixed Jewish-Arab municipal and rural councils, on a small scale and as numerous as possible, are the only realistic political measures that can eventually lead to the political emancipation of Palestine. (Arendt, 1948/1978b, p. 192)

Arendt's views were ignored, as were those of the Ihud association, and they led to her ostracism from the Jewish establishment. As a woman, and as a critic of the official Zionist position, Arendt was effectively silenced.

In May 1945, Zionists petitioned the United Nations and the British government to set up a Jewish state in Palestine. In June 1945, Zionists demanded entry of 100,000 displaced persons into Palestine. Proponents of the Biltmore Program and militarist elements in Palestine were aided in their cause by violence perpetrated against Jewish survivors of the Nazi Holocaust. The Haganah attempted the illegal rescue of survivors who came to Palestine to find safety.

The British responded by arresting Jewish political and religious leaders and closing down the Jewish Agency. In July 1946, the Irgun blew up the King David Hotel, site of the mandatory administration. Zionists continued to dispute proposed solutions, with the added factor of United States participation. The twenty-second Zionist Congress in Basel in December 1946 rejected negotiations with Great Britain and deposed Weizman. The matter was taken to the United Nations which, with Soviet and United States support, recommended partition. Palestinian Arabs continued to resist implementation of this plan.

The 1947–1948 war, which ended in the military and political collapse of the Arab nationalist movement, had devastating consequences, precipitating the flight of hundreds of thousands of Palestinian merchants, landowners, and community leaders. The Israeli state was heralded in the heat of massacres of men, women and children; desecration of the land and destruction of hundreds of villages; pillage and rape.

With the creation of the Arab League in March 1945, Arab states committed themselves to struggle for the independence of Palestine. A delegate of the Arab Higher Committee had been nominated to represent the Palestinian people in the League's Council. In November 1945, the League had demanded an end to the British Mandate and recognition of a democratically elected government with a legislative council based on proportional representation of Jews and Arabs. On the other hand, Abdallah, supported by the Hashemite rulers of Iraq and encouraged by the British, continued to pursue a "Greater Syria" with the partition of Palestine and construction of the Jewish state as the first phase. Distrust and disunity within the Arab movement were a major factor in the Zionist military victory.

CONCLUSION

Competition between Arab nationalists and Zionists in the late 1800s for control of Palestine was part of the larger struggle, particularly among the British and French, for control of the resources and access to sea routes of Greater Syria. The Balfour Declaration allowed the British to decide who would control the province of Palestine. Alliances of Arabs and Jews along class lines were disrupted and reorganized in this process.

Arab nationalist and Zionist movements were carriers of modernization. The expansion of capitalist–patriarchy required reordering of social organization and new standards of international law. Liberal humanism promoted rights of individuals, and promoted territorial rights, supporting nationalist movements in the name of protecting and preserving ethnic and cultural identity. In fact, modern nationalism reordered ethnic identity on the basis of class allegiances, thus protecting and preserving male rule. Just as liberal humanism conceals the power of men over women, so the concept of territorial rights

conceals the power of men over the earth. The "new world order" was a trans-
figuration and continuation of the old. In modern terms, women's liberation
meant participation as women in service to the male state in the new world
order. The expropriation of women's labor defining women's possibilities and
limitations in the modern era, utilized the existing class structure in which
women's subordination was maintained by a system of male alliances competing for control of women, resources, and the earth.

Zionists, particularly socialist Zionists of the late 1800s, emigrated to Palestine in order to change the structure of Jewish society, as well as to escape
persecution as Jews. Ber Borochov, for example, repudiated the relationship
between the Jewish capitalist and the Jewish worker. This exploitative relationship made Jews more vulnerable to exploitation from anti-Semitic forces
of the state. Many of the women Zionists of the Second and Third Aliyah had
worked with socialist movements in Russia. They shared the goal of eliminat-
ing competition and exploitative labor relations as the basis for social organization. Their analysis, like that of their male counterparts, did not include
exploitation of women's labor, paid or unpaid. Assuming that ending exploitative relations would necessarily bring equality for women, Zionist women
did not place their situation as women at the center of their political agenda.
Their political and social subordination continued to be the ground upon
which the state would be built.

There were other problems intrinsic to the socialist Zionist program. Zionist women espoused the guiding principle of settlement, conquering the land
for Jewish labor. Their socialist-nationalist principles were intrinsically misogynist. Women workers in pre-state Palestine lived this fact as they struggled for survival daily against the misogyny of the male controlled labor
movement. Excluded from the work of building the new state, women necessarily had a relationship to nationalism that was not the same as that of Zionist men. Their nationalist goals embedded them more deeply in their
socialization as women. Nationalism confirmed women in traditional roles,
for which women were not only rewarded, but to which women were forced
to retreat in order to survive. Protection by and benefits of the state, however
minimal, were contingent upon their allegiance to those roles. Women supported the nationalist agenda as wives and mothers, as cheap and unpaid
laborers; structurally this principle became the cornerstone of the new state.
Women served the state as domestics, wives, and mothers, as keepers of nationalist boundaries. The labor movement utilized Zionist women to see that
Jewish women and not Arab women were hired as domestics in their neighborhoods (Bernstein, 1987). They were told that plowing and loading crops
were too strenuous, and were, in fact, harmful to them (Izraeli, 1981). Reinforcing biological determinism, Zionists encouraged women's dependence
and co-optation. Each stage in the history of the Zionist Women Workers'
Movement bears that out.

The participation of Zionist women in the ideology of land and labor involved them in contradictory goals. The influx of cheap labor provided by Zionist women hurt Palestinian women, who were pushed out of jobs. Palestinian women had already experienced loss of land and livelihood in the late 1800s. Land reforms and imperialist politics forced them into the wage labor market. But what hurt Palestinian women was symptomatic of what was hurting Zionist women. Competition among women for scarce, low-paying jobs, for survival, was a consequence of devaluation and expropriation of women by the male-controlled economic infrastructure—whether Zionist, British, or Arab. Some Zionist women drew parallels between their situation and that of the Arab worker. But, liberal humanism protects individuals, not women, not exploited races. The worker of the Zionist movement, however, had a gender and a race. The male-controlled labor movement imported Yemenite Jews in order to elevate the status of Ashkenazi Jews. Ready now to escape the stigma of labor hidden in the reification of labor, Ashkenazi men utilized Yemeni men as cheap agricultural labor and Yemeni women as cheap domestic workers (Bernstein, 1987). Jewish women competed with one another for unskilled jobs; Ashkenazi women employed Oriental Jewish women, freeing themselves from the burden of continuous unpaid service required of them as wives, as women. Even when the Ashkenazi and Yemeni women both became "Israeli," their place in society was still determined by race and gender. What is meant by "Jew," then, in the Zionist ideology promoting self-determination for Jews, is "male" and "European." Socialist Zionists, by not addressing the misogynist basis of Zionist goals of land and labor, put themselves in the same camp as Zionists who identified their goals with those of the imperialist capitalist superstructure, to whom they eventually succumbed.

If the Working Women's Movement had placed women, rather than men, at the center of their agenda; if they had directly addressed male violence against women; if they had examined the ideology of nationalism from their vantage point, rather than from the vantage point of the "genderless" individual, it is plausible to conclude that a transformation would have had to occur in the evolution of the Zionist movement. The question of Jewish survival would have revealed itself as a question of women's survival; because anti-Semitism and woman-hatred are and always have been linked. It would have become necessary to recognize the impossibility of addressing and resolving the issue of Jewish survival without addressing and resolving the issue of violence against women, and against the earth.

What was done to ensure that Zionist women would not develop an analysis separating them from the misogynist goals of the Zionist project? Poor wages and lack of job opportunities kept women dependent upon men. Debilitating harassment of women workers discouraged many women from non-traditional work situations. When women formed their own construction crews, contracts were given instead to men. When training farms for women were successful, funds were withdrawn.

Many Zionist women chose to identify themselves with the male-controlled labor movement rather than with the women's movement to escape the stigma of their "inferiority" as women. Class and race hierarchy created cleavages between women whose survival depended upon contradictory goals. Class separation of women supported the conditions for their exploitation. Confined to unskilled work in the service sector, with no security, no benefits, and no prestige, women found rewards as wives and mothers whose unpaid work was critical to the survival of the state. Believing that the state would ultimately benefit them or that they could utilize the state to achieve equality, they committed themselves to its inception.

In the pre-state period and under British Mandate, Palestinian women, urban and rural, increasingly lost access to traditional modes of survival. Competition for control of land and of industry by the state and affiliated class of landholders and merchants, exacerbated women's vulnerability. Forced to produce for a foreign market, their workload increased. The vicissitudes of the foreign market often left them with no recourse but to take on low-paid service work or find other means of survival that were demeaning and dangerous. As Arab landholders sold land to Jews, the situation worsened.

Palestinian women were a target in the struggle between West and East. Protection of traditional mores fixing women's role as biologically determined to serve men and opposed to the immorality of the Western "free" woman was a smokescreen for competition among classes of men for access to new sources of wealth and power. It was a dangerous smokescreen, costing many women their lives. Hierarchical division of women of the West and East, aided by Arab nationalists (and Zionists) was critical to the success of the imperialist project.

Palestinian women from all classes utilized tools and power, and a long historical tradition of political involvement, within class contexts, to struggle against occupation. In the late 19th and early 20th centuries, women of Greater Syria utilized the press to address the connection between support of Arab nationalism and support of women in the modern era. They utilized their roles as wives and mothers to advocate for education, an approach supported by modernists among the Arab nationalists. Educated women were necessary to raise good citizens. Some women utilized westernization as an available ideology to fight against traditional restrictions of dress and occupation. Others relied upon retaining their "value" as women in traditional terms.

Palestinian women, facing Zionist settlers and the British administration, were on the front lines of the battlefield, their lives and livelihoods threatened daily by the weapons of politics, economics, and militia. Utilizing traditional and non-traditional roles, they resisted. Arab women organized welfare societies, produced magazines, organized demonstrations, and formed the

Arab Women's Executive Committee as an adjunct to the male-controlled Arab nationalist movement. They joined secret societies, carried weapons for male fighters, and hid rebels in their homes. In the context of nationalist ideology they sought a place for themselves in securing Palestine against Zionist and British intrusion.

As the struggle for control of Palestine solidified into a war of Zionism against Arab nationalism, "Jew" against "Arab," European Jewish women were pitted against Arab Jewish women, and both were pitted against Palestinian women. The British and the male-controlled Zionist and Arab nationalist movements, utilized women inter- and intracommunally to wage their wars. Neither British, nor Zionists, nor Arab nationalists, ever considered institutionalizing change in the exploitative power relations between men and women. While Zionist and Palestinian women faced one another across seemingly insurmountable barriers, they suffered similarly from political, sexual, and economic violence perpetrated against them. Palestinian women were driven from a land they had worked for centuries under conditions with limited options. Zionist women fled repressive conditions under which they suffered from misogyny intracommunally and intercommunally. The relationship of both groups of women to land depended upon compliance with the male-controlled social order. That Zionist women sought control over land at the expense of Palestinian women exemplified the role that hierarchical divisions among women play in sustaining capitalist–patriarchy. In the early 20th century, the potential existed for an analysis of the connections among expropriation of land, desecration of the earth, and violence against women, bringing into the foreground the common ground of Zionist and Palestinian women. Instead, the consequences of the antifeminism of nationalism would unfold in the institutionalization of the Israeli state on the land of Palestine.

Chapter Four
Consequences

Summer, 1985. Two women stand in the doorway. A one-room structure in the refugee camp Kalandia on the West Bank. I am a North American Jew staying in Jerusalem, conducting interviews with educators in Israel and on the West Bank. She is a Palestinian in her 80s, a survivor of the 1948 Arab-Israeli war.

It begins at Bir Zeit University. Before he takes us to meet his aunt in the refugee camp Kalandia, Zaid arranges for us to interview students and then to meet with women who have organized on campus. We find them in the cafeteria. In an afternoon I begin to learn what the nationalist struggle means to some of them: about confrontation with family; about alienation from the Muslim religious traditions; about finding strength and courage in Muslim traditions; about being arrested, detained, thrown in prison. Their socio-economic and religious backgrounds vary. Some are encouraged by brothers and parents to join the struggle; others suffer the disapproval or rage of family members. No one can feel secure in the current situation. The nationalist struggle is not an ideological exercise: It defines the parameters of their existence. It defines how or if they will even make it that day to the bottom of the long winding hill leading up to Bir Zeit. It defines whether or not, if they do, they will find open classrooms or what is more common, a ring of soldiers with poised rifles barring their entrance. It defines whether or not they will have food to eat; whether their friends, mothers, sisters, brothers, fathers, will return from work that day; whether their newborn children will be deformed by tear gas.

It continues at Kalandia, where Zaid has taken us to meet with his aunt. Surrounded by concrete barrels ringed with barbed wire, watchtower blocked by the minaret of the mosque, climb up the dirt path over pieces of stone, concrete and broken wire. Stop in front of this low stone enclosure, while Zaid enters, calling her name. As you go in, take a few minutes to adjust to the dim light eking through one small window. Zaid translates.

Saris, near West Jerusalem. It was the original village before we fled in 1948. First my brother fell as I clasped my ears against assault of gunfire and the sudden realization that . . . . Then we traveled to Beit Mahseer near our village. Carrying children, bags of hastily packed clothing that were dropped along the way, food for a day that extended into months, and then into years. Then my son died of thirst—he was 3—and other children died. Then we traveled to Haran near Bethlehem and we traveled to Kufr Aqab and stayed there for 2 years. Finally we stayed in Kalandia Refugee Camp. The family is scattered. There is nothing for me to do.

Later we sit with Zaid's mother eating bread she has baked, yogurt, grape jam, cucumber, egg, olive oil, and thyme. Zaid translates. We begin to know one another. We take note of each others gestures, interpret with our eyes. She stands in the doorway waving . . . she invites me to come back . . . it is better, she says, to learn Arabic from a woman.

Remember how she looks standing in the doorway; black dress and white keffiyah; weathered face . . . about Jews, she says " . . . I know not all the fingers on the hand are the same."

Summer 1986. North America. Here is the grandmother. The one who stares out of the picture with an angry, tired, defiance and fear, clasping one child while the other, a 3-year-old girl, shows us her back scarred with bullet wounds, angry red, craterlike holes. Here is the mother. She lies at night in the heat of the inner city grinding her teeth, clenching her fists, holding her stomach—or rails at the police, while the bullets fly by her bedside.

Turn the page . . . she is the last zero in the statistic this year, the one out of 10 whose breast hardened over that long anxious year that doctors told her the tumor was nothing to worry about. The one who lived next to the landfill, who could no longer ignore the rashes that plagued her children.

And she is the academic about whom, when she was not rehired, the dean said, "Good teaching is not a criterion for this job."

Turn the page . . . notice her unsteady gait . . . ask her name . . . this is the woman who was gang-raped and left to die only because, the experts say, it wasn't a few degrees cooler that day.

She who is marketed, cornered, sold, cajoled, who is hung out to grace the respectable house, the nation.

Begin to learn what the nationalist struggle means for some of them. The nationalist struggle that is not an ideological exercise, that defines the parameters of her existence. The nationalist struggle that determines how much will be cut from the welfare state this year to fund the new line of missiles at $7 billion each, that defines how the father will decide to prove his virility this week, that defines whether or not her child will be born drunk.

Remember how she looks standing in the doorway waving.

ISRAEL: A CASE STUDY OF SEXUAL POLITICS AND TERRITORIAL RIGHTS

Our Sages said, 'A man without land is not a man.' Only now that we have a state and a land of our own, can we be called both a nation and men. (Warhaft as quoted in Segev 1986, p. 90)

Wars and crises seemed not to be caused by capitalists but by 'nature': women, foreigners, the 'other,' the neighbour, the enemy, the Third World. (Von Welholf, 1988, p. 111)

The distinguishing features of pornography can be characterized as follows: 1) Female sexuality is depicted as negative in relationship to a positive and neutral male standard; 2) women are degraded and publicly humiliated; and 3) female sexuality is portrayed as an object of male possession and control, which includes the depiction of women as analogous to nature in general and the land in particular, especially with regard to imagery of conquest and domination. (T. Drorah Setel, 1985, p. 87)

And so the 1947–1948 Arab-Israeli war seemed not to be caused by phallocentric politics—the bloodshed, rape, pillage, ravaging, conquest, domination of the land . . . seemed not to be related to violent reduction of women to commodities to be marketed, sold, reproduced . . . seemed not to be related to murder, rape, enslavement of a majority of the peoples of South Africa . . . seemed not to be related to the 5-year-old girl–child who, playing outside the hut where she lived in the slums of Brazil, put soft white dust into her mouth and several agonizing hours later, died of radiation poisoning.

Instead, it seemed to be caused by the eternal hatred of Arab and Jew; by the impossibility of Arab and Jew, eternal enemies, to live side by side; by, according to some Jews, the lust of all Arabs to throw all Jews into the sea; by the power of justice, right, and moral good to save one despised race from another.

In 1947, alliances of men seeking fulfillment of the imperial goal of expanding the base of capital accumulation under the aegis of development, decided the fate of hundreds of thousands of Palestinian women and children. Confronted by the superior military and industrial base of France, Britain, and the United States, both Jewish and Arab nationalists had been engaged in diplomatic maneuvers for control of Palestine. The "great powers" sought allies in the Middle East: that is, each sought a monopoly over land and labor. Thus the British played off Arab and Jew, breaking promises and thwarting attempts of some Zionists and Arab nationalists at rapprochement.

Several factors contributed to Zionist victory in 1949. Along with intra-Arab conflicts, Arab leaders were involved in fighting for autonomy within borders created by the great powers. The British crushed the Palestinian nationalist movement, killing and deporting leaders and rebels. The Zionist leadership had developed a sophisticated infrastructure, with economic and military support of allies, British and American.

As a result of military success in the 1947–1948 war, the Zionists controlled 20,850 square kilometers or 77.4% of the land and water surface of the former mandated territory (Asadi, 1976). The Egyptian military ruled in the Gaza Strip, and the Hasemite monarchy in Transjordan annexed East Jerusalem and the remainder of the West Bank area. Wars in 1956, 1967, and 1973 would change the geographic map again, with the balance of power including an expanded land base, remaining in the hands of Israelis.

Raja Shehadeh, a Palestinian lawyer and refugee, writes of the ways in which Palestinians succumb to the trials of occupation. Daily humiliations, co-optation, and resistance leading nowhere foster intracommunal tensions and betrayals. It is the land, finally, that Shehadeh comes to feel has betrayed him:

> And I remember now how I looked about at the land he was pointing at, at the hills I had quietly loved while my more romantic dreams were fastened on Jaffa; and thought: you treacherous hills, lying there so modest and silent. Soft and unassuming, you are a harlot, slyly seducing these boys. And I remember how, from then on, I grew increasingly jealous, possessive and angry at the same time. I finally began thinking of his land as seducing us all into war—calling us into its lap to fall bleeding—a vampire that will suck our blood as we fight for it. You, who were only a temporary camp for us—now we will die for you— you have pulled these boys here as Jaffa pulled them—again we shall die for our land.
> I wondered at the beginning of the year when it was I learned the art of pornography. It was very early on. My language may have changed, but years later I feel exactly the same: this land is going to soak up our blood for generations to come—and I hate it for that. (Shehadeh, 1984, p. 124)

Colonization and pornography portray female sexuality as an object of male possession and control, portray nature in general and the land in particular as an object of male possession, conquest, domination. The pornography of colonization links rape of women and of the earth. The perpetrators of conquest and domination of land and of women, renamed "redemption of land and labor," posit an eternal enemy on the basis of which justice is created. And so, another well is closed off. Another aquifer dries up. Another home is demolished. The refugees move from place to place, displacing and creating new refugees: " . . . And now in Jamsin—renamed Givat Amal—live new residents, recently arrived via Cyprus, survivors of the camps of Europe . . . They sit around a long table, with one remnant of the abandoned furniture, and tell their tales . . . " (Davor quoted in Segev, 1986, p. 90) And now in Deir Yassin . . . renamed Givat Shaul Bet . . . they sit around a long table and tell their tales . . .

The program of the new State was " . . . judaisation of the conquered territory by military means" (Davis, 1977, p. 26).

> His [David Ben-Gurion] was a vision of a Jewish state that would not only carry the beacon of enlightenment and progress—the standard western, civi-

lized justification for conquest, domination and exploitation—into the barbaric hinterland of the Near East, but most ambitiously, betraying the chosen people's ethnocentricity, would posit a paradigm of enlightenment and liberation for the western world at large. The leading executive of the Jewish state had both his feet right in the mainstream of western civilization. (Davis, 1977, p. 26)

Polarization of West and East, a justification for Western conquest and exploitation, is sexual politics. Enlightened men bring rationality to ignorant women and natives. Enlightened men rape women and steal from natives to demonstrate their superior power to subdue.

Historian Tom Segev's documentation of cabinet meetings in the early days of statehood reveals the extent to which Israel's ministers had their feet " . . . in the mainstream of western civilization":

> In Cabinet sessions too the problem of looting was often discussed. Minister Shitrit reported thefts in Jaffa and Haifa, Minister Mordehai Bentov asked about a convoy of spoils which left Jerusalem and Minister Cizling said: . . . It's been said that there were cases of rape in Ramlah. *I can forgive rape, but I will not forgive other acts which seem to me much worse.* When they enter a town and forcibly remove rings from the fingers and jewelry from someone's neck, that's a very grave matter . . . Many are guilty of it. (Segev, 1986, pp. 71, 72) (emphasis mine)

Others were apparently able to forgive rape also because rape is the assumed right of the conquerer and because women suffering are fulfilling their nature. They were able to forgive rape because rape is the war against women, which is what war is. Those who could not publicly condone rape, covered up and denied. Women, witnesses to the slaughter of Palestinians of the village of Deir Yassin, must have been crazy when they broke down as they told Richard Catling:

> . . . There is . . . no doubt that many sexual atrocities were committed by the attacking Jews. Many young schoolgirls were raped and later slaughtered. Old women were also molested. One story is current concerning a case in which a young girl was literally torn in two. Many infants were also butchered and killed. (Sayigh, 1979, p. 76)

Deir Yassin . . . renamed Givat Shaul Bet. Violent expropriation of land and of women, renamed justice, economic development, progress, national rights, national pride. For the sake of cultural survival.

> Every race possessing a definite uniqueness seeks to become a nation, that is, to create for itself an economic, political and intellectual environment in which every detail will derive from its specific thought and consequently will also relate to its specific taste. A specific race can establish such an environment only in its own country, where it is the master. (Avishai, 1985, p. 125)

Nationalism assumes the divine right of men to rule. In the early days of statehood, as parties and interests aligned, secular and religious Jews reached a modus vivendi, clarifying justification of the state on the basis of "divine right." David Ben-Gurion, leader of the ruling Mapai party (Social Democratic Labor party, formed from the merger of Achdut Haavoda and Hapoel Hatzair), led the Jews into statehood. He was a pragmatist and a ruthless politician. In order to form a cabinet that did not interfere with his agenda, Ben-Gurion chose to align himself with the rabbinate, rather than with the Zionist left-wing opposition, represented by Mapam (Segev, 1986). On the other hand, was the "revolutionary" left really so far ideologically from the conservative Orthodox Zionists? The Hebrew word for labor is *avodah*, also the word for worship (Avishai, 1985). For example, one Orthodox Jew expressed the connection this way:

> Rabbi Abraham Isaac Kook . . . a disciple of the Orthodox Zionists, conceived of the advent of the Zionist labor movement as a strengthening of the vessels for Ruach Elohim, the "spirit of God." "The secularists will realize in time," he assured himself, "that they are immersed and rooted in the life—land, language, history and customs—bathed in the radiant sanctity that comes from above . . . All of its most cherished national possessions—its land, language, history and customs—are vessels of the spirit of the Lord. (Avishai, 1985, pp. 94, 97)

The Orthodox community legitimized the institutional character of the state. Thus it was Orthodox Rabbi Fishman, rather than his sister, Ada Fishman-Maimon, leader of the Zionist Working Women's Movement, who convinced Ben-Gurion of the rightness of his cause: "Israel will live according to the law of Moses, which needs not the slightest reform" (Fishman, quoted in Avishai 1985, p. 187). Hence, in 1951 religious courts won jurisdiction over marriage, divorce, burials, and inheritance in the secular democratic Jewish state. Furthermore women delegates to the National Assembly could not vote in elections to the Rabbinic Council, in spite of arguments that since the Rabbinic Council had jurisdiction over domestic relations and personal status, women ought to have a say in its composition (Maimon, 1962).

Of the 120 members of the first Israeli Knesset 75% were Eastern European Jewish men in their fifties and sixties. Eleven were women; three were Arab men (Segev, 1986). When the Arabs appeared in traditional dress, one member of the Jewish National Fund was insulted, questioning their allegiance to the state:

> Nevertheless, I do not want there to be many of them. Perhaps they will integrate into society. But it will take several generations before they become loyal to the state.
> Many shared that opinion: "The Arab minority is a danger to the state," said Yigael Yadin to Ben Gurion, "in time of peace just as much as in time of war." (quoted in Segev, 1986, p. 44)

Tewfik Toubi, Arab member of the Knesset, believed that if freedom and democracy were denied to a national minority, all citizens would be denied freedom and democracy (Segev, 1986). But justice and freedom for ruling-class men is what democracy is: Jewish women and Arab women and men in the Israeli state, occupied and holding on at the bottom rungs of the ladder, are "by nature," allowed to clamber for the top rungs. Few would make it.

The success of the imperial project depends upon two interrelated factors, control of land through disruption of women's relationship to the land, and control of indigenous peoples. Expropriation of Palestine depended upon bifurcation of Arab and Jew, a project carried out through destruction of the language, memory, associations, and projects of the indigenous inhabitants of Palestine. Once the state was established, European Jewish women acted as agents of modernization through their invisible labor, maintaining necessary services and cooperating in bearing the next generation of citizens at a rate that would ensure demographic security. Women in the army served as surrogate mothers for the state, working in transit camps with recent emigrees, " . . . pitching tents, digging drainage ditches . . . (providing) medical care, general instruction, (and) education of children—humane activities that carry a blessing for the State as a whole" (Hecht & Yuval-Davis, 1984, p. 190).

While extolling the role of women in supporting national rebirth, Ben-Gurion at the same time discounted the importance of the Women Workers' Movement and assigned the Women Workers' Council the role of " . . . watchdog guarding the interests of a 'minority' group" (Izraeli, 1981, p. 107). As for the other minority group to be contended with, Ben-Gurion " . . . viewed their plight with the same pragmatic purposefulness which generally characterized his national policy: ' . . . Land with Arabs on it and land without Arabs on it are two very different types of land,' he told his party's central committee, as if he were a real-estate agent discussing business" (Segev, 1986, p. 28). In the months and years to follow, it became clear what type of land the new state was to be.

EXODUS: STATE POLICY
AND LAND EXPROPRIATION

Ben-Gurion and others maintained that Palestinians had deserted their country and therefore had no claim to it. They maintained at once that Arab leaders told Palestinians to leave, and that they left of their own free will. One West Bank settler, expressing a commonly held perspective, equated Palestinians with negligent lovers. They, unlike Jews, did not know how to properly "cultivate" [their women] the land:

> The Jews, he said, had proved that the land was theirs by the way they lived on it. They loved it. They were tender toward it. They caressed it. They cultivated it. They planted in it. And the land, in turn, gave them its fruits. What had the Arabs done for the land? What kind of lovers were they? They neglected it. Their allegiance was to the village rather than to the land. (Quoted in Reich, 1984, p. 70)

While asserting the impotence of the negligent Palestinian, West Bank settler Medad Yisrael adds:

> And I genuinely believe that if we lived under Arab rule the situation for us would be much, much worse than the situation is for Arabs under Israeli rule. It would be a question of our very survival. We would be killed. It would be Hebron, 1929; it would be Kfar Etzion, 1948. (Quoted in Reich, 1984, p. 72)

Israeli revisionist historians have uncovered documentation showing that many Zionist leaders welcomed the exodus. In order to achieve Jewish hegemony they initiated policies ensuring refugees could not return. Zionist leaders condoned the use of the military to achieve the goal of expropriation of land and labor. The Haganah's Plan Dalet called for the destruction of villages, expulsion of the population, closing of transport and communication routes (Flapan, 1987). According to official records, and the testimony of Palestinians, soldiers raped, murdered, and looted, creating a mass panic. On July 12 and 13, 1948, for example, 50,000 Arabs were driven out of their homes in Lydda and Ramlah. Ben-Gurion hoped to keep the Arab population at not more than 15% of the Jewish population (Flapan, 1987). Martial rule, the razing of villages, laws turning land over to the government, all prevented the return of Palestinians, who were defined as "infiltrators." The army evacuated villages and transferred villagers to other parts of the country (Segev, 1986).

Military supervision imposed isolation of the Arab population from the Jewish population and isolated Arab populations from one another. The government formed Arab committees to facilitate the process of "normalization" or accommodation to new conditions, and then ignored their advice. Some Zionists had reservations about the treatment of the Arabs:

> Some of them [Arab advisors] had qualms about moving the Christian Arabs from their homes on the Carmel into the abandoned houses of the Moslem Arabs in Wadi Nisnas. "You can't gather 3,000 human beings as if you were gathering eggs," said one of them. "For decades there have been personal relations between the Arab and the Jewish population here . . . " (Segev, 1986, p. 55)

Ben-Gurion justified forced evacuation of Palestinians in military terms: " . . . There are about 17,000 Israeli-Arab refugees and infiltrators. How many of these are refugees and how many infiltrators? — Unclear" (Segev, 1986, p. 59). Villagers from Ikrit and Bir'em were particularly persistent in utilizing whatever channels possible to be allowed to return to their villages. In the end:

> On September 16, 1953, while the Bir'em petition was awaiting the decision of the High Court of Justice, airforce planes flew over the abandoned village and bombed it down to the ground. The villagers of Ikrit and Bir'em continued to fight for their right to return to their villages. After a time they were allowed to bury their dead there. (Segev, 1986, p. 59)

Yitzhak Avira, a founder of the Moaz Haim Kibbutz, was among those who protested treatment of the Arab refugees:

Recently, a new mood had pervaded the public—"the Arabs are nothing," "all Arabs are murderers," "we should kill them all," "we should burn all their villages," etc., etc. . . . I don't intend to defend the Arab people, but the Jewish people have to be defended from deteriorating into far-reaching extremism. (Flapan, 1987, p. 19)

Participants from Achdut Haavodah, in a meeting of Mapam, responded saying that:

. . . War has its own meaning and its own rules, they said, despite what might be morally indefensible in any other situation. A party secretary Avraham Levite " . . . could both justify and welcome as a matter of highest morality and political necessity every act of conquest—and the removal of every Arab settlement—dictated by the needs of war." While he agreed that " . . . every lawless act, all theft and looting, must be fought vigorously, up to and including the meting out of the death sentence," Levite considered " . . . the immoral behavior of the soldiers (was finally) a 'secondary question.' " (Quoted by Flapan, 1987, p. 22)

Knesset members who protested the immorality of the state's actions, continued to participate as perpetrators of the acts they criticized, even if by turning their backs. Beneath their protests lurked the "moralisms" of war, the power of the gun. Their protests were an attempt to maintain the respectability of the state, as the meaning of the male state unfolded.

The government officially imposed military rule in December, 1948, based on Emergency Regulations enforced by the British in 1936. Military authority prescribed who could leave or enter any Arab village. Soldiers denied permits to Arabs who needed to leave their villages, whether for work, health reasons, or visits, citing security considerations. Regulations allowed arrest, detention, and imprisonment, for any length of time deemed necessary. Fines and penalities could not be appealed (Jiryis, 1976; Lustick, 1980; Segev, 1986).

The Minister of Agriculture seized land under the Abandoned Areas Ordinance and the Waste Land Regulation, defining waste land as any land which was not cultivated, or " . . . in the opinion of the Minister of Agriculture, was not 'efficiently' cultivated" (Cattan, 1969, p. 80). The Absentee Property Regulations entitled the Custodian of Absentee Property to seize all property—land, buildings, possessions, money—of any citizen or resident of the Arab states or Palestine who had left her/his place of residence in Palestine, even if to take refuge from the war. Between 1948 and 1953, 350 of 370 new Jewish settlements were established on land classified as abandoned (Lustick, 1980, p. 57). In 1954, more than one-third of Israel's Jewish population lived on land classified as absentee property. Close to one-third of the new immigrants (250,000 people) lived in "abandoned" urban areas (Lustick, 1980). Furthermore, the Development Authority (Transfer of Property) Law empowered the government to sell or to lease acquired property only to the state, the Jewish National Fund, government institutions, or local authorities of the state.

One 12-year-old Palestinian, among those who left their villages, describes the consequences for women:

> We went to a village called Abu Sinan. We were a family, three girls, three boys, mother, father and grandfather, and we had nothing to eat. I used to take my younger brother and sister and creep back to get things from our home. My mother used to punish me for it, but I wasn't afraid of the Jews. I used to go in and get soap, flour, food to eat. One time when I was carrying a heavy sack of flour I trod on an electric wire which rang an alarm bell. That's when I fell and hurt my back. Another time the soldiers nearly caught us in our house, but we hid in a cupboard. It was our country, but we had become thieves in it!
>
> We used to get watermelon, okra, tomatoes and corn from our village. It was our land, we had sowed it, and we wanted to harvest it. Sometimes my mother and my aunt used to go at night—it was about eight or ten kilometres' walk. Once when they went, the guards saw them and shot my aunt through the head. You've seen her husband, Abu Saleh, and her daughter Amineh. What a hard life she's had! (Quoted in Sayigh, 1979, p. 88)

Most Palestinian women remaining in Israel were separated from their extended and often immediate family members who escaped to other Arab countries and were unable to return. While working the land was not an easy life for rural women, by confiscating their land the Israeli state forced Palestinian women to find other sources of support. Rural Palestinian women became more vulnerable to exploitation by men, as they became part of the cheap labor pool in agriculture and in the textile and food-processing industries or worked as domestics, the only avenues open to them.

While some Arab and Jewish villages arranged for harvesting to proceed, in the spring and summer of 1948 many fields were burned. The Israeli Defense Force shot hungry peasants returning to their fields for food and burned fields to prevent harvesting. Abandoned fields were given to Jewish settlements to harvest in an effort both to prevent Arabs from returning and to solidify the relationship of Jewish settlers to the land. The Druze in the north who had switched allegiance to the Jewish side were allowed to reap crops, while their Muslim neighbors went hungry (Morris, 1986). The Israelis bought loyalty through the right to harvest and gave a clear message that loyalty or exile were the two choices available to Palestinians.

PATRIARCHAL FAMILY LOYALTY: A FEMINIST ISSUE

Patriarchal family is a central institution upholding the male state. As the "central building block of the Israeli social order" (Bernstein, 1987, p. 169) the patriarchal family institutionalizes "equality–inequality," maintaining for the state the second-class-citizen status of women. Loyalty to the patriarchal family has been critical to women's survival: it is the institution that "protects" her in exchange for her services. Patriarchal family law gives her "rights" as a second-class citizen. Without it, she is an exile.

The intrinsic connection between nationalism and religion is acted out in control of family law by religious courts in Israel. State law and religion are linked: all Israeli citizens are classified as Jewish, Christian, or Muslim, whether or not they are "believers" (Rosenberg, 1977). Religious courts have jurisdiction over marriage and divorce, inheritance, familial relations. Historian Judith Wegner connects laws of religious courts governing women's status in Israel with gender prescriptions embedded in western law:

> Is there, for instance, any difference in principle between the perception of women's physical weakness in Jewish and Muslim traditions, which kept women largely confined to the home, and the attitude underlying western laws that continue to restrict women's employment? Does the same perception of women's moral weakness, which produced a talmudic rule that a traveling woman must be chaperoned by at least three men, underlie western laws that penalize prostitutes but not their patrons? Does the same assessment of women's intellectual weakness, which excluded Jewish and Muslim women from serious study of the sacred texts, underlie subtle pressures that continue to limit the entry of western women to the learned professions and to rigorous disciplines like mathematics and science? (Wegner, 1982, pp. 3, 4)

By religious-secular mandate, the second-class-citizen status of "women," "slaves," and "aliens" in Orthodox Judaism and Islam is institutionalized in modern terms in the structure and mores of Israeli society. The promulgation of legal jurisprudence defining women as property is the historical link between expropriation of women, land, and slaves, or colonized peoples, and economic power. In an interview with journalist Beita Lipman, one woman living in Jerusalem describes the consequences for women of the intersection of state and religion in the modern democratic Israeli state:

> The only way you can legally marry is with a religious ceremony. You go to the Rabbinate—it's a state institute: there they ask you a lot of questions, and they give you a lot of lectures about how you should behave before marriage and after marriage, what you should do with your husband; you should start lighting candles on a Friday evening. You have to say Yes, Yes, otherwise you get into complications. Then you have to have the ritual cleansing in the Mikve the night before your wedding. Often you have to tell them lies, because the cleansing is supposed to come a few days after the end of your period, and plans and dates go wrong. If the wedding falls during the days when you are still not regarded as 'clean,' you go there and you work out beforehand how to make it seem okay, otherwise you'd have to scrap the wedding day!
> I resented all this very much: I had the feeling I wanted to strike some of the stupid religious people who were sitting around at the Institute . . . but of course I didn't. I went, like a good little child, sat there and had to listen to all this rubbish because I knew that I had to go through with it if I wanted to be married. I did make one mistake: I began to argue with them. It took one and half hours, whereas Chananiah (her fiancé) was only in there ten minutes. They were trying to persuade me to be religious . . . I resented that very much, because of course by law I had to be there. It implies that the State, more and more, restricts my rights as a human being. I'm sort of, an extension of the State, instead of the State being a framework where I can choose my own way of life . . . (Quoted in Lipman, 1988, pp. 71, 72)

The wife is the "field" to be plowed and her child is the man's "harvest." "The Talmud explicitly compares the acquisition of a woman with the acquisition of a field . . . Centuries later, the same formal equation was made by Muslim jurists . . . of the Māliki school of Islamic law . . . that 'nothing so resembles a sale as does marriage'" (Wegner, 1982, p. 13). Following classical tradition, a wife is required to move to her husband's domicile. If she is unfaithful, a crime for women, but not for men, she forfeits the mohar (bride price) and loses her right to "maintenance." While the husband is required to provide for his wife, in return her "duty" is obedience. Neither Judaism nor Islam permits a wife to divorce a husband, although this is sometimes overlooked by the religious courts, where the verdict must be rendered. A man may or may not decide to "release his property" if a woman requests a divorce. Many women are unable to remarry because their husbands refuse to release them; but a husband may divorce his wife and refuse her support payment if she persistently refuses intercourse. If a wife refuses divorce, her husband may seek court approval to take a second wife. In everyday life the scenario looks like this. An Israeli Jewish woman from Tunisia had her first epileptic seizure when her husband threw a hot plate because supper was not ready one evening when he returned from work. Subsequently he introduced his "secretary" to the family and began including her in their daily lives. His wife refused divorce; the rabbinic courts granted permission for him to take a second wife because his first was epileptic. He then sold their home, to which his first wife found she had no rights, and set her up in an apartment legally belonging to his son (Lipman, 1988). Permission to take a second wife is not uncommon; it provides a way out for men, while the law forces women to remain in untenable situations:

> There are several hundred women in Israel who cannot get their divorce. They have marched through the streets of Jerusalem this week, and I spoke to two of them. One has been fighting for twenty-two years and has been unable to do anything, because when she first started the procedures her attorney told her to leave the house. That was a major mistake—she was immediately deprived of all her rights, even though she had left the house after being physically very badly treated by the husband. Her six months old baby was also molested. Since then he has said No to a divorce, and that's it . . .
>
> The only way marriage really works for Jewish women here is when it's happy! We are our husband's property . . . even though I earn more than Eli, I'm still the "second" wage earner.
>
> I'm his property even at Kupat Holim, at the health service. A friend of mine had been traveling abroad. She came back to Israel with their four children, a month ahead of her husband, and tried to renew their health insurance. They said "No, you will have to wait for him." She asked what would happen if one of them was ill in the meantime—kids fall ill all the time, don't they?—and was told there was nothing she could do. She did not exist as an independent entity without her husband. (Carmit Gie, a broadcaster, quoted in Lipman 1988, pp. 79, 80)

The Religious Affairs Ministry compiles a list of women who may not be married in a Jewish religious ceremony, and thus, if Jews, may not be married at all in Israel (in October 1989, there were 8,379 on the list) (Shapiro, 1990). Fabricated from rumors and unsubstantiated reports, the list includes divorcees who are alleged to have committed adultery and may thus not marry either former husbands or lovers; widows without children whose brothers-in-law must by law release them before they can remarry; converts whose authenticity is questioned; children of married women and a man not her husband (who are only allowed to marry children from the same). Some women listed have already satisfied requirements for marriage; most do not even know they are listed and cannot therefore refute false evidence (Shapiro, 1990).

Muslim men divorce through triple repudiation: a woman can divorce only under specific conditions (if her husband is proved impotent, has deserted or maltreated her, or refused to support her, and if stipulated in her marriage clause). Court cases often take years, given a bias in support of the male (Haddad, 1980).

Divorced or widowed women in Israel do not have the same rights of tax exemption as single men living with children. They do not receive the same amount of national insurance (Rosenberg, 1977). Technically a woman's income belongs to her husband, who controls the family resources and access to state resources. Income tax is filed in his name. A "non-compliant" woman is labeled rebellious; as such, she forfeits the "protections" of the state.

Women's dependence on the patriarchal family is reinforced by discrimination against them in the job market. In a 1989 interview with *New Outlook* editor Dan Leon, Professor Naomi Chazan, head of the African Studies Department at Hebrew University, noted that over the last decade the salary differential between men and women of the same rank has increased from 22% to 29%. No women work in the top three ranks of civil service, and only 5% to 8% of all professors are women (Leon, 1989, p. 12). While working women are technically guaranteed equal pay for equal work, this law is notorious for being circumvented. Women in civil service jobs receive lower benefits; promotion is difficult, job titles are reworded to justify lower pay. Women are getting poorer, according to Na'amat Secretary General Masha Lubelsky. Unemployment is higher among women than men, and there are 60,000 single parents, the majority of whom are women. Sixty-five percent of those who earn $500 a month are women, and women are only 9% of those earning $2,500 a month. Seventy percent of working women earn minimum wage, or below, particularly in the Israeli-Arab sector (Levavi, 1991). Palestinian women in the Israeli-Arab sector are 15% of the work force, many in part-time jobs. Twelve percent of agricultural workers in Israel are Palestinian women (Fishman, 1989). And Palestinian women fill jobs vacated by Jewish women who are promoted.

In every sector of the labor force, Palestinian women and Jewish women from Arab-speaking countries are the dhimmi of the dhimmi. Comprising the largest number of poor among women, many fill the role of domestics and unskilled laborers, as Ashkenazi women are moved up the ladder. Thirty-four percent of working women work in factories, predominantly textile: they are largely Palestinian and Jewish women from Arab countries. European women closer to the sources of capital have status, called equal rights. Ranking of women by race demonstrates that women are first of all separated out by the state, are intrinsically "other," meaning "less than"—and therefore must be entitled to (fight for) equal rights. Discrimination against African and Asian women clarifies the link between "woman," "Arab," "east" in the political ideology of the Israeli state. Israeli social values " . . . reflect the cultural mores of its European founding pioneer ruling elite, who saw and intended Israel to become a modern, technological, and western solution to the Jewish problem" (Davis, 1977, p. 34). Immigration from Middle Eastern countries bringing the population to a majority (60%) consisting of Jews from Arab countries was thus a serious problem for the founding fathers:

> The majority of Israel's post-1948 Jewish population (approximately sixty percent) is culturally Arab, and yet divorced from its Arab heritage and affiliation through being situated in Israel as second class citizens of a western extension, a settler colonial polity based on the distinction between Jew and Arab and on the exclusion and dispossession of the latter in the process of transforming Palestine into Israel. (Davis, 1977, p. 34)

Illiteracy among African and Asian women is attributed to "backward" sexual mores, for example, confinement of women to the home. This of course is a consequence of the "primitive" culture of the Middle East and is not a problem for women of the "advanced" western world. In fact, one critical reason why many Oriental Jewish women do not receive an education is the paternalism, in the form of Western ethnocentrism, that they face within the school system. An Ashkenazi 15-year-old woman attending a highly regarded Jerusalem high school describes the dynamic:

> I could stay in my present school and not transfer to a special High School, but I don't want to. What happens is that they keep the kids they want—he or she can stay without any exam, no matter what the school work is like or how good they are. And if they don't want a particular girl to stay, she won't stay. It's not based on how good they are in school, but mainly on background. If they don't want them—like most of the kids that come from Morocco—they don't let them stay in school, unless they're real bright.
>
> Most of them, they just tell them, "You don't fit into our school, and we don't want you here." And then they go to a different school of their own background. They wanted me to stay. I'm Ashkenazi, not Sephardi. I'm not from Morocco or Yemen or Algeria. My school work was very low, and there were many Moroccan kids whose school work was higher than me, but they didn't let them stay: they said, you'll not fit in; we want you to go.
>
> Unless you're very, very bright, you can't stay if you're a Moroccan Jew . . .

I want to meet Arabs, I want to see their way of living, to try and get them to be equal with us. In the book, they're supposed to—but they're not. If you live in Israel, you can see that they're not equal; they're not treated as equal . . . (Quoted in Lipman, 1988, pp. 58, 59)

Chaya Shalom is a fourth generation Sephardi Jew, born in Jerusalem in 1944:

I went to this public school called Alliance which was all Sephardic. I don't know the exact history of the school, but it had French support.
The children and the teachers were all Sephardic?
No, no. I'm talking about the children, Sephardim—actually Oriental. And most of the teachers were of European background. They were from France and came with this French education which was quite tough. The teachers beat the pupils. There was quite a gap between them and us. I don't know if they understood what all these people were about who were from a poor class, poor status. But you know, my parents, the old people admired the teachers because they were educated. Now the parents are more involved with what's going on in school. They, they gave all the power to the teachers. (Shalom quoted in Kaye-Kantrowitz & Klepfisz, 1986, p. 204)

Shalom describes her experience in an Ashkenazi Scouts movement, supported by the National Religious party, where she felt different and was compelled to hide her Sephardi background. She notes that many Sephardi try to change their accent to sound like Ashkenazim and often change their names to modern Hebrew names (Kaye-Kantrowitz & Klepfisz, 1986).

Furthermore, according to Shalom, statehood caused associations among Sephardi women to fall apart. Sephardi stories and songs were preserved by women; coping with their enormous workload, they would "sit together and to make it easier for themselves, they'd tell stories, personal stories, and they'd sing . . . " (Shalom quoted in Kaye-Kantrowitz & Klepfisz, 1986, p. 203):

. . . The women were together all day and they shared everything. They shared what they had, exchanged what they cooked, and also shared a lot of their personal life and feelings . . . What they described to me was really a women's community. (Shalom quoted in Kaye-Kantrowitz & Klepfisz, 1986, p. 202)

In Jerusalem, daily contact was disrupted as many of Shalom's neighbors moved from the Old City (in Jerusalem), and then under Jordanian administration, to the Israeli side. In addition, the "modern" generation, says Shalom, must cope with the invisibility of Sephardi culture—of women's world:

I am very angry because there were a lot of women there who were like doctors, healers. These women knew all about how—how you say—herbs and healing treatments. One was called Tsiporah La Polvera. Polvera is a powder. She knew how to heal eyes with a certain powder. Who knows how she made it. There were other women who really did miracles. In the house, you would see planted herbs which were good for a stomach ache or colds and other sicknesses. They also were midwives—like Bolissa Bekhora de Yehiel—and they had to be psychologists too because they prepared women for childbirth and raising children. The tradition was to want the first child to be a boy, and if a girl was born, these midwives helped the parents accept the girl baby. They even lived with the family for a few days and helped her with a lot of jobs. But at the time, nobody thought they were important enough to be remembered. They're not mentioned any place. (Shalom quoted in Kaye-Kantrowitz & Klepfisz, 1986, p. 203)

Association and cultural exchanges among Jewish, Muslim, and Christian women suffered similarly. Gazan political organizer Mary Khass describes the disruption of 1948:

I went to the English high school in Haifa—that was shared between Jews and Palestinians , both Muslim and Christian. There was a very good atmosphere until 1946, when demonstrations started . . . either Jewish or Palestinian students. I had many friends there, of all kinds. After 1948, and in spite of the war, it was impossible to stop seeing my friends—we used to sneak through the barbed wire and borders to see each other and be with each other . . . (Lipman, 1988, pp. 56, 57)

Zionists disrupted associations of Arab women in the countries of their origins as well, in the process of what the state termed the "in-gathering of the exiles." Once "resettled," Arab women would find their options for survival prescribed by their new status as Israeli Arab women. Associations of women continued to support women's survival, albeit in new forms, accommodating and supporting, resisting and attempting to influence the form of, women's entry into modernization.

IN-GATHERING OF THE EXILES

January 1949. In the camps, 28,000 immigrants waited for up to 6 months for settlement. By the end of that year the number had risen to over 90,000, one-tenth, or two out of three of the total number of immigrants (Segev, 1986). Tom Segev's *The First Israelis* (1986) is, to date, an unparalleled source of declassified documentation clarifying the formative period of the Israeli state. The transit camps, as they were called, were overcrowded and lacked sanitary facilities. Scarce food rations, inadequate nutrition, and unfamiliar foods caused health problems. There were no schools, and there was no work for the camp "inmates" (Segev, 1986). Women bore the brunt of the hardship, having to nurse, feed, and care for hungry and sick children, and generally take responsibility for making accommodations livable.

The newly arrived Jews were often blamed for the sordid living conditions in the camps, particularly if they were African or Asian:

In the [North] African corners of the camps you find filth, gambling, drunkenness and prostitution. Many of them suffer from serious eye diseases, as well as skin and venereal diseases. I have yet to mention robbery and theft. Nothing is safe from this anti-social element, no lock is strong enough . . . The [North]

Africans bring their ways with them wherever they settle. It is not surprising that the crime rate in the country is rising. In certain parts of Jerusalem it is no longer safe for a young girl, or even a young man, to go out after dark . . . Incidentally, they had often assured me that as soon as they had finished fighting the Arabs, they would go to war against the Ashkenazis. In one camp they planned a revolt, which entailed seizing the guards' rifles and murdering the local Jewish Agency functionaries . . . But above all there is one equally grave fact and that is their total inability to adjust to the life in this country, and primarily their chronic laziness and hatred for any kind of work. Almost without exception they are both unskilled and destitute. What can be done with them? How are they to be absorbed? Have we given sufficient thought to the question of what will happen to this state if this should be its population? And then, in addition, [other] Oriental Jews will eventually join them, too! What will happen to the State of Israel and its standards with this type of population? (Arye Gelblum, quoted in Segev, 1986, p. 160, 161)

Moroccan Jews, many of whom had been successful state officials, merchants, gold, copper, and silversmiths, were utilized in construction and agriculture as a cheap labor force, overworked and underpaid. Persian and Yemenite Jews were funneled into agriculture, where they competed with indigenous Arabs for seasonal work. Women replaced indigenous Arab women as domestics in the home of European settlers.

In 1949, the exodus of Yemenite Jews, Operation Magic Carpet, widely reported and acclaimed in the press, symbolized the fulfillment of the religious prescription supporting the creation of the state of Israel. "The newsreels showed them alighting from the airplanes, lying down on the landing strips and kissing the ground of the Holy Land" (Segev, 1986, p. 182). Portrayed as "overjoyed to be in Israel," in fact one observer described their arrival this way:

. . . Crowded, filthy, full of sores, their faces stare blankly, silently. Even after greeting them it is hard to get them to say a word, whether from exhaustion, they say they have been enroute for 15 days, or from apathy and fatalism, or fear of the future . . . This is the first night that this ancient Jewish race meets with the Jewish races of Europe and the Middle East. There is no joy in their faces, no sign of excitement, nothing to suggest a sense of relief and an end to trouble . . . (Quoted in Segev, 1986, p. 182)

One transit camp built for 500 people, with no kitchen, dining room or toilets, housed 12,000 Yemenites, many of whom did not have tents (Segev, 1986). Some Ashkenazi Zionists justified conditions in the camps by saying that " . . . if there had been toilets the people would not have used them" (Segev, 1986, p. 183). Officials forced some newly arrived Yemenites to take off their clothes, which were then burned "for fear of diseases and vermin."

My life has been hard; yes, it has been very hard. When the government in Yemen said we had to leave, we walked for many days to go to Aden, so that we could fly here. And do you know what they did when our plane landed? They sprayed us with DDT! Not just the aeroplane—they sprayed *us* . . . how dare they do that things to us, as though we were dirty? (Quoted in Lipman, 1988, p. 90)

The emigrees were then given Western-style clothes. Women whose traditional leggings worn under dresses were not replaced " . . . would crouch, hiding their legs in the sand, deeply ashamed" (Segev, 1986, p. 183). Zionist women who were assigned the task of acclimating immigrants to the new cultural norms coerced girls into having their hair cut and boys their sidelocks cut "for health reasons." One woman, particularly assiduous in carrying out this particular aspect of "seasoning" of immigrants, was dismissed from her post, because her zeal had too openly exposed the intentions of her superiors (Segev, 1986).

In one Yemenite camp soldiers ordered women stripped by medical orderlies, dusted the naked and crying women with DDT, and told them that they had too many children (Segev, 1986). The assessment that Yemenite women had too many children was dealt with in another manner.

In 1950 the Yemenite Association reported to the Ministry of Police a case of a baby girl who had been taken to a doctor for treatment and subsequently disappeared. Over 300 children vanished in similarly mysterious circumstances. Some suspected that the Yemenite babies had been given or sold for adoption in Israel or abroad. A report was submitted and a committee appointed, but the investigation was never completed (Segev, 1986). Had the Yemenite immigrants become a target for the international traffic in children and/or female sexual slavery? Studies of the international traffic in women and children by Janice Raymond, Kathleen Barry, Renee Bridel, and Gena Corea corroborate this hypothesis. Raymond documents procurement of children for adoption in Guatemala, Brazil, and Mexico, through a network of businessmen, lawyers, doctors, and other agents. Government officials take part in supplying false birth certificates and other papers. Adoption rings and agencies providing aid in developing countries act as covers for the international traffic in women and children (Raymond, 1989).

The Yemenite story fits the standard pattern uncovered by Raymond. Parents took their children to institutions for treatment or infant care homes. When they returned to take them home, they were told that the children had been transferred. But searching from one institution to another, parents could not locate their children. Death certificates for 316 children were eventually produced: the files of 22 children left in one infant home were never found. When the body of one child who had died and been buried without her parents being allowed to see her was exhumed, they discovered that the child was not theirs. The committee uncovered enough evidence that the children may have been sold for adoption abroad to recommend carrying out further investigation to the Knesset and the police. But the affair was dropped and forgotten (Segev, 1986).

Raymond notes that: "A primary cause of this trafficking in women and children is the ravaging of countries by U. S. supported military and civilian governments" (Raymond, 1989, p. 237). Sociologist Renee Bridel documents the enormous profits made from traffic in children, allowed by state bureaucracies and encouraged by businessmen and tourists globally. Newly formed and militarized nation–states form cooperative bonds utilizing the traffic in women and children as a source of financing. Children of families living in poverty, children in refugee camps without relatives, are ideal prey:

> The children will be bought or taken away from destitute Third World families, who, anyway have no means of knowing what will become of the child and who, often sell him or her themselves; they can also be caught in far away countrysides where the population can hardly find anything to eat; they will also be taken by false adoptions and disappear by the hundreds from refugee camps where a careful watch is lacking. (Bridel, 1984, p. 91)

Yemenites and other second-class citizens of North Africa and Asia were often placed in settlements close to borders and vulnerable to attacks. Of the 49,000 Yemenite Jews who came on the Operation Magic Carpet (there were 70,000 Yemenite immigrants), 70% were funneled into farming occupations (Segev, 1986). Many had been tradesmen or artisans in Yemen and felt that they had come down in the world. Discrimination in wages, harsh living conditions, and enforced assimilation produced alienation, despair, and resistance. Reporting to Ben-Gurion on the situation in Yemenite settlements in 1953, Knesset members asserted that: "If the Ashkenazi settlers thrive more, it is due to their initiative, their skills and adaptability, all of which provide them with better opportunities for managing their affairs, internally and externally" (Segev, 1986, p. 190). However, a study of one immigrant camp that later became a township stated:

> The forced reduction of social and cultural activities, the undermining of traditional authority, the lack of economic opportunity and the dependence on outside officials, all led to . . . aggressive behavior and at the same time to disease and physical debility . . . (Segev, 1986, p. 191)

Many of the Ashkenazi elite viewed the Yemenites and other Arab immigrants as commodities to be utilized, as raw material to be shaped, conditioned, seasoned. In general, the government's policy toward immigrants was self-serving. Zionist leaders were discriminating: they considered certain categories of people, including invalids, mentally disabled, and those people over 50, undesirable. Rabbis sought to exclude members of the heterodox Karaite community of Egypt. "Dr. Y. Meir, General Director of the Ministry of Health, said he had been 'horrified' to read in the newspapers that there was an intention to bring in the Falashas of Ethiopia. 'I hope that his report is unfounded,' he wrote to Giora Yoseftal" (Segev, 1986, p. 144). Among those immigrants considered undesirable were uncircumcised children, intermarried couples, journalists, and people over 50 who were not skilled workers (Segev, 1986). Although by 1951 the Law of Return had been enacted, granting automatic citizenship to any Jew who wished to settle in Israel, the Attorney General had to intervene when the Ministry of Interior refused entry to a group of old women from Bulgaria (Segev, 1986).

Treatment of Arab Jews reflected the masculinist, anti-women ideology supporting national identification. Over and over, European Zionists characterized the African and Asian Jew as an affront to the "dignity of man." "They approached it [the problem of immigrants from Arab countries] with appropriate academic rigor, their articles bearing titles such as 'Absolute Criteria' and 'The Dignity of Man'" (Segev, 1986, p. 157). One scholar proposed that to understand the mentality of these immigrants, one must compare them to the primitive expression of children, the retarded, or the mentally disabled. They treated them like women, incapable of full participation in society; not worthy of full benefits of social resources; undeveloped. Their paternalism concealed their true motivations. For example, Zionists maintained that Arab Jews left their countries of origin gladly and because of persecution. In fact, there was a range of reasons why they emigrated to Israel, not the least of which were incendiary Zionist activities within those countries. One Moroccan Jew, deciding to return to Morocco, asserted:

> We have never suffered in Morroco. If there was in Morocco any oppression, it was perpetrated by the French regime. The Arab policemen always treated us with great respect . . . Anyway you should know that we have always gotten on well with the Arabs. Wonderful people. It is only the Ashkenazim that we have never gotten on with. (Davis, 1977, p. 119)

WOMEN'S ASSOCIATIONS: CO-OPTATION, DEPENDENCE, RESISTANCE

Yemenite women, violently introduced to the values, customs, and belief systems of the Ashkenazi ruling classes, utilized traditional associations to accommodate to their new life and to resist exploitation.

Anthropologist Yael Katzir's study of Yemenite weavers from a rural village in Yemen relocated in a *moshav,* or cooperative agricultural settlement in Israel, affirms the historic importance of women's networks as a powerful social resource:

Middle Eastern women who are excluded from the formal cultural institutions have developed elaborate female networks based on kin, affinal, and neighborhood ties. Such networks serve for the exchange of political, cultural, and kinship information. They often function in economic exchange and for emotional support among the women. They are imperative in the arrangement of marriage, and they can channel cultural diffusion leading to cultural change. Middle Eastern female networks have well-established and ritualized mutual visiting patterns. (Katzir, 1983, p. 46)

Katzir notes that since the 1960s, anthropological literature on Middle East sex roles has confirmed that women's friendships are political. That is, women's friendships influence social mores and support women's entry into the domain of policy-making. Katzir's study, one of the few that examines Middle East Jewish immigrants' adaptation to the Israeli moshav, focuses on the 59 married couples, 4 widows and 1 widower from al-Gades in Yemen who comprised the 64 farm households resettled on a moshav in Israel in 1950. While this is an area for continuing study, Katzir's work contributes to our understanding of how women's networks can enhance women's social mobility and economic power. At the same time, Katzir's findings point to the limitations women face in attempting to restructure exploitative sex roles.

The moshav of Katzir's study was situated on the top of one of the rocky isolated hills near the Jordanian-Israeli border. The government established moshavim and other settlements along border areas for security reasons. Instead of integrating men from al-Gades into the regular army, the government utilized them as a border patrol. Another goal of moshav development was:

> . . . rapid sociocultural and technological integration of immigrants through planned change and development programs within easily supervised small moshav organizations . . . Concomitant with these practical considerations were the interests of the European political elite, to socialize the new immigrants into their particular pioneer, Zionist, socialist values and ideology and through economic dependence to gain their votes for the ruling political parties . . . (Katzir, 1983, p. 51)

The moshav was instituted as a unit of municipal government with municipal duties, including payment of taxes and dues. The skills of carpet weaving were no longer relevant in this situation, nor were they valued. Al-Gades men were forced to work as unskilled laborers within a cooperative economic arrangement controlled by the state, rather than as independent small traders.

Yemenite Jewish society of al-Gades was patrilineal; men controlled economic resources, as well as the education of sons, women's and children's labor, and activities. While second-class citizens, the Yemenite dhimmi were respected tradesmen who established important client–patron relations and networks with Muslim neighbors. Katzir documents the importance of friendships between Jewish and other Arab women for exchange of cultural information, and as informal agents of change:

> At the village springs, Jewish and Arab women struck long-lasting friendships and exchanged cultural information; as a consequence, women were often informal agents of change. These social networks with other Jewish and Arab women served as a crucial means of exchanging information and mediating between families. Thus while men had the authority, women could manipulate the power system indirectly in the areas of political, economic, and marriage decisions. (Katzir, 1983, p. 50)

In al-Gades, farming was not respected as an occupation, so that in the context of the moshav, men lost status, both as unskilled laborers and as farmers. However, men voted in the municipal council and retained control over resources and property as the new farm owners. National and moshav law redistributed privileges, changing the balance of power relations among men and among women, and between women and men. For example, national law recognizes and taxes the nuclear family as the basic unit of production, consumption, and socialization, rather than the extended kin family. State control of social relations provided a new set of rewards and privileges, as well as restrictions. National and moshav law " . . . raised the marriage age, forbade bridewealth, and provided the women with inheritance rights upon death and divorce" (Katzir, 1983, p. 53). But women could become moshav members and owners of farms only if they had sons who would inherit the property and title. The government decided the age at which a woman could marry, albeit by raising that age. State law reinforced pressure to marry; divorce laws supported control of women's bodies. Yemenite women found themselves enmeshed in a new set of requirements prescribing their status, or usefulness to the state. This new set of prescriptions was transmitted through Ashkenazi Israeli women on army assignment in the moshav who transmitted modern values to Yemenite women, including ideas about childrearing, hygiene, the status of women, their rights and duties in relation to men, and literacy skills (Katzir, 1983).

The initial productive activity of the al-Gades moshav, fruit production, shifted to egg production after the war of 1967 since the moshav could not compete with low prices of fruit produced on the Arab West Bank (Katzir, 1983). Women and children ran the chicken farm, but turned proceeds over to men. Alongside the produce marketed for the cooperative, women set up their own marketing enterprise with produce from their gardens and with eggs:

> In 1973 each woman carried as many as eight to ten 30-egg trays three to four times a week to Jerusalem, adding a total of roughly 3 million eggs to the free market. (Katzir, 1983, p. 54)

One Yemenite woman engaged in marketing describes the change in her life:

> Here in Israel I think I'm much happier than my man. You see, he stays on the moshav all the time. It is like he is afraid to go out: he just sits there when he is not working or at the synagogue. For me it is different: I like very much to come here and see my friends—some of them I know for nearly thirty years!

> Yes, I am selling my own vegetables: we are supposed to give the money to the moshav, but you know, it is very useful to have a little bit extra. The men keep the rules, but we don't always do like the men . . . yes. I am happy here, but he is not. (Quoted in Lipman, 1988, p. 90)

Women siphoned off money from selling eggs, thus controlling the amount of cash they could put into their own pockets. In this way they took charge of the daily household budget, since the men did not have access to surplus cash through the moshav system. Yemenite women became agents of change, investing in new household items to raise their standard of living.

Through their marketing, Yemenite women established close ties with a wide network of regular clients. Katzir notes that it is these contacts that have been most instrumental in their modernization:

> . . . they have acquired new values and ideas about child rearing, social mobility and living standards, using their women "friends" as a reference group . . . They consult the "friends" on technical and personal problems, get information about the acquisition of goods and about schools and jobs for their children, and arrange marriages for their daughters. (Katzir, 1983, p. 59)

Women utilize client ties to acquire access for their daughters to higher socioeconomic class status through marriage arrangements, pressure to continue schooling and to acquire vocations and urban living skills (Katzir, 1983).

> My own life? I left the school quite early—I could not see what to stay for. Of course I can read and write, I can do the money sums. I am married to a man from the moshav—we all come from Yemen there, so we understand each other. My parents fixed the marriage and it's quite all right. But I don't want my daughter to live on the moshav: it would be good if we could find a man with a business, in town. You know, life is much more interesting in the town. I spend a lot of money on her, on Rachel . . . today she wants some new shoes with high heels. It will be a matter of how much we sell today! (Quoted in Lipman, 1988, pp. 91, 92)

Katzir notes that the ability of Yemenite women to establish networks outside their immediate environment, as they were accustomed to doing in Yemen, continued to function as a way to manipulate a system benefiting and dominated by men. In their new situation, as mediators with outside society, women necessarily absorbed values that might enable them to achieve status in modern terms. Increasingly, however, moshav women became willing to give up the freedoms of an independent income in order to escape the low status accorded manual labor. For many of them, dependence on their husbands represented upward mobility. In this sense their activities were ultimately not a threat either to the national goal of immigrant acculturation, or to the male-dominated system. Male authority in the moshav continued to function as a form of control over women's activities and resources. The power of women's associations to bring about social change could be utilized to enable women to acquire privileges ultimately supporting male rule. The power of women's associations could also be utilized to address the common situation of women as women, across class and ethnic-racial formations meant to separate them, hence to diffuse that power.

Yemenite women benefited from exchanges with Ashkenazi women. But benefits acquired in exchange for loyalty to the state are limited, since the ways in which they are encouraged and allowed to serve the state are prescribed by their status as "Arab," as well as, as "woman." For example, military service is rewarded through monetary benefits (such as housing subsidies), and status. Arab women are for the most part excluded from both.

WOMEN AS RECRUITS

The structure of the Israeli military exemplifies the connection between control of women, of land, and of despised races. The Zahal, or Israel Defense Army, became a regular standing army (as opposed to a volunteer army) following the British model, in May of 1948. The women in Zahal belonged to Chen, the women's corps: its initials in Hebrew mean "charm." Nira Yuval-Davis quotes a 1973 army publication detailing the function of women in the military:

> . . . strengthening the fighting force by fulfilling administrative professional and auxiliary roles, in order to release male soldiers to combat roles; training women to defend themselves and their homes and integrating them in the security effort of Israel, even after the termination of their active military service. The female soldiers also help in the educational activity of Zahal—in the educational system as teachers, and in Zahal as a whole, in the areas of crystalizing the morale of the units and taking care of the soldiers of the units. (Yuval-Davis, 1985, p. 661)

The structure of the military exemplifies the social organization of the state. Sixty-five percent or more of Ashkenazi women do clerical work in the army, and 54.8% of women in the civilian labor force do clerical work (Yuval-Davis, 1985). The remaining women in the civilian labor force work in public and community service areas, occupations also relegated to army women.

Women boost the morale of the state by producing soldiers and through affiliation with and loyalty to their men. War widows receive a state salary comparable to that of a senior government officer (Yuval-Davis, 1985). The military, as an arm of the state, socializes women to identify with their procreative and wifely roles. Ben-Gurion, quoted by Yuval-Davis, puts it this way:

> There is no greater mission in life, and nature decreed that only a woman can give birth to a child. This is woman's task and her blessing. However, a second factor must be remembered: the woman is not only a woman, but a personality in her own right in the same way as a man. As such, she should enjoy the same rights and responsibilities as the man, except where motherhood is concerned. (Yuval-Davis, 1985, p. 670)

The 1969 National Security Law states that every Israeli citizen or permanent resident must be recruited (men who are 18–29 years of age, and women
who are 18–26 years of age; physicians and dentists up to age 38). However,
Palestinians are excluded, and 51.5% of Jewish women were recruited in 1976
to 1977 (Yuval-Davis, 1985). Religious women are exempted from service
as a concession to the religious parties who tried to keep women out altogether
because women, according to them, are immoral by nature, and corrupt men.
Two-fifths of the women excluded did not meet Hebrew language requirements, had insufficent level of education, and/or poor performance on psy-
chotechnic tests, or had criminal records. Married women, pregnant women,
or women with children are released; they are performing their service to
the state by fulfilling their reproductive role (Yuval-Davis, 1985). The majority
of these women are from Arab countries, and are confined in higher numbers to unskilled labor outside the home, and to reproductive labor within
the home. They produce more children for the state and are excluded from
more of its benefits. The contempt behind reification of motherhood is exposed as mothers are encouraged in a role for which they are punished. By
excluding them from benefits, the army reinforces the degraded status of Arab
women. The army reinforces the "inferiority" of all women and the mandate
of service to men through the ways in which it incorporates as well as rejects
women.

Women in the army fulfill roles, then, like those of women in civilian life.
They free men for combat, supporting militarism; they provide wifely and sexual services, both literally and figuratively; they educate or inculcate the
uninitiated in state mores. Women excluded from the privileges and status
of army service are those who are furthest away from centers of power, women
denied formal education, women of the "wrong" extraction. In this way army
women, representing the elite, help to maintain the image of the military and
its desirability as a career goal.

Women in Zahal receive status—that is compensation from the state in
the form of wages—commensurate with the "value" of their "nature," intrinsically less than that of a man. Furthermore, as Palestinians continue to be excluded from sensitive occupations associated with state security, Jewish
women are increasingly moved into these positions, which offer higher salaries and status. In this way women become invested in maintaining the
status quo.

THE MARRIAGE EXCLUDING WOMEN:
NATIONALISM AS ORTHODOXY

Nationalism and religion: nationalism itself a religion, and religion itself
a center of bureaucratic power, shape the inner and outer lives of Israel's
citizens. Struggles of Zionist women to participate in nation-building within

the framework of the male establishment convinced many women that the rhetoric of civil rights did not lead to practical application of the principle of equal rights. They also found that rule by European elite men ensured that women's interests would conflict across race and class lines.

In the last days of the first Knesset, 1951, women from the World Zionist Organization introduced the Women's Equal Rights Law (WERL), " . . . designed to erase any legal sanctioning of sex roles" (Lahav, 1977, p. 195). The bill that was passed did reduce discrimination in some areas by granting married women the right to handle property, equal rights to child custody, and by stating that " . . . with regard to any legal act, the same law shall apply to a woman and a man and any provision of law that discriminates against women shall be of no effect" (Section 1). Sections 5 and 6 respectively provide that the new law shall not derogate from the laws applied to marriage and divorce and from laws " . . . protecting women as women" (Lahav, 1977, p. 195). However, WERL has in no way challenged the tenets of the religious system regarding women's status and role, so that " . . . the legal system recognizes both the principle of sex equality and the principle of sex-based discrimination" (Lahav, 1977, p. 204). Religious courts are reluctant to accept secular supervision and are unlikely to become an agent for social change. As Lahav points out, revisioning social norms is meaningful only if institutions with the power to legislate change are sympathetic.

Conflicting responses of various groups of women to the problematic Section 6 of WERL, which protects women as women, further reveal the power of the male state to institute self-perpetuating norms. While Ada Maimon, for example, recognized the danger of Section 6 in legitimating sex roles, a strong coalition of women within the labor movement opposed any attempt to " . . . equalize the present system" (Lahav, 1977, p. 207). Section 6, for example, prohibits women from working at night and provides for an earlier retirement age; both stipulations protect women's role in the family. That women are at risk working at night because the state supports a view of women that encourages attacks by men (a fact of women's status not touched by law constructed from within the framework of misogynist ideology) does not enter the argument.

WOMEN/PALESTINIANS: EXPLOITABLE RESOURCES

Underrepresented in all Israeli parties, women have limited access to important political positions. According to Knesset member Ora Namir, the power of the religious parties in the Knesset limits women's options:

> Think of it: we have a government of 25 Ministers and members of the Cabinet, and there isn't a single woman there. They still all believe that as long as we have our woman's organization in the Histadrut it will be enough. Let the women play women's business. They will not share power with us.

If I take the Knesset as an example: we are not many women, we are ten women here from different parties, and I think that if you compare the women's activities in the Knesset to the men's activities in the Knesset, in each party they are more devoted, they are more sensitive . . . you will see them more at work in the plenary, in the committees, on tours, touring the country, meeting people far more than the men. So we do the hard work but when it comes to power or representation men and men alone rule. It is not only the question of the religious parties in Israel and their power. Yes, the religious ones are more powerful than their number warrants, but they derive the power from the proportional representation system of election in Israel; because of the coalition, because of the fact that the public has never given any majority either to the Labor, or to the Likud, and when we form a coalition we always have to take them into it. Their price is very high.

In Israel the power of the religious parties in the Knesset and the power of religion over the life of women is linked. If they did not have the strength to keep a government ruling the country, they would not be able to force so much religious law on to women either . . . . Nowhere does religion and orthodoxy go together with the advancement of women, it just doesn't. For them a woman is second, for them a woman should stay at home, be almost constantly pregnant, bring children into the world and that's it . . . cook well, clean well, bake well, press well, do laundry well. That goes with their way of thinking. (Lipman, 1988, p. 116)

Along with structural factors in the political system that bar women's access to political power, social mores absorbed through formal and informal education ensure that women will make choices maintaining sex-role assignments. Occupational segregation of Israeli women as housewives and mothers, as secretaries and service workers (47.4% of the female labor force) discourages women from participation in the male political arena. Since the sixth Knesset there have been no women on the Committee for Foreign Affairs and Security, and other than the fourth Knesset, no women have sat on the Finance Committee. Out of 27 women representatives in local government in 1950, only 2 were not Ashkenazi; in 1955, only 4 out of 32; in 1959, 6 out of 34; in 1965, 5 out of 31, with no change in 1969. Although more women of African-Asian or Israeli origin have been recruited since the sixth Knesset, this has not changed the overall representation of women in local government (Weiss & Yishai, 1980).

Like Israeli women, Palestinian women and men are treated on a separate legal basis as a linguistic, religious, and cultural class with minority status. There is no legal basis in Israeli law for intermarriage between Jew and Palestinian. The Law of Return guarantees automatic citizenship to Jews, and not to Palestinians, as a way of ensuring demographic superiority. Barred from military service, Palestinians cannot take advantage of subsidized housing and other benefits afforded those who have served in the army. On the basis of the 1953 National Insurance Law created to encourage families to bear many children, Israeli mothers received 20 Israeli pounds per child. When it was discovered that Palestinians, who tended to have larger families, benefited more than Jews, the law was changed to confer family allowances based on military service. Palestinian mothers were denied benefits (Lustick, 1980).

Palestinian women live in Arab municipalities that receive a third of the funding received by Jewish municipalities. In mixed cities (Akka, Haifa, Yaffa, Lydd), they live in separate quarters unable to develop and build schools and recreation centers. Palestinian women risk losing sick children because they must travel to Jewish centers: while they might receive Histadrut health insurance there are no clinics in Arab centers (Pederson, 1983).

In 1962, before becoming Minister of Defense and leader of the Labor party, Shimon Peres characterized the Palestinian population as: "The indifferent resigned; the actively hostile; the hostile resigned" (Lustick, 1980, p. 67). Peres asserted that it was up to the government to decide which of these groups would dominate the Palestinian community. The Koenig memorandum (drafted by Israel Koenig, "Arabist" in the Ministry of Interior) asked for creation of a new political force in the Arab sector controlled by the government. Koenig advocated the adoption of: " . . . tough measures at all levels against various agitators among college and university students," and economic discrimination against Palestinians to deprive them of the "social and economic security that relieves the individual and the family of day-to-day pressures, [and] grants them, consciously and subconsciously, leisure for 'social-nationalist thought' " (Lustick, 1980, p. 69).

Using tactics similar to those of the British and French to suppress Arab nationalism, the Israeli government separates Muslim, Druze, and Christian through a system of rewards and punishments. The government refuses to identify the Druze as Arab in spite of protests from the Druze community. The Druze receive more help in the form of government subsidies and local development programs and are allowed a modest role in the military, which qualifies them for further benefits.

Like the British, Israelis have kept intact the *hamula* (kinship or extended family) system as a means of controlling villages and co-opting leaders. This policy works to the detriment of Palestinian women, who must now cope with a new set of restrictions on decision making and mobility within their communities.

Separation in education by ethnic-religious community under the mandatory government and in Israel has been another strategy for control of Palestinians. Classes in Palestinian communities are crowded due to lack of government assistance. Curriculum is shaped by Zionist ideology: Palestinian children must learn Hebrew, but Jewish children are not required to learn Arabic. Palestinian students are channeled into "women's" occupations, such as teaching, and away from areas considered "security risks," such as electronics and aeronautics. Lack of teaching materials on Palestinian history and tradition leaves the Jewish population disposed to the characterization of and reduction of Palestinians to a potentially subversive security risk—a threat to the state.

At the end of the British Mandate, only a third of school-age Palestinians attended school, 85% in towns and 20% in rural areas where 80% of the population lived. Of the one-third attending school, 7% were women; 95% of villages had no schools for women and 50% had no schools at all. Secondary education was, for the most part, available only through private schools (Pederson, 1983).

In 1980, although 90% of "non-Jewish" women in Israel went to primary schools, only 75% finished; and of 37% attending secondary school, only 20% finished. In 1974 to 1975, only 2% of Arabs in Israel attended universities: 5% of these were women (Pederson, 1983).

Women are disadvantaged by lack of facilities in Arab sectors, unequal distribution between urban and rural areas, and biases affecting how they are treated, and what areas of employment they are allowed to pursue. For example, as noted, Palestinians are limited to occupations that do not represent a security risk in the eyes of the Israeli government, so that while women have benefited from an increasing emphasis on the importance of education to a refugee population (Palestinians are among the most highly educated of Arab peoples), within Israel their options for education are limited.

Like Israeli women, Palestinians are barred from positions of power within those institutions and organizations that control the state. The separation and treatment of Israeli women and of Palestinians (both women and men) as classes or as "special interest groups" conceals the critical connections between the exploitation of both. Furthermore, colonialist and nationalist ideologies define gender, class, and race from a male perspective. Expropriation of the land, of women's labor, and of the Palestinians as an identity group is related. Bringing into the foreground the parallels in the struggles of Israeli women and of Palestinians as a class clarifies connections between the Zionist nationalist project and the politics of capitalist economics.

The Palestinian nationalist movement is similarly informed by male supremacist ideology. Yet, the critical connections between the exploitation of Israeli women and the exploitation of Palestinian women disappear as each group of women is identified and identifies itself with the men to whom they are connected, with whom they are in alliance, and who control their survival. Identification with male-controlled nationalist movements and ideology is dangerous for women, even as the nationalist struggle provides a site for women's political engagement. The challenge is to transform the nationalist struggle by examining the ground of nationalist ideology: a ground that is fast becoming a cesspool filled with the poisons of wars.

THE ISRAELI ENVIRONMENT

The history of cultivation of the soil is a history of sexual exploitation. Zionists, for example, claim land and exploit women, on the basis of "redemption." Zionist women, supporting redemption of the land, find that men, displacing indigenous farmers and controlling the labor of women, control the earth and tools of cultivation. Palestinian women and European Jewish women become commodities whose sale is dependent upon the value given to them by the producer and controller of the means of production. The meaning of culture in the 20th century unfolds, a struggle with, for, and against expropriation of the soil and of the tools, including hands, of cultivation.

The land of Palestine, traversed by men seeking goods, power, access to other lands, trade routes, building military posts, is situated at the meeting place of three world vegetation zones: the Mediterranean, Irano-Turanian, and Saharo-Arabian phyto and zoo-geographic region (Whitman, 1988). The topography is marked by limestone mountains of the north (Galilee) and Judean hills; the fertile valleys of upper Jordan, Jezreel, and Bet Shean; the Mediterranean coastal plain with its sandstone ridges, sand dunes, and rich alluvial soils; the Dead Sea in the east, in the north the fresh water of Lake Kinneret and in the south, the Gulf of Eilat and the Red Sea (Whitman, 1988). In the coastal plain and alluvial valleys, farmers have tended citrus orchards and field crops for centuries.

In the 20th century, tools of cultivation are engineered to meet the production goals of an economic system based on utilization of land, air, water, minerals, soil, and women as resources for capital gain. This process depends upon and breeds violence against women, against indigenous cultivators who are displaced, as well as women utilized in other social strata, and colonialist women who accommodate, collaborate, and resist. Expropriation of the land and the tools of cultivation dictated by the ideology of unlimited growth, violently disrupts the entire ecosystem upon which the productivity of the land depends. Some of the consequences are disruption of inter- and intracommunal relations through forced evacuation of farming villages, civil wars, factionalism, escalation of the use of force by arms, and mutilation of women's bodies and of the earth.

The Ministry of the Interior, in cooperation with the Environmental Protection Agency, an arm of the government, is publisher of a report by Joyce Whitman on the environment in Israel. Whitman's book is the only comprehensive source available detailing the process of development in Israel–Palestine. While Whitman supports the official view of the benefits of development, her documentation is a tale of devastation to the environment and to the populace. Moreover, the facts make clear the interrelationship between the politics of ecology and of race and sex.

The coastal plain along the Mediterranean Sea has become the site of the country's expanding industrial base, hence, highly urbanized. Between 1948 and 1988, the population expanded from under 600,000 to 4.3 million. The population density rose from 43.1 persons per square kilometer in 1948 to 196.3 in 1987, concentrated in 40% of the landbase; 79% of the population live in towns of over 10,000 inhabitants; 50% live in towns of over 50,000 (Whitman, 1988).

Because of highly technicalized methods, only 6% of the population are employed in agriculture. Agriculture has grown at the unprecedented annual rate of 7%. To achieve this, Israel has utilized all existing water resources and arable land. The widespread use of fertilizers and pesticides is a result of Zionist ideology of redemption of land and labor:

> The ideological motivation for setting up rural settlements and for experimentation in communal settlements has led to a wide distribution of rural settlement in previously sparsely settled, environmentally sensitive areas, especially in the mountainous regions. These experiments, as positive as they are from a national and societal perspective, exact an environmental cost that is expressed mainly in the widespread expansion of development activities to sensitive areas of unique ecological value. (Whitman, 1988, p. 33)

Overutilization of water has been one of the most devastating consequences of rapid development in communications and transport systems, as well as urban residential and commercial development. The war over water is the central factor in the Israeli occupation of South Lebanon.

The Israeli government maintains a military presence in South Lebanon, attempting to control the vital water source of the Litani River. The military controls the vital aquifers of the West Bank. As early as 1919, Zionist leaders recognized Israel's critical need for renewable sources of water. In 1920, Chaim Weizmann, Israel's first President, " . . . tried frantically to impress on British Foreign Secretary the necessity for including the Litani River within the borders of the draft Mandate [conferred on Britain, shortly after, by the League of Nations]" (Skutel, 1986, pp. 22, 23).

The Israeli government, like the French in South Lebanon at the turn of the century, supports certain (co-optable) elements within the population against others. Control of water depends upon indigenous cooperation. Journalist H. J. Skutel quotes from the diaries of former Israeli Prime Minister, Moshe Sharett:

> To him [Dayan] the only thing that's necessary is to find an officer, even just a Major. We should either win his heart or buy him with money, to make him agree to declare himself the savior of the Maronite population. Then the Israeli army will enter Lebanon, will occupy the necessary territory, and will create a Christian regime which will ally itself with Israel. (Skutel, 1986, p. 23)

Thus the security zone established by Israel to protect Israeli citizens from the ever-present scourge of Arab hatred is in fact a front for a strategy to control access to water. Furthermore:

> Published maps of the security zone in no way reflect its actual range of application, The Israelis and [South Lebanese Army, SLA] reserve the right to attack suspected terrorist bases many kilometers beyond its stated limits. (Skutel, 1986, p. 24)

Along with control of water, the military controls agriculture through expropriation of land owned by Arabs for Jewish settlement and through introduction of single-cash-crop farming. In the Gaza Strip, for example, Jewish settlements affiliated with the National Religious party, structured as moshavim, or agricultural communities, produce tomatoes for export in hothouses, utilizing high levels of artificial irrigation and large quantities of water from local wells. Overdraining of water from the fertile oasis for hundreds of families between Rafah and Yamit makes the oasis unfit for traditional vegetable cultivation. The only available water for the Arab population must be obtained by digging into the dunes; but use of bulldozers is forbidden other than for the construction of new Jewish settlements or for the destruction of Arab villages and farms. Single-crop production and intensive irrigation cause soil erosion and increased salination and pollution, ensuring that eventually the productivity of the land will be used up and destroyed (Davis, 1979).

The Israeli government has also disrupted the main industry in the Gaza, orange plantations. A military order in 1967 made it mandatory for Gazans to obtain a license from the area commander to utilize wells and irrigation installations, including those operating prior to 1967 (Dillman, 1989). Since applications are frequently refused and water quotas have been cut, the groves do not have enough water to produce. High fines are levied when allowable water usage is exceeded, charted by water meters put on every source of water and plot of land. Similar policies instituted in the West Bank ensure Jewish control and ensure deprivation for Palestinians whose access is severely curtailed, if not altogether eliminated. Extensive well digging in the West Bank has lowered the water table to the extent that many springs and Palestinian owned wells have dried up. Palestinians have not been allowed to develop any wells for irrigation (Davis, 1979; Dillman, 1989; Skutel, 1986).

Development of recreational facilities disrupts fragile ecosystems. In 1977, when villagers from Bir'em in the Galilee asked to return to their village as they had been promised by Prime Minister Menachim Begin, the area was declared a nature reserve. The Society of the Protection of Nature, working with the Ministry of Agriculture (headed at that time by a former general and one of the leaders of the Greater Israel Movement), forbids settlement in Israel's nature preserves by "foreigners," or Bedouins. Although Israeli Arabs are officially citizens of Israel, the term foreigner is applied to them nonetheless (Davis, 1979).

In the northern Negev and in the Galilee, the Green Patrol ensures that "foreigners" will not return to farm their land. The so-called foreigners are Bedouin living in the northern Negev, native inhabitants of the land dispossessed by foreigners. The Green Patrol, sons of veteran kibbutzim and moshavim, notorious for the brutality with which they keep Arab farmers from their land,

> ... brings in jeeps and lorries, mounts a whole herd of sheep on lorries, throws people out, collects the tents, takes them hundreds of kilometers south and leaves the families looking for their herds, contacting the police and finally paying enormous fines before they can get their herds back. (Davis, 1979, p. 16)

Seventy-five to 80% of Israel's water resources are used for high-production agriculture (Dillman, 1989, p. 47). Water sources include freshwater streams and rivers, only a few of which flow regularly; they include Lake Kinneret, the only freshwater lake in Israel, and reservoirs storing floodwater and treated wastewater. Sixty percent of water used is groundwater, "... that invisible underground sea which is recharged by rain that percolates through the pores of soil and in places moves into fractures of bedrock ... it surfaces at lakes, streams, rivers, the wetlands, ponds and the ocean" (Hynes, 1989, p. 77).

Chemical fertilizers, pesticides, seawater intrusion resulting from overpumping, domestic and industrial wastewater discharged without proper treatment into streams and *wadis* (channels through which water flows during the rainy season)—all contribute to the deterioration of groundwater quality. Toxic levels of nitrates from chemical fertilizers seep into the coastal aquifer. Overpumping of groundwater has led to seawater intrusion and increased salinity in wells. By the year 2000, according to an Israeli environmentalist, West Bank aquifers will be completely destroyed (Skutel, 1986).

Domestic wastewater, treated and stored in septic tanks and cesspools located above groundwater sources, highly toxic industrial pollutants that cannot be broken down by biological processes, the threat of oil pollution from storage tanks and transmission lines laid over the coastal aquifer—all continually reduce groundwater quality and, hence, threaten life. In a 1973 survey, 45% of wells did not meet recommended standards for drinking water (Whitman, 1988).

No comprehensive policy exists to prevent pesticide poisoning of food, water, soil, and air. In 1981, agribusiness utilized 17,661 tons of chemicals, including herbicides, fungicides, and insecticides (Whitman, 1988, p. 211). While the use of DDT has been banned, some Israeli farmers still use it. Residues in food, water, soil, and air introduce a regime of death through gradual if not immediate poisoning of organs and organisms necessary to life.

H. Patricia Hynes, an environmental engineer, traces the uses and consequences of pesticide poisoning in *The Recurring Silent Spring,* her feminist analysis of Rachel Carson's groundbreaking work, *Silent Spring.* Hynes emphasizes the connection that Carson makes between militarism and agribusiness:

> The habit of dominance and conquest, she said, drives man's intensive use of chemicals to eliminate the parts of nature which interfere with his progress.

She showed that war on people and war on nature employ the same weapons: nerve gases developed for World War II were used as pesticides in agriculture after the war. Likewise, herbicides developed for agriculture before the Vietnam War were used as defoliants in that war. The destruction of people and nature with chemical poisons constitutes the same failure to solve problems other than by force. (Hynes, 1989, p. 15)

In 1990, in a startling example of the use of pesticides as a political weapon, Israeli Jewish settlers damaged 150 olives trees in an Arab village by spraying them with chemicals. In September of 1990 alone, 792 trees were uprooted in the West Bank by settlers or by the army. Since the beginning of the intifada, 92,025 trees have been uprooted in retaliation for alleged stone throwing, or during house demolitions, road widening, or building of military checkpoints (Palestine Human Rights Information Center, 1990). The uprooting of trees as punishment has another significance. That the politics of race colonization and devastation of the land are interwoven is clarified by the statements of Menachim Begin in whose mind Palestinians exist as "two-legged vermin," and of Israeli Prime Minister Shamir describing Palestinians as "grasshoppers" (Said, 1989, p. 12).

Hynes points out:

. . . The insecticidal properties of certain synthesized compounds were discovered when they were being tested on insects for use in chemical warfare during World War II. When that war ended, the chemical industry declared war on insects and weeds and opened up a whole new market for chemical biocides. (Hynes, 1989, p. 74)

High levels of pesticides accumulating in the soil year after year are absorbed into the tissues of plants and insects (not just those targeted), disturbing the balance in nature necessary for soil fertility. Chemical synthetics cause cancer in animals and humans; their use in agriculture has been, since World War II, a major factor in the increase in environmental diseases from toxic substances (Hynes, 1989).

Hynes cites field studies confirming Carson's findings: " . . . the chemical method of insect control results in damage to natural insect controls and ultimately causes worse infestation and aggravated crop losses than were experienced before broad-scale, exclusive use of synthetic chemical pesticides" (Hynes, 1989, p. 109). The use of biocides in modern agribusiness:

. . . eliminates an abundant variety of plant and insect life, and thus many of nature's own mechanisms to resist disease and insect attack. Cultivating a single crop through vast acres creates a vulnerability to insect and weed problems. Biological control methods focus on the particular problem insect without harming other insects and without poisoning the web of life in which the insect lives. (Hynes, 1989, p. 111)

Most pesticides are not regulated in Israel, and testing of local produce is sporadic and voluntary (Whitman, 1988).

Hyne's documentation points to the deception inherent in the concept of permissible standards. Government agencies "regulating" pesticide levels allow for a slow level of poisoning in order not to disrupt economic policies supporting unlimited growth. Policies of the Ministry of Health, responsible for monitoring and testing of food products, support national goals of high-speed production for profit at the expense of health and longevity.

Negligent storage of pesticides is pervasive in Israel. Of the warehouses in the Beersheva region alone, 65% were in substandard condition in 1988. Storage of empty, inadequately cleaned pesticide containers next to food supplies is a serious health hazard (Whitman, 1988). Hynes points out that "Many of the major ecological disasters of the past two decades [Bhopal, Chernobyl, and the Rhine River] have occurred in the manufacture, storage, use, and disposal of pesticides or chemical compounds with deadly biocidal components" (Hynes, 1989, p. 13). Chemical fires at pesticide warehouses reflect inefficient licensing and managerial procedures and lack of knowledge and equipment to deal with chemically induced accidents (Whitman, 1988). Hyne's analysis underscores an observation of Rosalie Bertell, nuclear analyst and author of *No Immediate Danger: Prognosis for a Radioactive World*:

> Bertell observes that in the race to test and manufacture weapons in order to protect ourselves from outside enemies, polluted air, food and water become "enemies" within one's own country. (Hynes, 1989, p. 53)

It is not only the use of synthetic chemicals that threatens air, food, and water in Israel, but the weapons industry to which Bertell refers, particularly the nuclear arms buildup. Israel's enormous expenditure on arms puts modern technology to use in the service of perpetuating violence, rather than in the service of " . . . the development of peacetime economies and biophilic technologies" (Hynes, 1989, p. 54). Mordechai Vanunu, an Israeli and former technician at the Israeli plutonium extraction plant near the Negev town of Dimona, was charged with treason and sentenced to 18 years of isolation for disclosing the nuclear capabilities of the Israeli government, " . . . sufficient to build ten atomic bombs according to advanced specification" Israel has assembled " . . . at least 200 nuclear weapons of varying destructive power" (Cobban, 1988, p. 416). Nuclear, chemical, and biological weapons in the Middle East represent the ultimate consequence of phallocentric politics. From a feminist perspective, it is clear that the antinuclear movement must become a central focus of the peace movement.

The population most directly affected by the environmental and health hazards of a nuclear presence in the Negev are the Bedouin, who have cultivated that land for centuries. Disruption of the ecosystem and disruption of the ecology of interethnic relations, for example, the complementarity between nomadic and sedentary populations, are parallel developments. In order to control the Negev desert and the Arab population there, the Israeli government has instituted policies expropriating Bedouin lands and resettling Bedouins in closed areas. Settled tribes are easier to tax, to control, and to incorporate into plans for developing the national economy. Sedentarization of tribes has disrupted ancient reciprocity among pastoral and nomadic populations and urbanites who support one another's way of life through exchange of goods in a process often described as an ecological trilogy (Chatty, 1978).

The area around Dimona in the Negev has been targeted as a site of industrial development, with science-based and petrochemical factories and an airport, as well as intensive agriculture (Falah, 1989). To acquire the land, the government utilized the Ottoman Land Law of 1858 requiring official registration of lands, and the British legislation of 1921 prohibiting acquisition of state land through cultivation. In spite of documentation of taxes paid, the Bedouin have no legal claim to lands they have farmed for centuries. The Land Acquisitions Law of 1951 empowered the state to confiscate private lands for "urgent needs." In 1976, the government proposed to recognize 12.5% of Bedouin land claims, if ownership could be proved. Later recognition was given to 20% of the land claims. Thirty percent of the total claims were to be covered by compensation at 65% land value, and the remaining 50% of the land expropriated. Negotiations were suspended with the 1977 elections. In 1979, there were 3,200 registered cases of land disputes; in 1986, 5,944 Bedouin houses considered illegal, were scheduled for demolition (Falah, 1989).

Seven Bedouin townships have been planned, with four currently inhabited. Bedouins are allowed to lease, but not to own land. The state can enter at any time for any reason, and the Bedouin have no legal way to oppose changes in the size or boundaries of their lots (Falah, 1989). Prohibited from pursuing agriculture or animal husbandry, the Bedouin have been forced into low-paying jobs, or are unemployed. The townships lack adequate infrastructures, electricity, roads, telephone connections, and health services.

Anthropologist Smadar Lavie writes about the effects of occupation, both by the Israelis and by the Egyptians, on the Mzeina Bedouin of the South Sinai desert (Lavie, 1990). The Israelis utilize and strain customary gender relations as they carry out the occupation. For example, respecting customary practices, soldiers are forbidden to enter Bedouin houses when no man is present. But when bulldozer spare parts disappear, Israelis break into and search houses. Bedouins speculate that the military governor assumed that the thieves would have hidden the parts in houses where the men would be away, so that the soldiers would not enter. In another example, fathers attempt to form alliances based on economic security in the face of shifting geo-political developments, making women more vulnerable to unwanted marriages (Lavie, 1990).

Bedouin men appointed as local officials by the military governor act as a conduit for civil or military projects affecting the entire community. They supplement insufficient earnings from this "job" with migrant labor work and are often absent for days at a time (Lavie, 1990). Bedouin women, led by the "old women," violate mores governing gender roles as they deal with officials, tourists, and other kinds of intruders. In the face of foreign rule, Bedouin women attempt to turn exploitation to their advantage. They host tours into their inner yards, allow tourists to take their pictures, and demonstrate traditional cooking:

> My husband calls me a prostitute when I let tourists in and show them things from our old ways of life. He hit me on my back once for it. But when it comes to the tourists' money, he spends it without a qualm. (Quoted in Lavie, 1990, p. 189)

A post-menopausal woman, called al-'Ajuz, or the old woman, has greater latitude in confronting military and other intruders because she is no longer restricted by prohibitions on her actions. Loss of sexual status (reproductive status) allows her more freedom. In this context old women have been able to trade favors, benefiting their communities. Lavie notes that old age may have always been a liberation from traditional women's roles (Lavie, 1990). But a woman's freedom at the end of her life is bittersweet, particularly in the context of foreign occupation, where she must substitute one set of confining mores for another.

CONCLUSION

1948. The Israeli newspaper *Haaretz* reported that the sexual offenses plaguing the country were " . . . among the manifestations of demoralization caused by war among both winners and losers to the same degree" (Segev, 1986, pp. xvi, xvii). During those same months Israeli Prime Minister, David Ben-Gurion " . . . had been informed of murderous acts—or 'slaughter' as he put it—and rape, which were committed by Israeli soldiers. Such reports intensified the panic and flight of the Arabs" (Segev, 1986, p. 26). Minister of Agriculture Aharon Cizling, his entire being shaken because " . . . now Jews too have behaved like Nazis . . . " insisted on concealing these actions, and investigation of them, from the public (Segev, 1986, p. 26). Neither the sexual offenses committed against Jewish women in Israel, nor the rape and murder of indigenous Palestinian women, would be revealed to the world: neither would be considered cause for concern.

Zionist women and indigenous Palestinian women had, however, cause for concern, and their concerns crossed over nationalist boundaries. In fact, the cause of their common concerns had and continues to have a locus in nationalist ideology supporting strategies for control of natural resources and for reduction of women to natural resources to be exploited and mined.

The relation of women and land is exemplified in the plight of Palestinian

women who have been dispossessed of their land through historical developments of the 18th and 19th centuries, culminating in the institutionalization
of the Zionist state of Israel. Zionist women who emigrated to Palestine believed in the redemption of land and labor as the vehicle for and answer to
Jewish persecution and instability. The nationalist solution promising reclamation of land isolates women who, on either side of the nationalist debate
(colonizer or colonized), become the ground upon which the flag is staked.

The experience of Zionist women and Palestinian women in the early years
of the Israeli state depended upon association with nationalist movements,
race, or racial formations as instituted by the practices of the state, class affiliation, and sex-class status, that is whether or not a woman was married, single, divorced, heterosexual, or lesbian. Whatever her affiliation—Jewish,
Muslim, Christian—the fact that a woman globally is " . . . reified and degraded
for the utilitarian value she represents as a sex commodity . . . " (Barry, 1979,
p. 218) is institutionalization of sex, race, and class hierarchy in the new state.

Journalist Leslie Hazelton, analyzing Zionist ideology as supporting male
aggression, notes that the verb in Hebrew meaning "to take up arms" also
means "to have sexual intercourse" (Hazelton, 1977, p. 96). The war against
women, depletion of the earth's resources, and destruction of the ecosystem
are perpetrated by ideologies supporting male rule and kept in place through
what Barry describes as sex colonization.

Sex colonization ensures women's loyalty to men and to the male state.
Women's bodies are colonized through strategies of co-optation, enforced dependence, and sexual slavery, which require a wide range of alliances and
cooperation among men. The male state not only profits from colonization
of women, its existence depends upon it. The experiences of Zionist women
in pre-state Palestine and of Palestinian women under the Israeli state within
and outside of the green line illustrate the connection between nationalist-
militarist ideology, the formation of the male state, and the traffic in and
"seasoning" of women.

Zionist women seeking equality as well as freedom from oppression as
Jews by emigrating to Palestine, were immediately taught what equality means
for women. The overriding strategy of the male-dominated Zionist labor movement was to put them in their place. Confined to the domestic sphere, refused entry into the skilled labor market, refused access to learning new skills,
women were, in fact, starved into submission. Zionist men warned that if
women worked in the field with men (particularly, of course, Arab men), they
would lose their honor. Instead they put them out on the streets where they
were forced to utilize pimps to acquire work in kitchens, where their employers harassed and sometimes raped them. Women had no choice but to
stay in situations where they were humiliated, degraded, utilized as cheap
labor, and sexually used. The creators of the Zionist state, like those of all
modern states, utilized and/or condoned the traffic in women, as a necessary

condition for the formation of the state. National and increasingly corporate labor, exemplified by the Histadrut (Jewish Federation of Labor Unions), relied on women as unpaid and cheap laborers within and outside the home. Economic and physical coercion ensured that they would fall into place.

In the face of these harsh and discouraging conditions, Zionist women made valiant efforts to acquire skills, participate in the formation of the state, and thus to survive. Through the support of an international network of women's organizations, they were able to establish training farms and collectives for women. Associations of women outside and within Palestine saved the lives of countless numbers of women.

That women in the Israeli state suffer from confinement to the home, lower wages, fewer educational and job opportunities, marginalization in politics, violence within and outside the home, makes it clear that the Working Women's Movement was not able to significantly alter the situation of women. Two interconnected factors affected this outcome. First, the majority of women in the movement resisted defining themselves " . . . as engaged in a struggle against male oppression" (Izraeli, 1981, p. 113). The incorporation of the Working Women's Movement into the Histadrut where the Women Workers' Council was removed from its constituency, and where ultimately the feminist movement became " . . . the largest voluntary social service and, later, welfare organization in the Yishuv . . . helped to perpetuate the myth of equality and to discourage the emergence of alternative definitions around which women could organize" (Izraeli, 1981, p. 114).

Second, it was not only, as Daphne Izraeli maintains, that identification with a larger movement constrained the development of feminist ideology, but also that the larger movement was itself antifeminist. The failure of Zionist women to identify the antifeminism of nationalism was connected to their failure to connect their situation to that of Palestinians in general, and to Palestinian women in particular.

That Zionist women in pre-state Palestine viewed Arabs as their enemy was a function of their inability to recognize the antifeminism of Zionist ideology. Zionist women, in raising guns against Arabs, were defeating their own cause. They were supporting the demonization of the "other" and participating in expropriation of the earth justifying male rule. Demonization of the other, the biological determinism of racism and misogyny, had been the justification for vilification of Jews for centuries.

The consequences are lived out in the structure, practices, and day-to-day life of women and men in the Israeli state and in the occupied territories. Holocaust pornography brings together the demonization of race and sex. Jewish men participate in ideologies that support their own destruction. "In pornography women are portrayed as supersexed beings who will devour or destroy men . . . They are the fantasy of men's fear and loathing of women and as such must be subdued; sexual aggression and violence are the means to bring them under control" (Barry, 1979, p. 196). Arabs are also portrayed as supersexed beings who will devour or destroy; sexual aggression and violence are the means to bring them under control. Racism is a feminist issue. Colonization of women and of the earth can only lead to the hopelessness of the "final solution."

In 1980, Samar Hawash and other Palestinian women split off from the Nablus Seamsters Union, formed in 1958, to create a separate unit for women. Samar was a member of the Administrative Committee of the Palestinian Working Women's Committees organizing women in the occupied territories. Women in workshops in Jerusalem earning one-third what men earned listened to arguments familiar to Zionist women attempting to enter the labor force: men produce more than women, men have more experience:

> Often when we visit sewing workshops, owners will tell us that women produce less than men, and they usually cite biological reasons. It is ridiculous, because in the villages women are working in the fields while men sit unemployed in the village coffee house drinking tea. Women get lower wages because they are seen as inferior. (Hilterman, 1987, p. 8)

Palestinian women have developed a range of strategies to address their situation as women. Some advocate increased participation of women in the male-controlled unions; others advocate separate committees for women. The Nablus Union of Working Women, facing indifference of the male leadership, must cope at the same time with the reluctance of women to join them, as well as the difficulties encountered by women who would like to join them. For many women, travel is difficult, family pressures may prohibit leaving the home for meetings, and if working outside the home, they may not have the time or energy for organizing. Nonetheless, activists encouraged and created associations of women in sewing classes, for example, where women can discuss their situations. As one organizer of the Palestinian Women's Committees explained: "A woman cannot fight the occupation if she is not even convinced that she has rights, for example the right to leave the house" (Hilterman, 1987, p. 8).

When Palestinian women leave their houses, they confront sex colonization outside the home: on their way to work some will be shot and many will be arrested and detained in prison where they will be sexually humiliated. Furthermore, most male-dominated unions, struggling to survive, have been shut down under Israeli occupation. The destruction of the fragile economic infrastructure of Palestinian society by the Zionist state ensures male hegemony along lines of race and class, reinforcing the sex-class system from which Palestinian women have labored to emerge. Intimidation of Palestinian men is accomplished through the sexual brutalization of Palestinian women.

Some Zionist women attempted to address racism as a feminist issue. In pre-state Palestine, for example, some made connections between their plight and that of Arab workers. But Zionist officials continually thwarted their efforts. Some Ashkenazi Zionist women decried the utilization of Oriental Jewish women to make their lives easier. They condemned the separation of women that racism is. The Zionist strategy of divide and conquer, utilized to subdue and control the Palestinian population and to thwart all attempts at rapprochement between men across ethnic-racial boundaries, is a feminist issue.

The sexual politics of nationalist movements polarizing East and West set women of the West against women of the East, facilitating the exploitation of both. But the sexual mores prescribing women's status, roles, possibilities, whether those women are, for example, Jewish or Muslim, are linked. Men are men because they are honorable: their honor is sexual domination and control of women. For both, marriage is the locus of that control:

> Where in the Arab world a woman may be murdered in the most extreme acts of honor, in the West murder of women in snuff films (where women are actually murdered in the climax of sexual pleasure) represents the most extreme condition of the act of male sexual freedom. (Barry, 1979, p. 196)

Nationalist movements encourage women to identify with men and male-based ideology and politics as a way of separating themselves from the struggles and from the degradation and from the daily violence perpetrated against women.

Jewish and Palestinian women suffering sexual abuse by fathers, brothers, and other male relatives in the home, suffering wife beating, suffering marital rape, forced by social mores and/or by the state into staying in life-threatening situations, thrown out into the streets where they are at the mercy of other men, become silent actors hidden from one another, shadows of each other's destinies.

That both Zionist and Palestinian nationalist movements have responded to autonomous women's movements as a threat tells us about the kinds of social organization both movements represent, implement, and/or intend to implement. But Israeli and Palestinian women involved in grass-roots and official nationalist movements continue to form separate women's organizations, some attempting to address occupation as a feminist issue. The power of women's associations that have for centuries supported women's survival in the Middle East may prove to be the bridge, not only between Jew and Arab but also to the 21st century.

Epilogue

... Therefore it is essential that our categories and concepts are such that they help us to transcend capitalist patriarchy and help us construct a reality in which neither women, men, nor nature are exploited and destroyed. But this presupposes that we understand that women's oppression today is part and parcel of capitalist (or socialist) patriarchal *production relations,* of the paradigm of ever-increasing growth, of ever-increasing forces of production, of unlimited exploitation of nature, of unlimited production of commodities, ever-expanding markets and never-ending accumulation of dead capital. (Mies, 1986, p. 23)

... State power, embodied in law, exists throughout society as male power at the same time as the power of men over women throughout society is organized as the power of the state. (MacKinnon, 1989, p. 170)

Sunday, October 21, 1990. Early evening. I turn on the radio to catch the news. This is what I hear. An Israeli woman soldier, 18 years old, was stabbed to death, along with a 43-year-old gardener and a 29-year-old policeman who tried to help. The Palestinian accused of the crimes is 19 years old. He claims he was seeking revenge for the massacre of 22 Palestinians by the Israeli army at Al-Aska mosque two weeks earlier. What will be the response of Jews and others in North America, seeking an end to this cruel spiral of violence, murder, revenge, murder, revenge? What will be the response of Israelis and Palestinians across a spectrum of political positions?

Thursday, August 2, 1990. National Palace Hotel, East Jerusalem. Women and Peace, including Women in Black, Shani, Women's Organization for Political Prisoners, the Women's Network (Reshet, formed after the Brussels conference), Palestinian women's organizations from the territories and independent Palestinian women, make their way into the room. The purpose of the meeting, run jointly by women from within and outside of the green line, is to plan an International Peace Conference, based on a feminist model, for negotiation of the Israeli-Palestinian conflict. Slogans for the Conference are presented: "Down with the occupation," "Two states for Two People," "Right of Return." A woman notes that none of these slogans has the word "woman" in it. Another says that the slogan "Feminist Agenda for Two States" provides for this. Someone points out that the conference's title is "Women Go for

Peace." At the end of the day, in an atmosphere of hope and conviction, the women walk out into the streets of their battle-torn land. These meetings represent a new level of participation of Palestinian and Israeli women in the ongoing attempt to develop a feminist analysis of the nationalist struggle ravaging Israel–Palestine.

The knowledge that women as a class have common cause, and that nationalism and the exploitation of women, of nature, of the "colonies" are inextricably interlinked, is the beginning of breaking the spiral of violence. Facing the actual condition of women, the interdependence of the privilege of elite women and the deprivation of women of the underclasses, facing what women must do to secure privilege and to survive in the underclasses, exposes the truth that " . . . only the freedom of all women protects any women" (Dworkin, 1983, p. 231). The process of taking control over our lives can illuminate new possibilities for social organization based on ecological principles of relating to and surviving on this earth.

Feminist analysis asks the critical question that is so often ignored—what are the consequences of androcentric historical developments for women? The exodus of the Palestinian population in 1948, for example, creating a refugee population in other countries of the Middle East, is particularly hazardous for women within those countries who are subject to an increased demand for sexual services. Androcentric double-speak condemns Israeli women from Arab countries for having too many children, while supporting conditions ensuring that they will provide enough children to supply the cheap labor force. Those who utilize the Holocaust as a justification and rationale for Jewish hegemony in Palestine ignore the crucial link between genocide of the Jews and hatred of women. Rivalry between groups of men for the monopoly over sexual prowess, the sexualization of power, is at the core of what women and despised races suffer. In this context, what equality is for women in the male state is acceptance of her "inferiority"; women are of social worth only as what men construct women to be. The state institutionalizes and protects male control of women's bodies, whether in the home, in the streets, or in the workplace. An Israeli soldier puts it this way:

> . . . We were standing there at a checkpoint. Along came a good-looking woman, well dressed and proud, in a way that succeeded in making my commander nervous. Although he usually exhibited extraordinary control and sensitivity, he suddenly became very angry, and got into the "taming of the shrew" syndrome. Her pride was interpreted as a personal assault against us. The fact that they are standing on their legs without being afraid seems like a revolt against us. It is necessary to humiliate them, not because we are sadists, but to make it clear who is the adult and who the child. It is not good that there is such confusion and the pyramid must be re-erected on its foundation. Such a woman, walking proudly, tears down the whole system. (Palestine Human Rights Information Center, 1990, p. 102).

The state is male power over women, ensuring their exclusion from the state polity:

In 1968, I worked during the elections for the Likud—the National Right Party—and voted for them. Having no idea and consciousness of what I was doing, I reacted swiftly to the call that Israel needs a strong man, Menachim Begin, to restore the political situation. An incident in the office of one of the heads of the Herut Party didn't change my mind. Being alone in the office with him exposed me to sexual harassment: only my physical insistence saved me from being raped. Later on he served as a Minister in the government. Now he is in a key position in the Knesset. (Shalom, 1990)

These are the words of a lesbian-feminist political activist, a Sephardi Israeli who did eventually change her political position. They expose what women who join political movements from right to left are up against—whether in the form of physical or verbal assault of their "sexuality." In the face of this threat:

The social politics in Israel in the early seventies and the post Yom-Kippur war had shifted my mind. That time I was working in Jerusalem University where the political activities of the students were at a height. Having friends from the so called left and knowing some in the non-Zionist radical left exposed me to a whole new area. It was the first time in my life that I opened my mind and was able to criticize. In my youth, I had a very traditional closed education in an Alliance girls' school where they taught women to obey. Having a patriarchal-traditional home, just strengthened this education.

In 1980 when I joined the Women's Center in Jerusalem and at the same time I came out as a lesbian, I exposed myself to feminism, where I found the most just reply to many questions I've asked myself then about social and national relations. It was such a relief to my oppression as a woman. *Being stimulated by other women and the new culture of women brought me to act out and take responsibilities and actions to change this world.* (Shalom, 1990) (Emphasis mine)

The media in North America do not report that women—Israeli citizens, Jewish, Muslim, Christian, and others, as well as Palestinian women who are "stateless"—are changing their minds. It takes work and commitment, as women encourage one another, addressing fears, misconceptions, taking risks, face to face. Fighting against illegal laws designed to thwart their efforts, Women in Black won the right to wear buttons with two flags, Palestinian and Israeli, later adopted by Peace Now, the mainstream of the movement. How women conduct themselves, the issues that women bring up, can become a model for the general peace movement (Shalom, 1990).

Among those women, lesbians struggle against silencing outside of and within the peace movement. The myth of the free speech of women is nowhere more evident than in the suppression of lesbian speech and lesbian recognition, as well as lesbian analysis. At the December 1988 conference, "Empowerment of Jewish Women," a lesbian who thanked lesbians for their contribution to the conference met with both encouragement and disapproval. Suppression of lesbians in the peace movement is another form of lesbian exploitation. The power of the peace movement to effect change depends upon addressing social and economic terrorism directed against lesbians. The struggles of lesbians for economic survival, physical safety, and recognition, clarify the tenacity with which the male state defends its right to power over women.

Critical to lesbian survival, associations among lesbians have the potential for analysis of and action against phallocentrism, whether in the form of exploitation of women, of the earth, or of despised races. Silencing and suppression of lesbians ensures the separation of women, of women's associations intra- and intercommunally, demanded by the male state:

> Fat'ma smiles. She speaks in a halting but sound English. "I acknowledge it not to be a popular subject," she says, "but we do exist. I do not imagine me." She tells me an Arab proverb I have heard before: "When a woman loves a woman, it brings no shame to her father and no swelling to her belly." She adds dryly, "This is not the favorite proverb of Arab men." She specifically asks that I tell the women I write to and for that she exists. Not as openly as she would like, she murmurs, then gives me a long look. "But I was fortunate to study for one year, when I was younger, at university in your Colorado. It was not very open or acceptable there, either. Is it so very different for a lesbian woman anywhere?" (Morgan, 1989, p. 264).

Breaking down the isolation of women from women that characterizes women's lives globally, European, Israeli, and Palestinian women came together on December 29, 1989. Women Go for Peace held a conference, a vigil in which 3,000 women participated and a historic march of 6,000 women. On December 30, a legal demonstration of thousands forming a chain around the walls of the Old City suddenly turned into a lesson in brutality for many Israelis and others who had not yet been subjected to tactics of the police "anti-terrorist unit":

> A few minutes before the demonstration was due to end, some Palestinians at Herod's Gate raised on their shoulders a seven-year-old girl, who was holding a Peace Now poster and was dressed in a camouflage uniform like the ones worn by the PLO fighters. The police officer on the spot regarded this as a final proof that the demonstration is "in support of anti-Israeli terrorism," and ordered his men to charge. Within seconds, the whole two kilometer stretch between Damascus and Herod's Gates became the scene of total police rampage; police horsemen galloped and their clubs landed on heads; heavy tear gas clouds filled the air; fleeing demonstrators were shot in the back with "plastic" bullets. The police's "anti-terrorist unit" busily smashed the cameras of press photographers and beat them up; several Knesset members were beaten as well. Some Italian demonstrators fled into the nearby "Pilgrim's Palace" Hotel, followed by the police's relentless water cannon; strong water spouts broke the hotel windows, and one of the flying glass splinters tore out the right eye of 40-year-old Maritza Manno. The police did not rest until all demonstrators had escaped—except for the dozens who were either detained or hospitalized. ("Time for Tear Gas," 1990, p. 11)

Refusing to be daunted, on the morning of May 20, 1990, as news broke out of the massacre of Gazan day laborers in Rishon le-Tzion, peace activists took to the streets, refusing to wait five days for a police permit. University lecturers stopped their lectures, Jewish and Arab trade unionists held a rally, Israeli solidarity delegations visited Palestinian leaders on hunger strike ("Protests and Dilemmas," 1990). These activities are not unusual. They are the everyday work of a peace movement that grows while its invisibility in the media silences. Hundreds of Druze, conscientious objectors, fill Israeli military prisons. Youth Against Occupation connects the struggle of youth for their rights ("In the schools, we work to create alternative student councils, which will really fight for their constituents rather than be the principal's rubber stamp") with the struggles of Palestinians under occupation (Wagner, 1990, p. 12). As early as 1945, before the official founding of the state of Israel, a peace group, International Movement of Conscientious Objectors, began the work of providing a site for resistance to militarism. One aspect of their work is to inform Israeli women of their legal right to exemption from military service on the grounds of conscience.

In 1982, some Israeli men formed an organization, Yesh Gvul (There is a Limit) to support resistance to serving in the Israel–Lebanon war. "For the first time, Israeli patriots questioned the hitherto unchallenged motives of the army and war. Terms like 'security' and 'self-defense' formerly unquestioningly accepted, were examined and criticised" ("Conscientious Objection in Israel," 1990, p. 6). Since the outbreak of the intifada, Yesh Gvul has focused its resistance on occupation of the West Bank and Gaza. One hundred and eleven objectionists have served prison sentences. Many return to prison two and three times, rather than serve in an occupation they do not support. Over 1,500 men and women have signed Yesh Gvul petitions. One spokesman for Yesh Gvul put it this way: "We provide a moral political alternative to the traditional model of blindly following and obeying orders" ("Conscientious Objection," 1990, p. 6). Another, while in prison, wrote this:

> Discussion about who is right is at this minute irrelevant. There are absolute situations, situations which nothing in the world can make relative. An armed soldier confronting a child is such an absolute situation, and what led to that situation, what it is all about and who is in the right does not affect the unequivocal wrongness of the situation . . . Anyone who today agrees to serve in the Occupied Territories in the role of the occupier may find himself in such a situation, even against his will . . . Let the exceptional people talk about the nation. Common mortals and rank and file soldiers should attend each to one's own conscience. ("Conscientious Objection," 1990, p. 7)

All these movements help to create an environment conducive to social-political reorganization. They represent the discomfort, and, at times, the rebellion of men who experience the down side of the dynamic of dominance and subordination. But they do not address the sexualization of power from which that dynamic unfolds, and from which men continue to profit.

Can a nationalist resistance movement become a site for exposing and challenging violence against women and against the earth embedded in nationalism itself? Can a "people's" revolution be a liberatory movement for women? What are we asking for when we ask for peace and justice in the Middle East?

Asking these questions shifts the focus of political discourse and political struggle. The concepts of equality, peace, and justice are rooted in a hierarchical, dualistic framework of polar opposites which is in turn rooted in the historical fact of male power and phallocentric politics. Sexism, racism, repression, are women's experience of equality. Our view of the Israeli-Palestinian conflict is shaped by social-political constructions of sex, race, and class.

The Israeli-Palestinian struggle is to clear away misconceptions, lies, and strategies of colonization disrupting the ecosystem, as well as to clear away exploitative race/sex/class relations continued in the era of the Israeli state. With a feminist praxis, this struggle can become liberatory.

References

INTRODUCTION

Abbott, Nabia. (1941). Pre-Islamic Arab queens. *The American Journal of Semitic Languages and Literatures, 58*(1), 1–22.

Baron, Salo. (1983). *A social and religious history of the Jews* (Vol. 18). New York: Columbia University Press.

Barthes, Roland. (1975). *The pleasure of the text,* quoted in Phillip Wexler, Structure, text and subject: A critical sociology of school knowledge. In Michael W. Apple (Ed.), *Cultural and economic reproduction in education.* London: Routledge and Kegan Paul.

Beinin, Joel. (1989). From Land Day to Peace Day . . . and beyond. In Zacharay Lockman & Joel Beinin (Eds.), *Intifada: The Palestinian uprising against Israeli occupation.* Boston: South End Press.

Boullata, Peter. (1989). Intifada. In Zachary Lockman & Joel Beinin (Eds.), *Intifada: The Palestinian uprising against Israeli occupation.* Boston: South End Press.

Bowerstock, G. W. (1988). Palestine: Ancient history and modern politics. In Edward Said & Christopher Hitchens (Eds.), *Blaming the victims.* London: Verso.

Cutler, Allan, & Cutler, Helen. (1986). *The Jew as ally of the Muslim: Medieval roots of anti-Semitism.* Notre Dame, IN: University of Notre Dame Press.

Dworkin, Andrea. (1983). *Right-wing women.* New York: Perigree Books, Putnam's Publishing Group.

Goldberg, Harriet. (1979). Two parallel medieval commonplaces: Antifeminism and anti-semitism in the Hispanic literary tradition. In P. E. Szarmach (Ed.), *Aspects of Jewish culture in the Middle Ages.* Albany: State University of New York Press.

Griswold, William J., with Ayad al-Qazzaz. (1975). *The image of the Middle East in secondary school textbooks.* Tucson, AZ: Middle East Studies Association of North America.

Hazelton, Leslie. (1977). *Israeli women: The reality behind the myth.* New York: Simon & Schuster.

Hoagland, Sarah Lucia. (1988). *Lesbian ethics.* Palo Alto, CA: Institute of Lesbian Studies.

Hodgson, Marshall. (1974). *The venture of Islam* (Vol. 1). Chicago: University of Chicago Press.

Hynes, H. Patricia. (1989). *The recurring silent spring.* Elmsford, NY: Pergamon Press.

Lerner, Gerda. (1986). The origin of prostitution in ancient Mesopotamia. *Signs, 2*(2), 237–254.

March 8th—International Women's Day: A salute to Palestinian women. (1989, March). *Palestine Aid Society, 9*(3), 1.

Merchant, Carolyn. (1980). *The death of nature—Women, ecology and the scientific revolution.* San Francisco: Harper & Row.

Mies, Maria. (1986). *Patriarchy and accumulation on a world scale: Women in the international divison of labour.* London: Zed Books.

Mies, Maria, Bennholdt-Thomas, Veronika, & Von Werlhof, Claudia. (1988). *Women: The last colony.* London: Zed Books.

Morgan, Robin. (1989). *The demon lover: On the sexuality of terrorism.* New York: W. W. Norton.

Porath, Y. (1975). *The emergence of the Palestinian-Arab national movement, 1918–1929.* London: Frank Cass.

Raymond, Janice G. (1986). *A passion for friends: Toward a philosophy of female affection.* Boston: Beacon Press.

Reuther, Rosemary R., & Reuther, Herman J. (1989). *The wrath of Jonah—The crisis of religious nationalism in the Israeli-Palestinian conflict.* San Francisco: Harper & Row.

Said, Edward. (1988, September/October). Identity, negation and violence. *New Left Review, 171,* 47–69.

Shahak, Israel. (1989, April-June). History remembered, history distorted, history denied. *Race and Class, 30*(4), 80–86.

Terry, Janice C. (1985). *Mistaken identity: Arab stereotypes in popular writing.* Washington, DC: American Arab Affairs Council.

CHAPTER 1: THE INTIFADA

American-Israeli Civil Liberties Coalition, Inc. [newsletter]. (1990, Summer). B'tselem. *10*(2), 5.

Antonelli, Judith. (1987, April). Analyst decries pornographic images in Israeli mass media. *The Jewish Advocate,* p. 1.

Antonious, George. (1946). *The Arab awakening.* New York: Putnam Press.

Antonious, Soroya. (1980). Prisoners For Palestine: A list of women political prisoners. *Journal of Palestine Studies, 9*(3), 29–80.

Beinin, Joel. (1989). From Land Day to Peace Day . . . and beyond. In Zachary Lockman & Joel Beinin (Eds.), *Intifada: The Palestinian uprising against Israeli occupation.* Boston: South End Press.

Brinkley, Joel. (1990, September 23). For Israelis, appeal of occupied territories grows. *New York Times,* p. 6.

Chomsky, Noam. (1990). The art of evasion—Diplomacy in the Middle East. In *Occupation and Resistance.* New York: The Alternative Museum.

Cossali, Paul, & Robson, Clive. (1986). *Stateless in Gaza.* London: Zed Books.

Cox, Sophie. (1984). Land before honour. *Spare Rib, 139,* 26–28.

Davis, Uri. (1977). *Israel, Utopia incorporated: A study of class, state and corporate kin control.* London: Zed Books.

Dworkin, Andrea. (1989). *Pornography: Men possessing women.* New York: E. P. Dutton.

Fishman, Alex. (1989, June/July). The Palestinian woman and the Intifada. *New Outlook, 32*(6/7), 9–11.

Galilee, Lily. (1989, June/July). Rendezvous in Brussels. *New Outlook, 32*(6/7), 27–29.

Giacaman, Rita, & Johnson, Penny. (1989). Building barricades and breaking barriers. In Zachary Lockman & Joel Beinin (Eds.), *Intifada: The Palestinian uprising against Israeli occupation.* Boston: South End Press.

Haddad, Yvonne. (1980). Palestinian women: Patterns of legitimation and domination. In Khalil Nakhleh & Elia Zureik (Eds.), *Sociology of the Palestinians.* New York: St. Martin's Press.

Hazelton, Leslie. (1977). *Israeli women: The reality behind the myth.* New York: Simon & Schuster.

Hilal, Jamil. (1977, Winter). Class transition in the West Bank and Gaza. *Journal of Palestine Studies, 6*(2), 67–179.

Hourani, Albert H. (1946). *Syria and Lebanon*. London: Oxford University Press.

Khouri, Ibtihaj. (1990, July). "I laid a rose on my husband's grave" (An Arab Woman in Black). *Challenge*, pp. 10–12.

Lempert, Leslie I. (1990, Summer). Update on the Intifada. *American-Israeli Civil Liberties Coalition, Inc.* [newsletter], *10*(2), 3.

Lipman, Beita. (1988). *Israel: The embattled land—Jewish and Palestinian women talk about their lives*. London: Pandora.

Mansour, Lina, & Giacaman, Rita. (1984, March). The West Bank women's movement. *Off Our Backs, 16*(3), 7.

Ma'oz, Moshe. (1984). *Palestinian leadership on the West Bank— The changing role of the Arab mayors under Jordan and Israel*. London: Frank Cass.

Mies, Maria. (1988). Capitalist development and subsistence production: Rural women in India. In Maria Mies, Veronika Bennholdt-Thompsen, & Claudia Von Werlhof (Eds.), *Women: The last colony*. London: Zed Books.

Morgan, Robin. (1989). *The demon lover: On the sexuality of terrorism*. New York: W. W. Norton.

Najjab, Salwa. (1989, April). *Notes on women and health in occupied Palestine*. Unpublished paper.

Ostrowitz, Rachel. (1989, June/July). Dangerous women: The Israeli women's peace movement. *New Outlook*, pp. 14–15.

The Other Israel. (1986, 1987, 1988, 1989, 1990). [Newsletter of the Israeli Council for Israeli-Palestinian Peace, Herzl Schubert, Fd.]. Tel-Aviv, Israel.

Palestine—A study of Jewish, Arab and British policies (Vol. 1). (1947). Published for the ESCO Foundation for Palestine, Inc. New Haven, CT: Yale University Press.

Palestine Human Rights Information Center. (1990, September). Data base project on Palestinian human rights. *Human Rights Update, 3,* 10.

Palestinian Federation of Women's Action Committees in the Occupied Territories. (1988). *The program and internal platform of the Palestinian Federation of Women's Action Committees in the Occupied Territories*. P.O. Box 51284, Jerusalem.

Palestinian Federation of Women's Action Committees, West Bank and Gaza Strip. (1989, December). *Newsletter*, p. 4.

Peteet, Julie. (1986, January/February). Women and the Palestinian movement—No going back? *Middle East Report*, 21–24.

Raymond, Janice. (1989, May 25). To end violence, women must be seen as humans. *Greenfield Recorder*, p. 8.

Rockwell, Susan. (1985, Winter). Palestinian women workers in the Israeli-Occupied Gaza Strip. *Journal of Palestine Studies, 14*(2), 114–136.

Roy, Sarah. (1987, Autumn). The Gaza Strip: A case of economic de-development. *Journal of Palestine Studies, 17*(1), 56–88.

Sabbagh, Suha. (1990, April/May). Yassar Arafat on the role of Palestinian women. *Return*, 9–11.

Sayigh, Rosemary. (1983). Encounters with Palestinian women under occupation. In Nasseer H. Aruri (Ed.), *Occupation: Israel over Palestine*. Belmont, MA: Association of Arab American University Graduates.

Sayigh, Rosemary. (1985, Spring). The Mukhabarat state: A Palestinian woman's testimony. *Journal of Palestine Studies, 14*(3), 18–31.

Smith, Barbara. (1990, November 7). Jogger rape: Ask a black feminist. *The Guardian*, p. 18.

Union of Palestinian Medical Relief Committees. (1988). *Health professionals united to save Palestinians under occupation fact sheet*.

Women and Peace, Women's Peace Movement. (1988, June). *Fact sheet*. P.O. Box 61128, Jerusalem.

Women and peace. (1989, June/July). *New Outlook,* 30–33.

Women for Support of Political Prisoners—Jerusalem. (1989). *Objectives and activities.* P.O. Box 31811, Tel Aviv.

Women's Organization for Political Prisoners. (1989: March, May, June, August). [Newsletter]. P.O. Box 31811, Tel Aviv.

Yuval-Davis, Nira. (1989). National reproduction and "the demographic race" in Israel. In Nira Yuval-Davis & Floya Anthias (Eds.), *Woman—Nation—State.* New York: St. Martin's Press.

CHAPTER 2: WOMEN SUPPORTING WOMEN'S SURVIVAL

Abbott, Nabia. (1941). Pre-Islamic queens. *The American Journal of Semitic Languages and Literatures, 58*(1), 1–22.

Abbott, Nabia. (1941). Women and the state on the eve of Islam. *The American Journal of Semitic Languages and Literatures, 58*(3), 259–284.

Abbott, Nabia. (1942). *Aishah, the beloved of Mohammad.* Chicago: University of Chicago Press.

Adler, Rachel. (1977). A mother in Israel: Aspects of the mother role in Jewish myth. In Rita M. Gross (Ed.), *Beyond androcentrism: New essays in women and religion.* Missoula, MT: Scholars Press.

Ahmed, Leila. (1986). Women and the advent of Islam. *Signs, 2*(4), 665–690.

Ayalon, David. (1979). *The Mamluk military society.* London: Galliard.

Baron, Salo. (1943). *A social and religious history of the Jews* (Vol. 3). Philadelphia: The Jewish Publication Society of America.

Braude, Benjamin, & Lewis, Bernard. (Eds.). (1982). *Christians and Jews in the Ottoman Empire: The functioning of a plural society* (Vols. 1–2). New York: Holmes & Meier.

Beeston, A. F. L. (1952). The so-called Harlots of Hadramaut. *Oriens, 5,* 16–22.

Brooten, Bernadette J. (1982). *Women leaders in the ancient synagogue.* Chico, CA: Scholars Press.

Carella, Michael J., & Sheres, Ita. (1988). Hebraic monotheism: The evolving belief, the enduring attitude. *Judaism, 37*(2), 229–239.

Davis, Fannie. (1986). *The Ottoman lady: A social history from 1718 to 1918.* Westport, CT.: Greenwood Press.

Dengler, Ian. (1978). Turkish women in the Ottoman Empire: The classical age. In Lois Beck & Nikki Keddie (Eds), *Women in the Muslim world.* Cambridge, MA: Harvard University Press.

Deshen, Shlomo, & Shokeid, Moshe. (1982). *Distant relations: Ethnicity and politics among Arabs and North African Jews in Israel.* New York: Praeger.

Deshen, Shlomo, & Zenner, Walter. (1982). *Jewish societies in the Middle East.* Washington, DC: University Press of America.

Epstein, Mark. (1980). *The Ottoman Jewish communities and their role in the fifteenth and sixteenth centuries.* Freiburg, Germany: Klaus, Swartz Verlag.

Fiorenza, Elizabeth S. (1979). Word, spirit and power: Women in early Christian communities. In Rosemary Reuther & Eleanor McLaughlin (Eds.), *Women of spirit: Female leadership in the Jewish and Christian tradition.* New York: Simon & Schuster.

Gerber, Haim. (1980, November). Social and economic position of women in an Ottoman city, Bursa, 1600–1700. *International Journal of Middle East Studies, 12*(3), 231–244.

Goitein, S. D. (1978). *A Mediterranean society: The Jewish communities of the Arab world as portrayed in the documents of the Cairo geniza* (Vols. 1–4). Berkeley: University of California Press.

Goldschmidt, Arthur, Jr. (1983). *A concise history of the Middle East.* Boulder, CO: Westview Press.

Grosz, Katrina. (1989). Some aspects of the position of women in Nuzi. In Barbara S. Lesko (Ed.), *Women's earliest records, from ancient Egypt and western Asia*, Proceedings of the conference on Women in the Ancient Near East, Brown University, Providence, Rhode Island, November 5–7, 1987. Atlanta, GA: Scholars Press.

Hatem, Mervat. (1986, Summer). The politics of sexuality and gender in segregated patriarchal systems: The case of eighteenth and nineteenth century Egypt. *Feminist Studies, 12*(2), 251–274.

Hodgson, Marshall. (1974). *The venture of Islam* (Vol. 1). Chicago: University of Chicago Press.

Hoffman, Anat. (1990, July). Women in Black will not be intimidated: Are you a "Woman in Black?" *Challenge*, pp. 10, 11.

The interpreter's Bible (Vol. 2). (1953). New York: Abingdon Press.

Katzir, Yael. (1982, April). Preservation of Jewish ethnicity in Yemen: Segregation and integration as boundary maintenance mechanics. *Comparative Studies in Society and History, 24*(2), 264–279.

Lerner, Gerda. (1986). The origin of prostitution in ancient Mesopotamia. *Signs, 2*(2), 236–253.

Lewis, Bernard. (1973). *Islam in history.* London: Alcove Press.

Lewis, Bernard. (1984). *The Jews of Islam.* Princeton, NJ: Princeton University Press.

March, Kathryn S., and Taqqu, Rachelle L. (1986). *Women's informal associations in developing countries: Catalysts for change?* Boulder, CO: Westview Press.

Marmorstein, Emile. (1954). The veil in Judaism and Islam. *Journal of Jewish Studies, 5*, 1–11.

Meyers, Carol. (1978, September). The roots of restriction: Women in early Israel. *Biblical Archeologist, 41*(3), 91–103.

O'Leary, D. L. (1927). *Arabia before Muhammad.* London: E. P. Dutton.

Oschorn, Judith. (1981). *The female experience and the nature of the divine.* Bloomington: Indiana University Press.

Raymond, Janice. (1986). *A passion for friends: Toward a philosophy of female affection.* Boston: Beacon Press.

Rich, Adrienne. (1986). Compulsory heterosexuality and lesbian existence. In *Blood, bread, and poetry: Selected prose, 1979–1985.* New York: W. W. Norton.

Salkin, Jeffrey. (1986, Summer). Dinah, the Torah's forgotten woman. *Judaism, 35*(3), 284–288.

Setel, T. Drorah. (1985). Prophets and pornography: Female sexual imagery in Hosea. In Letty M. Russell (Ed.), *Feminist interpretations of the Bible.* Philadelphia: Westminster Press.

Shalom, Chaya. (1990, September). *To be a lesbian-feminist activist in the women's peace movement.* Unpublished manuscript.

Smith, W. R. (1903). *Kinship and marriage in early Arabia.* Boston: Beacon Press.

Staples, William P. (1937, April). The Book of Ruth. *The American Journal of Semitic Languages and Literatures, 53*(3), 145–157.

Starhawk. (1987). *Truth or dare: Encounters with power, authority and mystery.* San Francisco: Harper & Row.

Stern, Gertrude H. (1939, July). The first women converts in early Islam. *Islamic Culture, 13*(3), 290–305.

Stillman, Norman. (1979). *The Jews of Arab lands.* Philadelphia: Jewish Publication Society of America.

Teubal, Savina. (1984). *Sarah the priestess.* Athens, OH: Swallow Press.

Vriezen, T. C. (1963). *The religion of ancient Israel.* London: Lutterworth Press.

Watt, W. Montgomery. (1974). *The majesty that was Islam.* London: Sidgwick & Jackson.

Weinstein, Mario. (1990, July). Conscientious objection in Israel. *Challenge*, pp. 10, 11.

Wiebke, Walther. (1981). *Women in Islam.* London: George Prior.

CHAPTER 3: WOMEN'S RIGHTS AND INTERETHNIC RELATIONS

Ahmed, Leila. (1984). Early feminist movements in the Middle East: Turkey and Egypt. In Freda Hussain (Ed.), *Muslim women.* New York: St. Martin's Press.

Antonious, George. (1946). *The Arab awakening.* New York: Putnam.

Arendt, Hannah. (1978a). *The Jew as pariah: Jewish identity and politics in the modern age* (Ron H. Feldman, Ed.). New York: Grove Press.

Arendt, Hannah. (1978b). To save the Jewish homeland. In *The Jew as pariah: Jewish identity and politics in the modern age* (Ron H. Feldman, Ed.). New York: Grove Press. (Original work published 1948)

Arendt, Hannah. (1978c). Peace or amistice in the Near East? In *The Jew as pariah: Jewish identity and politics in the modern age* (Ron H. Feldman, Ed.). New York: Grove Press. (Original work published 1950)

Barry, Kathleen. (1979). *Female sexual slavery.* New York: New York University Press.

Ben-Zvi, Rachel Yanait. (1989) *Before Golda: Manya Shochat.* New York: Biblio Press.

Bernstein, Deborah. (1987). *The struggle for equality—Urban women workers in prestate Israeli society.* New York: Praeger.

Buber, Martin, & Magnes, Judah. (1972). *Toward union in Palestine—Essays on Zionism and Jewish-Arab cooperation in Palestine.* Westport, CT: Greenwood Press.

Cohen, Amnon. (1973). *Palestine in the eighteenth century.* Jerusalem: The Magnes Press.

Davis, Fannie. (1986). *The Ottoman lady: A social history from 1718 to 1918.* Westport, CT: Greenwood Press.

Drumont, Paul. (1982). Jewish communities in Turkey during the last decades of the nineteenth century in the light of the archives of the Alliance Israelite Universelle. In Benjamin Braude & Bernard Lewis (Eds.), *Christians and Jews in the Ottoman Empire* (Vol. 1) . New York: Holmes & Meier.

Feldman, Ron H. (Ed.). (1978). Introduction. In Hannah Arendt, *The Jew as pariah: Jewish identity and politics in the modern age.* New York: Grove Press.

Flapan, Simha. (1979). *Zionism and the Palestinians.* New York: Barnes & Noble Books.

Goldschmidt, Arthur, Jr. (1983). *A concise history of the Middle East.* Boulder, CO: Westview Press.

Gran, Peter. (1941). *Islamic roots of capitalism, Egypt, 1760–1840.* Austin: University of Texas Press.

Halpern, Ben. (1969). *The idea of the Jewish state.* Cambridge, MA: Harvard University Press.

Hodgson, Marshall. (1974). *The venture of Islam* (Vol. 3). Chicago: University of Chicago Press.

Hourani, Albert H. (1946). *Syria and Lebanon.* London: Oxford University Press.

Issawi, Charles. (1982). The transformation of the economic position of the millets in the nineteenth century. In Benjamin Braude & Bernard Lewis (Eds.), *Christians and Jews in the Ottoman Empire* (Vol. 1). New York: Holmes & Meier.

Izraeli, Daphne N. (1981, Autumn). The Zionist women's movement in Palestine, 1911–1927: A sociological analysis. *Signs, 7*(1), 87–114.

Jayawardena, Kumari. (1986). *Feminism and nationalism in the Third World.* London: Zed Books.

Kandiyoti, Deniz. (1989). Women and the Turkish state: Political actors or symbolic pawns? In Nira Yuval-Davis & Floya Anthias (Eds.), *Woman—Nation—State.* New York: St. Martin's Press.

Karpat, Kemal. (1974). *The Ottoman state and its place in world history.* Leidan: E. J. Brill.

Karpat, Kemal. (1982). Millets and nationality: The roots of the incongruity of nation and state in the post-Ottoman period. In Benjamin Braude & Bernard Lewis (Eds.), *Christians and Jews in the Ottoman Empire: The functioning of a plural society* (Vols. 1–2, pp. 141–169). New York: Holmes & Meier.

Katznelson-Shazar, R. (Ed.) (1975). *The plough woman: Memoirs of the pioneer women of Palestine.* New York: Herzl Press.

Kohn, Hans. (1962). *The age of nationalism.* New York: Harper & Row.

Laskier, Michael. (1983). *The Alliance Israelite Universelle and the Jewish communities of Morocco: 1862–1962.* Albany: State University of New York Press.

Lesch, Ann Mosley. (1980). *Arab politics in Palestine, 1917–1939.* Ithaca, NY: Cornell University Press.

Lewis, Bernard. (1984). *The Jews of Islam.* Princeton, NJ: Princeton University Press.

Maimon, Ada. (1962). *Women build a land.* New York: Herzl Press.

Mandel, Neville J. (1976). *The Arabs and Zionism before World War I.* Berkeley: University of California Press.

Ma'oz, Moshe. (1968). *Ottoman reform in Syria and Palestine, 1840–1861.* Oxford, England: Clarendon Press.

Mernissi, Fatima. (1982, Fall). Women and the impact of capitalist development in Morocco. *Feminist Issues, 2*(2), 69–104.

Mernissi, Fatima. (1987, Spring). Professional women in the Arab world: The example of Morocco. *Feminist Issues, 7*(1), 47–65.

Miller, Ylana. (1985). *Government and society in rural Palestine, 1920–1948.* Austin: University of Texas Press.

Mogannam, Matiel. (1937). *The Arab woman and the Palestine Problem.* Westport, CT: Hyperion Press.

Muslih, Muhammad. (1987, Summer). Arab politics and the rise of Palestinian nationalism. *Journal of Palestine Studies, 16*(4), 7–94.

Owen, Roger. (1981). *The Middle East in the world economy, 1800–1914.* London: Methuen.

Palestine—A study of Jewish, Arab and British policies (Vols. 1 & 2). (1947). Published for the ESCO Foundation for Palestine. New Haven, CT: Yale University Press.

Patai, Raphael. (1974). *Encyclopedia of Zionism and Israel.* New York: McGraw-Hill.

Phillip, Thomas. (1978). Feminism and nationalist politics in Egypt. In Lois Beck & Nikki Keddie (Eds.), *Women in the Muslim world.* Cambridge, MA: Harvard University Press.

Porath, Y. (1974). *The emergence of the Palestinian Arab national movement, 1918–1929.* London: Frank Cass.

Reinharz, Shulamit. (1984). Toward a model of female political action: The case of Manya Shohat, founder of the first kibbutz. *Women's Studies International Forum, 7*(4), 275–287.

Rogers, Barbara. (1980). *The Domestication of women: Discrimination in developing societies.* London: Tavistock Publications.

Ro'i, Yaacov. (1982). The Zionist attitude to the Arabs. In Sylvia Haim & Elie Kedourie (Eds.), *Palestine and Israel in the 19th and 20th centuries.* London: Frank Cass.

Ruppin, Arthur. (1934). *The Jews in the modern world.* London: Macmillian.

Sayigh, Rosemary. (1979). *Palestinians: From peasants to revolutionaries.* London: Zed Books.

Sisters of exile: Sources on the Jewish woman. (1973). Ichud Habonim, Labor Zionist Youth. New York.

Smelansky, Moshe. (1972). Citrus growers have learned to cooperate. In Martin Buber & Judah Magnes, *Toward union in Palestine—Essays on Zionism and Jewish-Arab cooperation in Palestine* (pp. 57–65). Westport, CT: Greenwood Press.

Swedenburg, Ted. (1989). *Palestinian women in the 1936–39 revolt: Implications for the Intifada.* Paper presented at the "Marxism Now: Tradition and Difference" Conference, University of Massachusetts, Amherst, December 2, 1989.

Tucker, Judith E. (1985). *Women in nineteenth century Egypt.* Cambridge, England: Cambridge University Press.

Von Werlhof, Claudia. (1988). On the concept of nature and society in capitalism. In Maria Mies, Veronika Bennholdt-Thomsen, & Claudia Von Werlhof (Eds.), *Women: The last colony.* London: Zed Books.

CHAPTER 4: CONSEQUENCES

Asadi, Fawzi. (1976, Autumn). Some geograpic elements in the Arab-Israeli conflict. *Journal of Palestine Studies, 6*(1), 79–91.

Avishai, Bernard. (1985). *The tragedy of Zionism.* New York: Farrar, Straus, & Giroux.

Barry, Kathleen. (1979). *Female sexual slavery.* New York: New York University Press.

Bernstein, Deborah. (1987). *The struggle for equality: Urban women workers in prestate Israeli society.* New York: Praeger.

Bridel, Rene. (1984). Traffic of children. In Kathleen Barry, Charlotte Bunch, & Shirley Castley (Eds.), *International feminism: Networking against female sexual slavery.* Distributed by The International Women's Tribune Centre, Inc., New York.

Cattan, Henry. (1969). *Palestine, the Arabs, and Israel: The search for justice.* London: Longman.

Chatty, Dawn. (1978). Changing sex roles in bedouin society in Syria and Lebanon. In Lois Beck & Nikki Keddie (Eds.), *Women in the Muslim world.* Cambridge, MA: Harvard University Press.

Cobban, Helena. (1988, Summer). Israel's nuclear game: The U.S. stake. *World Policy Journal, 5*(3), 415–433.

Davis, Uri. (1977). *Israel, Utopia incorporated: A study of class, state and corporate kin control.* London: Zed Press.

Davis, Uri. (1979, June). Settlements and policies under Begin. *MERIP, 9*(5), 12–18.

Dillman, Jeffrey D. (1989, Autumn). Water rights in the occupied territories. *Journal of Palestine Studies, 19*(1), 46–71.

Falah, Ghazi. (1989, Winter). Israeli state policy toward bedouin sedentarization in the Negev. *Journal of Palestine Studies, 18*(2), 70–91.

Fishman, Alex. (1989, June/July). The Palestinian woman and the intifada. *New Outlook, 32*(6/7), 9-11.

Flapan, Simha. (1987, Summer). The Palestinian exodus of 1948. *Journal of Palestine Studies, 16*(4), 3–26.

Haddad, Yvonne. (1980). Palestinian women: Patterns of legitimation and domination. In Khalil Nakhleh & Elia Zureik (Eds.), *Sociology of the Palestinians.* New York: St. Martin's Press.

Hazelton, Leslie. (1977). *Israeli women: The reality behind the myth.* New York: Simon & Schuster.

Hecht, Dina, & Yuval-Davis, Nira. (1984). Ideology without revolution: Jewish women in Israel. In Jon Rothschild (Ed.), *Forbidden agendas: Intolerance and defiance in the Middle East.* London: Al Saqi Books.

Hilterman, J. R. (1987, June). Women organize themselves. *Voice of Palestinian Women,* Nos. 9 & 10 (3rd year), pp. 7–8.

Hynes, H. Patricia. (1989). *The recurring silent spring.* Elmsford, NY: Pergamon Press.

Izraeli, Daphne N. (1981). The Zionist women's movement in Palestine, 1911–1927: A sociological analysis. *Signs, 7*(1), 87–115.

Jiryis, Sabri. (1976). *The Arabs in Israel.* London: Monthly Review Press.

Katzair, Yael. (1983). Yemenite Jewish women in Israeli rural development: Female power versus male authority. *Economic Development and Cultural Change, 32*(1), 45–62.

Kaye-Kantrowitz, Melanie, & Klepfisz, Irena. (1986). An interview with Chaya Shalom. *Tribe of Dina: A Jewish women's anthology.* Montpelier, VT: Sinister Wisdom 29/30.

Lahav, Pnina. (1977, Autumn). Raising the status of women through law: The case of Israel. *Signs, 3*(1), 193–209.

Lavie, Smadar. (1990). *The poetics of military occupation—Mzeina allegories of bedouin identity under Israeli and Egyptian rule.* Berkeley: University of California Press.

Leon, Dan. (1989, June/July). The Israei woman—Myth and reality. An interview with Naomi Chazan. *New Outlook, 32*(6/7), 12-13.

Levavi, Lea. (1991, January 1). Women's situation worse than before. *The Jerusalem Post.* Quoted in *American-Israeli Civil Liberties Coalition, Inc.* [newsletter], *11*(1), 4.

Lipman, Beita. (1988). *Israel: The embattled land—Jewish and Palestinian women talk about their lives.* London: Pandora.

Lustick, Ian. (1980). *Arabs in the Jewish state.* Austin: University of Texas Press.

Maimon, Ada. (1962). *Women build a land.* New York: Herzl Press.

Morris, Benny. (1986, Autumn). The harvest of 1948 and the creation of the Palestine refugee problem. *The Middle East Journal, 40*(4), 671–685.

Palestine Human Rights Information Center. (1990, September). *Human Rights Update, 3,* 10.

Pederson, Birgitte R. (1983). Oppressive and liberating elements in the situation of Palestinian women. In Bo Utas (Ed.), *Women in Islamic societies.* New York: Olive Branch Press.

Raymond, Janice. (1989). Children for organ export. *Reproductive and Genetic Engineering, 2*(3), 237–245.

Raymond, Janice. (1989). The international traffic in women: Women used in systems of surrogacy and reproduction. *Reproductive and Genetic Engineering, 2*(1), 51–57.

Reich, Walter. (1984, June). A stranger in my home. *Atlantic Monthly, 54*–90.

Rosenberg, Bernard. (1977, Fall). Women's place in Israel—Where they are, where they should be. *Dissent, 408*–417.

Said, Edward W. (1989). Intifada and independence. In Zachary Lockman & Joel Beinin (Eds.), *Intifada: The Palestinian uprising against Israeli occupation.* Boston: South End Press.

Sayigh, Rosemary. (1979). *Palestinians: From peasants to revolutionaries.* London: Zed Books.

Segev, Tom. (1986). *The first Israelis.* New York: Free Press.

Setel, T. Drorah. (1985). Prophets and pornography: Female sexual imagery in Hosea. In Letty M. Russell (Ed.), *Feminist interpretations of the Bible.* Philadelphia: Westminister Press.

Shapiro, Haim. (1990, May 15). Rabbinate marriage blacklist based on unproven reports. *Jerusalem Post.* In *American-Israeli Civil Liberties Coalition, Inc.* [newsletter], *10, 2,* 4.

Shehadeh, Raja. (1984). *Samed: Journal of a West Bank Palestinian.* New York: Adama Books.

Shipler, David. (1986). *Arab and Jew: Wounded spirits in a promised land.* New York: Times Books.

Sik, Toma. (1990, April-May). Conscience and the army. *The Other Israel,* p. 41.

Skutel, H. J. (1986, July-August). Water in the Arab-Israeli conflict. *International Perspectives,* pp. 22–24.

Von Werlhof, Claudia. (1988). On the concept of nature and society in capitalism. In Maria Mies, Veronika Bennholdt-Thomsen, & Claudia Von Werlhof (Eds.), *Women: The last colony.* London: Zed Books.

Wegner, Judith. (1982). The status of women in Jewish and Islamic marriage and divorce law. *Harvard Women's Law Journal, 5,* 1–33.

Weiss Shevach, & Yishai, Yael. (1980, Spring). Women's representation in Israeli political elites. *Jewish Social Studies, 42*(2), 165–176.

Whitman, Joyce. (1988). *The environment in Israel.* Israeli Ministry of the Interior.

Yuval-Davis, Nira. (1985, Fall). Front and rear: The sexual division of labor in the Israeli army. *Feminist Studies, 2*(3), 649–676.

EPILOGUE

Barry, Kathleen. (1979). *Female sexual slavery.* New York: New York University Press.

Conscientious objection in Israel. (1990, July). *Challenge,* pp. 6–7.

Dworkin, Andrea. (1983). *Right-wing women.* New York: Perigree Books, Putnam's Publishing Group.

MacKinnon, Catharine A. (1989). *Toward a feminist theory of the state.* Cambridge, MA: Harvard University Press.

Mies, Maria. (1986). *Patriarchy and accumulation on a world scale: Women in the international divison of labour.* London: Zed Books.

Morgan, Robin. (1989). *The demon lover: On the sexuality of terrorism.* London: W. W. Norton.

Palestine Human Rights Information Center. (1990). An Israeli soldier's description of soldier and settler behavior in Jazalon refugee camp. [From *Ha'aretz,* March 11, 1988.] Chicago: Author.

Protests and dilemmas. (1990, July/August). *The Other Israel,* p. 3.

Shalom, Chaya. (1990, September). *To be a lesbian-feminist activist in the women's peace movement.* Unpublished manuscript.

Time for tear gas. (1990, January/February). *The Other Israel,* pp. 10–11.

Wagner, Ronnie. (1990, January/February). Youth in protest. *The Other Israel,* pp. 11–12.

Index

Abandoned Areas Ordinance, 166
Abbott, Nabia, 24, 78–79, 87
Abdel Hadi, Isam, 49
Abram, 81
Absentee Property Regulations, 166
Abu Jihad, 49
Achdut Haavoda, 136, 137, 144, 150, 166
Adler, Rachel, 83
Ahmed, Leila, 88, 94, 117–118
Aisha, 87, 88
Alami, Musa, 149
Al-Fajr, 59
Al-Gades (Yemen), 178–179
Algeria, 49
Al-Wuhsha, 97
Alliance Israelite Universelle, 115, 116, 118
Amal, 38
Androcentric discourse, 18–21, 200
Androcentric historiography, 3–7, 22, 23–24, 53, 75–76, 81, 93, 105
Ansar prison, 45
Anti-Arab ideologies, 17, 115, 166, 171, 173, 174, 177, 185, 191
Anti-feminism, 7, 17, 74, 196
  and anti-Semitism, 16–18
Anti-Jewish ideologies, 16, 36, 37, 115, 128, 129
Antonelli, Judith, 36
Antonious, George, 139, 140
Antonious, Soroya, 29, 49
Arab Ladies Association, 145
Arab League, 153

Arab nationalism, 122, 123, 124, 125, 126, 127, 128, 130, 140, 144, 145, 146, 147, 153, 156. *See also* Women
Arab queens, 78, 79
Arab Revolt of 1936, 146, 147, 148
Arab Women's Council (U.S.), 59
Arab Women's Executive Committee, 145, 146, 147, 157
Arab women's society, 144
Arad, Nava, 53
Arafat, Yasser, 48, 49
Arendt, Hannah, 129, 130, 151–152
Arieli, Dana, 61–62
Asadi, Fawzi, 161
Ashkelon prison, 44
Ashkenazi "as a term," 13, 70
Ashrawi, Hanan. *See* Mikhail-Ashrawi, Hanan
Association of Labor Committees, 41
Association of Palestine Women, 48
Association of Women Academics in Gaza, 50
Association of Working Palestinian Women, 48
Associations of women, 76–107
  disruption of, 14, 22, 51, 58, 60, 61, 72, 70, 76, 81, 86, 90, 93, 107, 109, 118, 119, 138, 139, 149, 150, 155, 157, 172, 184
  economic, 80, 96, 98, 99, 100, 103, 114, 118, 179, 180
  familial-kin-communal, 75, 76, 81, 100, 127, 172, 177, 178

Associations of women (*continued*)
  historical, 21, 22, 45, 76, 77, 104, 105
  intercommunal, 77, 90, 91, 95, 96,
      97, 101, 105, 106, 138, 145, 149,
      173, 179, 180, 181, 199, 200,
      201, 202
  political, 4, 8, 29, 30, 34, 35, 40, 43–
      58, 74, 86, 106, 122, 123, 127,
      132, 135–138, 145, 146, 147,
      150, 183
  religious, 41, 71, 79, 80, 86, 87
Assyrians, 13, 24–25, 78
Aviad, Janet, 62
Avishai, Bernard, 162, 163
Ayalon, David, 106

Babatha, 23–24
Balfour Declaration, 139, 140
Barbari, Yussra, 50
Barguty, Siham, 44
Baron, Salo, 24–25, 99
Barry, Kathleen, 120, 175, 195, 198
Barthes, Roland, 18
Bedouin, 3, 189, 190, 193, 194
  and environment, 192, 193, 194
Beeston, A. F. L., 86
Begin, Menachem, 189, 191
Beinin, Joel, 21, 73
Ben-Gurion, David, 28, 150, 161, 162,
      163, 164, 165, 176, 181, 194
Bernstein, Deborah, 134, 135, 137, 148,
      149, 154, 167
Bertell, Rosalie, 192
Biltmore Program, 151, 152
Biological determinism, 3, 22
Bir Zeit University, 4, 46, 158
Borochov, Ber, 129, 154
Boullata, Peter, 11–12
Bowerstock, G. W., 23–24
Braude, Benjamin, 102
Bridell, Renee, 192
Bridge, The (Gesher Leshalom), 56, 71
Brith Shalom, 148
British Mandate, 141, 143, 144, 145,
      146, 148, 151, 152, 153
Brooten, Bernadette, 79, 80, 83, 88

Brussels Conference, 53
B'tselem, 30–31
Buber, Martin, 148–149

Cairo Genizas, 95, 96, 97, 107
Caliphate, 99
"Call for Peace, A" (conference), 57
Canaan, 23, 78, 81
Capitalist-patriarchy, 12, 13, 22, 66, 109,
      117, 118, 119
Carella, Michael, 90
Cattan, Henry, 166
Central Park jogger, 32, 33
Chatty, Dawn, 193
Chazan, Naomi, 170
Chomsky, Noam, 28
Christian Public Charity Society for
      Ladies, 127
CLAF (Community of Lesbian-Feminists),
      58
Class systems, 4, 6, 12–16, 18, 30, 38,
      45, 47, 48, 52, 58, 66, 67, 69, 72,
      84, 92–96, 98, 99, 101–104, 106,
      109–113, 115, 117–119, 122, 126,
      127, 129, 131, 134, 138, 139, 141,
      143, 144, 148, 149, 152–156, 176,
      178, 179, 180, 186, 187, 189, 195,
      199. *See also* Sex-class status; Sexual
      regulation and class; Racism
Client-patron relations, 102
Cobban, Helena, 192
Committee of Union and Progress, 121,
      122, 126, 127
Corea, Gena, 175
Cossali, Paul, 38–43, 66
Cox, Sophie, 35
Culture, 10, 11
  separation from nature, 14
Cutler, Helen and Alan, 17

Davis, Fannie, 100–101, 121
Davis, Uri, 70, 161, 171, 177, 189,
      190
Deborah, 83, 84
De-development, 66
Defense Emergency Regulations, 28

Deir Yassin, 161–162
Democratic Front for the Liberation of Palestine, 48
Democratic Movement for Israeli Women, 39
Democratic Women in Israel. *See* Tandi
Dengler, Ian, 103–104
Deportations of Palestinian women and children, 29, 72
Deshen, Shlomo, 102
Dhimmi, 94, 95, 101, 102, 105, 107, 111, 112
Dillman, Jeffrey, 189, 190
Dimona, 192–193
Dinah, 90, 91
Dines-Levy, Gail, 36
Drumont, Paul, 112
Druze, 3, 167, 185, 203
Dualism, 3, 14, 20, 22, 71, 119
Dworkin, Andrea, 7, 36–37, 200

East for Peace, 59
Education, 99, 122, 123, 185
    under British, 143, 185, 186
    Eurocentric bias, 22–23
    Islamic, 41
    in Israel, 171, 185
    Zionist movement and, 143, 185
Elkana, Dalia, 60
Employment. *See also* Women, in work force
    in agriculture, 65, 188
    of Arab Jews in Israel, 176, 179
    of Israeli women, 63, 72, 170, 171, 179, 181, 183, 184
    of Palestinians in Israel, 170, 185, 186
    of Palestinians in occupied territories, 1, 64, 65, 67
    in prestate Palestine, 131, 132, 133, 134, 135, 137, 138, 141, 143, 144, 149
Environment, Israeli, 187–194
Epstein, Mark, 102
Equal Rights, 6, 8, 15, 124
Eurocentrism, 23, 162, 171, 172

Faiza, 40
Falah, Ghazi, 193
Falastin, 127
Fatah, al-, 48, 49
Fedayeen, 39
Female friendship, 21, 22, 40, 44, 45, 57, 76, 77, 79, 80–83, 86, 88, 90, 97, 100, 101, 105, 106, 114, 118, 138, 139, 172, 178, 180, 181, 198, 199, 200, 202
Feminist analysis, 4, 5, 6–16, 31–34, 35–37, 52, 53, 54, 57, 63, 66–74, 76, 77, 81–84, 86, 90–94, 104–107, 108–110, 116–119, 122–124, 131, 135, 136–138, 148, 150, 151, 153–157, 161, 162, 164, 167–173, 175, 176, 177, 180, 181–187, 190, 191, 193, 194–198, 200–204
Fiorenza, Elizabeth S., 80
First Arab Women's Congress of Palestine, 144, 145, 146
Fishman, Alex, 48, 50, 170
Flapan, Simha, 126, 144, 148, 149, 151, 165, 166

Galilee, Lily, 53, 54
Gaza Strip, 1, 6, 35–36, 38–43, 50, 64–69, 161, 189
    day laborers in, 1, 202
    de-development of, 66
    women in, 38–43, 65, 66, 67
Gender
    and race, 12, 13, 16, 52, 62, 70, 72, 116, 119, 138, 149, 171, 184, 186, 195, 196, 197, 200, 204
    social constructions of, 4, 13, 16, 45, 52, 74
General Union of Palestinian Women, 49
Geneva Conventions, 28
Genya, 57
Gerber, Haim, 103
Gesher Leshalom (The Bridge), 56
Giacaman, Rita, 45–48, 51
Gie, Carmit, 60, 169
Goitein, S. D., 95–100

Goldberg, Harriet, 17
Goldschmidt, Arthur, 92, 139
Gordon, Yael, 136
Gran, Peter, 117
Grosz, Katrina, 98
Gush Emunim, 59
Gyn-affective scholarship, 22
Gynocentric customs, 77, 78

Ha'am, Ahad, 129
Haaretz, 194
Haddad, Yvonne, 170
Haganah, 150, 152, 165
Hagar, 81, 82
Halpern, Ben, 130
Hamas, 50
Harem, 85, 88
"Harlots" of Hadramaut, 86
Hatem, Mervat, 76–77, 105, 106, 107
Hawash, Samar, 47, 197
Hawatmeh, Nayef, 48
Hazelton, Leslie, 14, 37
Health care, 26, 29, 30, 34, 35, 185
    of Palestinian women, 29, 30, 34–35,
        185
Hecht, Dina, 164
Herzl, Theodore, 129, 151
Hetero-patriarchy, 76
Hetero-relations, 76, 103, 104
Hijawa, Sulafa, 54
Hilal, Jamil, 64
Hilterman, J. R., 197
Hind bint Utbah, 87
Hind, 79
Hirr, 86
Hirschman, Irene, 62–63
Histradut, 44, 63, 136, 137, 144, 149,
    150
Hoagland, Sarah Lucia, 14
Hobbes, Thomas, 15
Hodgson, Marshall, 16, 77, 85, 121
Holocaust, 2, 19, 20, 36, 200
Hourani, Albert, 139, 140
Humanism, 15
Huri, Ruqayya, 146
Hynes, H. Patricia, 22, 190, 191, 192

Ihud Association, 148
Ikhwan al-Qassam, 146
Imperial politics, 16, 23–24, 27, 116,
    126, 139, 140
Incest, 8, 34
Institute for Arab Women's Studies, 48
International Alliance of Women for Suf-
    frage and Equal Citizenship, 147
Intifada, 2, 7, 11, 12, 26, 28, 29–33, 35,
    44, 45, 50, 51, 54, 68, 69, 74
    Israeli women and, 44, 54, 55, 56, 57,
        199, 200, 202. See also Women,
        Palestinian, in resistance move-
        ments
    Palestinian women and, 6, 7, 28, 29,
        30, 31, 32, 33, 35, 44, 45, 50, 51,
        59–63, 64, 66, 68, 69, 70, 197,
        199, 200, 202
Irgun, 151, 153
"Iron Fist" policy, 54, 73
Islam, 41–42
Islamic Association for the Employment
    of Ottoman Women, 123
Islamic fundamentalism, 62, 71
Islamic University of Gaza, 41
Isma'il, Miriam, 32
Israel
    founding of, 151–153, 157, 160, 161–
        167, 172, 173
    Jewish immigration into, 173–177
    treatment of Arab and North African
        Jews in, 59, 72, 73, 171, 172, 181
    treatment of Palestinians in, 1, 2, 33,
        36, 37, 44, 45, 72, 163, 165, 166,
        167, 171, 184, 185
Israel Women's Alliance Against the
    Occupation, 57
Israeli Defense Forces (IDF), 27. See also
    Zahal
Israeli Information Center for Human
    Rights, 30–31
Israeli youth, 19, 20, 21
Israelites, 23–24, 89, 92
Issawi, Charles, 112
Izraeli, Daphne, 133, 134, 135, 136,
    137, 149, 150, 154, 164, 196

Jabalaya refugee camp, 39, 42
Jabotinski, Vladimir, 129–130
Jael, 83, 84
Jahiliya, 92, 186
Jayawardena, Kumari, 107–108
Jewish family law, 45
Jewish Secular Cultural Community
    Center, 53
Jewish-Arab tribes, 77, 84
Jiryin, Sabri, 166
Johnson, Penny, 51

Kahinah, 78
Kalandia Refugee Camp, 158, 159
Kamal, Zahira, 47
Kandiyoti, Deniz, 111, 112, 122, 123–
    124
Karpat, Kemal, 111
Katzir, Yael, 105–106, 177, 178, 179,
    180
Katznelson-Shazar, R., 132–133, 138,
    139
Kaye-Kantrowitz, Melanie, 172
Khan Yunis refugee camp, 42
Khass, Mary, 173
Khelil, Najat, 59–60
Khouri, Ibtihaj, 56–57
Kira, 101
Kira, Ester, 100
Klepfisz, Irena, 172
Knesset, 163, 166, 183, 184
Koenig, Israel, 185
Kohn, Hans, 120

Lahav, Pnina, 183
Land confiscation, 27, 36, 37, 65, 66,
    73, 140, 160, 161, 164, 165, 166,
    187, 191, 193
Land Law of 1858, 113, 114
Langer, Felicia, 40
Laskier, Michael, 115
Lavie, Smadar, 193, 194
Law of Return, 177, 184
Lazare, Bernard, 130
Lebanon, 188, 189
Lempert, Leslie I., 28

Leon, Dan, 170
Lerner, Gerda, 12–13, 94
Lesbians, 58, 77, 106, 201, 202
Lesch, Ann, 143
Levavi, Lea, 170
Lewis, Bernard, 85, 102
Lipman, Beita, 60, 61, 62–63, 168, 169,
    172, 173, 175, 180, 184
Lustick, Ian, 166, 185

Magnes, Judah, 138, 148
Maha, 42
Maimon, Ada, 131, 136, 137, 163
Majda, 41
Malchin, Sarah, 132, 133
Malul, Nissim, 148
Mamaea, 78
Mamluks, 77
Mamorstein, Emile, 93
Mandel, Neville, 122, 126, 127
Mansour, Lina, 45–48
Ma'oz, Moshe, 111
Mapai, 163
Mapam, 163
Mapat Hashalom, 55
March, Kathryn, 76
Mechanistic, 13
Merchant, Carolyn, 13–15
Mernissi, Fatima, 118
Meyers, Caroline, 93
Mies, Maria, 8–10, 69
Mikhail-Ashrawi, Hanan, 54
Militarism, 9, 10, 27–29, 31, 35, 36, 37,
    63, 73, 92, 93
Miller, Ylana, 143
Millets, 101, 102, 107, 108, 111, 112
Miriam, 79
Mogannam, Matiel, 127, 143, 144, 145–
    146, 147
Mona, 42–43
Morgan, Robin, 6, 47, 51, 52, 64, 70–
    71, 202
Morris, Benny, 167
Moscobiyeh Interrogation Center, 35
Moshav, 178, 179
"Mothers of the Believers," 88

Muhammad, 84–88, 92
Muslih, Muhammad, 125
Mwallima, 99, 100

Na'amat, 44
Nabila, 39–40
Nablus, 47
Najjab, Salwa, 29–30, 34
Namir, Ora, 183
Naomi, 82, 83
Nation-state, 3, 6, 16, 69, 73, 108
Nationalist politics, 3, 7, 8, 10, 11, 13,
    19, 31, 91, 92, 104, 108, 109, 120,
    122, 123, 124, 125, 139–141, 151–
    157, 160–164
    and religion, 168, 169, 182
Nazis, 36, 37, 61
Neve-Tirza (prison), 43, 45
New Outlook, 59, 170
Nova (magazine), 54
Nuclear bombs, 192

Occupation, 2, 8, 10, 28, 29, 30, 31,
    34, 38–43, 46, 58, 60, 61, 74, 161,
    198
Occupied territories, 1, 4, 7, 20, 26, 27,
    28, 29, 30, 44, 46, 48, 62, 64–69,
    158, 159, 189. See also Gaza Strip;
    Health care; Water; Intifada; Pales-
    tinians; Settlements
O'Leary, D. L., 77, 78
Oriental Jews, 59, 60, 70, 170–171
Orthodox Judaism, 52, 71, 135, 140,
    141–142, 163, 168
Oschorn, Judith, 89, 91, 93
Ostrowitz, Rachel, 54, 55, 58
Ottoman Arab Brotherhood, 122
Ottoman Decentralization Party, 122,
    128, 130
Ottoman Empire, 101, 107, 108, 110,
    112, 113, 139, 142
Ottoman Family Code Law of 1917,
    123
Ottomanism, 110, 120, 125
Owen, Roger, 111–112, 113
Oz V'shalom/Netivot Shalom, 55

Palestine Aid Society, 7
Palestine Arab Workers Society, 144
Palestine Human Rights Information
    Center, 28, 68
Palestine Jewish Colonization Associa-
    tion, 138
Palestine Liberation Organization, 48,
    49, 53
Palestine National Council, 48, 50
Palestine, 23, 78, 131, 132, 140, 141,
    142, 153, 160, 161, 187
Palestinian Communist Party, 48
Palestinian Declaration of Independence,
    48
Palestinian Federation of Women's
    Action Committees, 64
Palestinian Women's Association, 50
Palestinians. See also Employment; Gaza
    Strip; Health care; Israel, treatment
    of Palestinians in; Women, Pales-
    tinian
    killed and injured during intifada, 1,
        26, 28, 29, 31, 32, 33, 35, 37
    in Israel, 163, 165, 166, 167, 168,
        170, 171, 182, 184, 185, 186,
        191, 195, 197
Patai, Raphael, 129
Patriarchal state, 13, 167, 195
Patriotism, 11, 63, 120
Peace Now, 39, 61–62
Peace Quilt, 55
Pederson, Birgitte, 185, 186
Peres, Shimon, 185
Personal status laws, 72, 168, 169, 170,
    183
Peteet, Julie, 51
Phallocentric politics, 6, 7, 8, 18, 20, 22,
    23, 60, 89
Phillip, Thomas, 122
Plan Dalet, 165
Platonism, 14
Poalei Zion, 130, 133, 136
Popular Front for the Liberation of Pales-
    tine, 48
Porath, Yehoshua, 24, 126, 140, 142
Pornography, 8, 35, 37, 160, 161

Qassam, Shaykh 'Izz al-Din al-, 146

Rabin, Yitzhak, 73
Racism, 12, 13, 28, 33, 34, 36, 37, 52–
  53, 59, 61, 64, 66, 67, 70–75, 91,
  115, 119, 128, 129, 138, 143, 149,
  155, 156, 162, 163, 165, 171–177,
  182, 184, 185, 186, 191, 197
Ramadan, 44
Ramallah, 46
Rape, 32, 33, 54, 70, 73, 149, 162
Raymond, Janice, 21–22, 33, 76, 79, 86,
  175, 176
Red Crescent, 21–22, 49
Refugee camps, 1, 33, 60, 68, 158, 159
Reich, Walter, 164, 165
Reshet, 54
Reuther, Rosemary, 23, 80
Riots of 1929, 144
Rishon Lezion, 1, 202
Robson, Clive, 38–43, 66
Rockwell, Susan, 65, 66, 67, 68
Rogers, Barbara, 116
Ro'i, Yaacov, 130
Rosenberg, Bernard, 168, 170
Roy, Sarah, 66
Ruppin, Arthur, 129
Russian Compound, 30, 31
Ruth, 82, 83

Saba, Lily, 50
Sabbagh, Suha, 48
Safiyah bint Huayy, 88
Said, Edward, 21
Salkin, Jeffrey, 90–91
Salwa, 41
San Remo Conference, 140
Sarah, 81, 82
Sayigh, Rosemary, 45, 143, 146, 147,
  162, 167
Sedjera Collective, 132, 133
Segev, Tom, 20, 160, 161, 173–174,
  175, 176
Self-determination, 2, 3, 6, 9, 50, 51, 63,
  74
Sephardi "as a term," 70

Serri, Bracha, 59, 60
Setel, T. Drorah, 91
Settlements
  Gaza, 189
  West Bank, 27, 28, 62
Sex-class status, 4, 7, 8–10, 13, 15, 38,
  52, 63, 64, 65, 67, 72, 91, 92, 93,
  94, 97, 103, 104–106, 108, 114,
  116–119, 123, 131, 133, 135, 137,
  138, 145, 149, 150, 154, 156, 167,
  169, 170, 171, 176, 178, 181–185,
  194, 195, 197, 198
Sexual regulation and class, 12, 13, 93,
  94, 105
Shahak, Israel, 19–20
Shakdiel, Leah, 55
Shalom, Chaya, 58
Shalvi, Alice, 63
Shamir, Yitzhak, 191
Shani (Women Against the Occupation),
  55
Shapiro, Haim, 170
Shari'a, 45, 52, 85
Sharrett, Moshe, 188, 189, 190, 192
Shaykh 'Izz al-Din al-Qassam, 146
Shechem, 90, 91
Shehadeh, Raja, 161
Sheres, Ita, 90
Shochat, Manya, 132, 133, 138
Skutel, H. J., 188, 189
Slave markets, 1
Smelansky, Moshe, 148
Smith, Barbara, 33
Smith, W. R., 78, 92
Staples, William P., 82
Starhawk, 86
Stereotypes, 2, 16, 17, 18, 20, 36, 59,
  74, 115, 116, 166, 171, 173–174,
  176, 177, 185, 186, 191, 197
Stern, Gertrude, 85, 88
Stillman, Norman, 85, 106
Supreme Women's Council (PLO), 48
Susskind, Simone, 53
Swedenburg, Ted, 146–148
Sykes-Picot Agreement, 139
Szold, Henrietta, 138

Tamir, Alice, 63
Tandi (Movement of Democratic Women in Israel), 56
Tanzimat, 110, 111, 112
Taqqu, Rachelle, 76
Taudi, 43
Terrorism, 21, 61
Terry, Janice, 18
Teubal, Savina J., 81
Toubi, Tewfik, 163–164
Traffic in children, 176
Traffic in women, 10, 12, 18, 104, 106, 117, 176
Transit camps, 164, 173–175
Tucker, Judith, 114

Ulama, 85
Um Jihad, 49
Umma, 85
Umm Qirfah Fatimah bint Rabi'ah, 87
Umm Sadir Sajah bint Aws ibn Hiqq, 87
Umm Zim Salma bint Malik, 87
Union of Palestine Medical Relief Committees, 26, 27, 29, 73
Union of Palestinian American Women, 60
United Nations Universal Declaration of Human Rights, 28
Universal Declaration of Human Rights, 28
UNRWA (United Nations Relief and Works Agency), 41, 43, 52, 57

Vanunu, Mordechai, 192
Von Welhof, Claudia, 110, 117, 160
Vriezen, T. C., 89

Waqf, 102, 114
Waste Land Regulations, 166
Water, 27, 46, 188, 189, 190
    in Gaza, 189
    in West Bank, 62, 189
Watt, Montgomery, 84, 85, 92
Wegner, Judith, 168
Weiss, Shevach, 184
Weizmann, Chaim, 130, 151, 188

Whitman, Joyce, 187–88, 190
Witches, 14
Women. See also Women, Jewish; Women, Palestinian
    as "agents of change," 124, 164, 175, 180
    and Arab nationalism, 144, 146–149, 150, 156. See also Arab nationalism; Women's work committees; Palestinians, in resistance movements
    Bedouin, 193, 194
    Canaanite, 90, 91
    Christian, 70, 71, 80, 95, 96, 97, 98, 99, 102, 103, 109, 122, 173
    colonization of, 9, 34, 74, 118, 195, 197
    domestication of, 93, 94, 110, 117, 124, 170, 175, 180
    Egyptian, 9
    Jewish-Christian, 80
    and labor, 63, 64, 65, 67, 72, 118, 131, 154, 155, 156, 164, 170, 171, 182, 184, 186, 197
    and nature, 9, 12, 13–16, 22, 31, 35, 161
    as occupied territory, 6, 7, 8, 10, 15
    as property, 1 3, 85, 89–94, 105, 124, 131, 161, 169
    and reproduction, 8, 9, 10, 37, 68, 91, 92, 123, 131, 182
    violence against, 4, 5, 8, 9, 10, 12, 14, 15, 22, 27, 28, 29, 30–37, 40, 44, 54, 55, 57, 58, 60, 61, 64, 67, 68, 71, 72, 73, 78, 91, 157, 162, 167, 194, 195, 198, 200, 202
Women, Jewish
    Arab, 138, 139, 149, 171, 173
    Ashkenazi, 13, 55, 155, 171, 172, 181
    and Holocaust, 35
    in Israel, 167–172, 183, 184
    North African, 169, 171, 174
    Orthodox, 6, 62
    in peace movements, 4, 43, 44, 46, 53–59, 62, 199–202
    Sephardi, 55, 73, 138, 139, 149, 172

Women, Palestinian
  imprisoned, 29, 31, 32, 37, 39, 40, 43, 44, 45
  in Israel, 184, 185, 186, 197
  Muslim, 41, 70, 71, 95, 96–99, 102–106, 109, 122, 170, 171, 173
  Muslim fundamentalist, 7, 41, 50, 62, 170, 173
  in occupied territories, 1, 6, 7, 29, 35, 38–43, 64–67, 158
  in resistance movements, 4, 7, 29–31, 33–40, 44, 45–53, 56, 57, 59, 69, 73, 156, 157, 197, 199, 200, 202
  and Zionism, 39, 42, 138, 139, 150, 154, 156, 167, 184, 186, 195, 196, 197, 200
Women Against Occupation, 34, 43
Women Against Violence, 43
Women and Health, 29, 30, 34
Women for Peace, 54
Women for Support of Political Prisoners, 30
Women Go for Peace, 202
Women in Black, 4, 55, 56, 57, 58, 59
Women's Association for Social Works, 48
Women's Committee for Peace and Equality, 44
Women's Committee for Political Prisoners, 30
Women's Equal Rights Law, 183
Women's Health Project, 29–30, 34–35
Women's International League for Peace and Freedom, 56
Women's Organization for Cultural Work in Palestine, 134

Women's Organization for Political Prisoners, 30, 31, 32, 33, 36, 37
Women's Work Committees (Palestinian), 4, 8, 29, 46, 47, 48, 49, 51, 52, 197
Women Workers' Council, 137–138, 150, 164, 196
Working Women's Committees, 4, 29, 39, 44, 47
World Federation of Democratic Women, 56
World Zionist Organization, 183

Yadin, Yigael, 23, 163
Yael, 57
Yesh Gvul, 203
Yeshai, Yael, 184
York, Steve, 26
Young Ottomans, 121
Young Turk Revolution, 119
Yuval-Davis, Nira, 72, 164, 181, 182

Zahal, 20, 27, 60, 61, 181, 182
Zainab, 87
Zamili, Amal, 50
Zenner, Walter, 102
Zenobia, queen of Palmyra, 78
Zionist movement, 62, 124, 125, 126, 128, 129, 130, 132–139, 143, 148, 149, 151–157
  and eurocentrism, 23
  Working Women's Movement, 131, 132, 133–139, 150, 155, 156, 164, 196
Zionist Women, 131, 132, 133, 134, 135, 139, 141, 142, 149, 150, 151, 152, 154, 155, 156, 157, 182, 187, 194, 195, 196, 197, 198

About the Author

Dr. Elise G. Young has published, prepared curriculum, and spoken widely on the Israeli-Palestinian conflict. She was assistant professor at City College of the City University of New York, and was visiting assistant professor at Hampshire College in 1989–1990. Her poetry has appeared in journals and anthologies. She is a member of the Middle East Peace Coalition, Northampton, Massachusetts, and is currently working on a research project on Palestinian women and health care under occupation for the Institute on Women and Technology.

Photo by Alice Stanislawski

DUE DATE